TEACHING THE BIBLE
WITH UNDERGRADUATES

RESOURCES FOR BIBLICAL STUDY

Editor
Davina C. Lopez, New Testament

Number 99

TEACHING THE BIBLE
WITH UNDERGRADUATES

Edited by

Jocelyn McWhirter and Sylvie Raquel

SBL PRESS

 **PRESS**

Atlanta

For those in every generation who have instructed us

CONTENTS

Part 1. Learning Outcomes

Part 2. Reading

Part 3. Engaging Gen Z

Part 4. Going Online

LIST OF FIGURES

ABBREVIATIONS

AAHEB	*American Association for Higher Education Bulletin*
ABD	Freedman, David Noel, ed. *Anchor Bible Dictionary*. 6 vols. New York: Doubleday, 1992.
AE	*American Educator*
AEL	*The Australian Educational Leader*
AIL	Ancient Israel and Its Literature
AJPC	*Australasian Journal of Popular Culture*
AmSchol	*The American Scholar*
AP	*Aslib Proceedings*
APS	*The Asia-Pacific Scholar*
AsianSocSci	*Asian Social Science*
ASV	American Standard Version
BC	*Brain Connectivity*
BHS	*Biblica Hebraica Stuttgartensia*
BJET	*British Journal of Educational Technology*
BJPS	*The British Journal of Political Science*
CE	*Cogent Education*
Change	*Change: The Magazine of Higher Learning*
CHB	*Computers in Human Behavior*
CLR	*Clinical Law Review*
Compass	*Compass: Journal of Learning and Teaching*
CompEd	*Computers and Education*
CRAAP	Currency, Relevance, Authority, Accuracy, and Purpose
CSTS	The Critical Social Thought Series
CT	*College Teaching*
Didaktikos	*Didaktikos: Journal of Theological Education*
DK	*Digital Kompetanse*
EJ	*The English Journal*
ELTHE	*ELTHE: A Journal for Engaged Educators*
EPR	*Educational Psychology Review*
ER	*Educational Researcher*
ESV	English Standard Version
FE	*Frontiers in Education*

FM	*First Monday*
GBS	Guides to Biblical Scholarship
HE	*Higher Education*
HERD	*Higher Education Research and Development*
IHE	*Internet and Higher Education*
IISIT	*Issues in Informing Science and Information Technology*
IJESE	*International Journal of Environmental and Science Education*
IJHAC	*International Journal of Humanities and Arts Computing*
IJSHE	*International Journal of Sustainability in Higher Education*
IJSSS	*International Journal of Social Science Studies*
IL	*Informal Logic*
Int	*Interpretation*
JAAL	*Journal of Adolescent and Adult Literacy*
JAH	*Journal of Adolescent Health*
JBL	*Journal of Biblical Literature*
JCSD	*Journal of College Student Development*
JEE	*The Journal of Economic Education*
JG	*Journal of Geography*
JGHE	*Journal of Geography in Higher Education*
JHHE	*Journal of Hispanic Higher Education*
JHLSTE	*Journal of Hospitality, Leisure, Sport and Tourism Education*
JHLT	*Journal of Hispanic/Latino Theology*
JILS	*Journal of Information and Learning Sciences*
JIME	*Journal of Interactive Media in Education*
JIOL	*Journal of Interactive Online Learning*
JLE	*The Journal of Law and Economics*
JM	*Journal of Marketing*
JPD	*Journal of Psychoactive Drugs*
JPSE	*Journal of Political Science Education*
JSOT	*Journal for the Study of the Old Testament*
JTD	*Journal of Trauma & Dissociation*
JTSW	*Journal of Teaching in Social Work*
JWA	*The Journal of Writing Assessment*
KDPLS	The Kappa Delta Pi Lecture Series
KIEJ	*Kennedy Institute of Ethics Journal*
KJV	King James Version
KULA	*KULA: Knowledge Creation, Dissemination, and Preservation Studies*
LAI	Library of Ancient Israel

LE	*Liberal Education*
LEAP	Liberal Education and America's Promise
LEB	Lexham English Bible
LSJ	Liddell, Henry George, Robert Scott, Henry Stuart Jones. *A Greek-English Lexicon*. 9th ed. with revised supplement. Oxford: Clarendon, 1996.
LXX	Septuagint
MEACTS	Merrill Education ASCD College Textbook Series
MERLOT	*MERLOT Journal of Online Learning and Teaching*
MBPS	Mellen Biblical Press Series
MP	*Monitor on Psychology*
MS	*Motivation Science*
MT	Masoretic Text
NA^{26}	*Novum Testamentum Graece*, Nestle-Aland, 26th ed.
NA^{28}	*Novum Testamentum Graece*, Nestle-Aland, 28th ed.
NACTAJ	*NACTA Journal*
NASB	New American Standard Bible
NET	New English Translation
NIDB	Sakenfeld, Katharine Doob, ed. *New Interpreter's Dictionary of the Bible*. 5 vols. Nashville: Abingdon, 2006–2009.
NIV	New International Version
NJDL	*Nordic Journal of Digital Literacy*
NKJV	New King James Version
NRSV	New Revised Standard Version
NTTSD	New Testament Tools, Studies, and Documents
OH	*On the Horizon*
OralHist	*Oral History*
OTL	Old Testament Library
Phaedr.	Plato, *The Phaedrus*
PN	*Philosophy Now*
PSA	*Psychological Science Agenda*
PSE	*Postdigital Science and Education*
PSP	*Political Science and Politics*
RBS	Resources for Biblical Study
ReadRep	Reading Report
REE	*Race, Ethnicity, and Education*
RelEd	*Religious Education*
RHE	*Review of Higher Education*
RPA	*Rhetoric and Public Affairs*

RR	Research Report
RRE	*Review of Educational Research*
RT	*The Reading Teacher*
SC	*Sociology Compass*
SemeiaSt	Semeia Studies
SG	*Simulation and Gaming*
SIJE	*Shanlax International Journal of Education*
SLULJ	*St. Louis University Law Journal*
SRBS	*Systems Research and Behavioral Science*
SSJ	*The Social Science Journal*
StABH	Studies in American Biblical Hermeneutics
SWC	*Social Work and Christianity*
T@C	Texts@Contexts
THE	*Teaching in Higher Education*
THL	Theory and History of Literature
ThTo	*Theology Today*
TLH	Teaching and Learning in Higher Education
TPE	*Technology, Pedagogy, and Education*
TS	*Teaching Sociology*
TTR	*Teaching Theology and Religion*
USQR	*Union Seminary Quarterly Review*
VCTEFP	*Visual Communication and Technology Education Faculty Publications*
WabJT	*Wabash Journal on Teaching*
WP	*World Psychiatry*
W&P	*Writing and Pedagogy*
WPEL	*Working Papers in Educational Linguistics*
WW	*Word and World*

Introduction

JOCELYN MCWHIRTER AND SYLVIE T. RAQUEL

The generation now coming of age has been variously labeled Post-Millennials, iGeneration, and Generation Z. Commonly known as Gen Z, it includes those born after 1996.[1] The first Gen Z undergraduates matriculated in or around 2015, so that since 2019 they have made up the majority of college students. Their youngest instructors belong to the ranks of Millennials, who, together with their Gen X and Baby Boomer colleagues, were recently teaching the youngest of their generation. Most professors may therefore know little about the distinct characteristics of their current students.

Gen Z differs from previous generations in demographics, sensibilities, aspirations, expectations, preferred ways of learning, and overall emotional health. For many professors, pedagogical techniques that worked well with Gen Xers and Millennials tend to fall flat with Gen Z. This situation has driven undergraduate education to a crossroads. Unless instructors learn more about this new generation of students, the topics that inspire them, and the pedagogies that engage them, they stand to lose Gen Z's attention. Programs that wish to survive in a market with fewer college-age students and higher tuition rates would do well to give their attention to Gen Z.[2]

More than any previous generation, Gen Z is ethnically diverse. About half (50.9 percent) identify as white. A quarter are Latinx, and 13.8 percent

---

1. Kim Parker and Ruth Igielnik, "On the Cusp of Adulthood and Facing an Uncertain Future: What We Know about Gen Z So Far," Pew Research Center, 14 May 2020, https://tinyurl.com/SBL03108a. Parker and Igielnick did not set an end date. Other Gen Z researchers work with slightly different dates.
2. Jeffrey J. Selingo, "The New Generation of Students: How Colleges Can Recruit, Teach, and Serve Gen Z," *The Chronicle of Higher Education*, 2018, https://tinyurl.com/SBL03108b.

are black.[3] Nearly one-third (29 percent) are first- or second-generation immigrants. The vast majority graduate from high school, and nearly half enroll in four-year baccalaureate programs. More than half of those aim to be the first in their family to earn a bachelor's degree.[4] Although Gen Zers agree on the importance of a college education, many come from families that know little about the values and systems of higher education.[5]

In addition, most Gen Zers care little for one of higher education's traditional vehicles: books. They are more accustomed to videos and brief snippets of text. The oldest were born into a world of handheld devices. According to a 2018 survey, about 95 percent of high school students had access to smartphones, laptops, desktops, and tablets. If they were not watching videos or following social media, they might have been playing video games. Forty-five percent reported that they were "constantly" or "almost constantly" online.[6]

The online habits of Gen Zers may have affected their mental health. Another 2018 survey shows that nearly one-third of young adults described their mental health as "fair" or "poor."[7] As Terry Doyle and Todd Zakrajsek have noted, "The brain was not built for constant sensory stimulation."[8] Continuous exposure to rapidly shifting auditory and visual input, along with social media platforms that allow for cyberbullying and tally "friends" and "likes," seems to be one of the causes.[9]

So does social and political unrest. Gen Zers have been growing up in the shadow of the September 11, 2001, attacks on the Pentagon and the World Trade Center. As of the time of this writing, none can recall a year when the United States did not have troops stationed in the countries deemed responsible. Many Gen Zers also lived through the Great

---

3. William Frey, "Now, More than Half of Americans Are Millennials or Younger," *The Avenue*, 30 July 2020, https://tinyurl.com/SBL03108c.

4. Parker and Igielnik, "On the Cusp."

5. "Fourth Installment of the Innovation Imperative: Portrait of Generation Z," Northeastern University, 18 November 2014, 9.

6. Monica Anderson and Jingjing Jiang, "Teens, Social Media, and Technology: 2018," Pew Research Center, 13 May 2018, https://tinyurl.com/SBL03108d.

7. Sophie Bethune, "Gen Z More Likely to Report Mental Health Concerns," *MP* 50 (2019): 20.

8. Terry Doyle and Todd Zakrajsek, *The New Science of Learning: How to Learn in Harmony with Your Brain* (Sterling, VA: Stylus, 2013), 26.

9. In 2018, 27 percent of high school students agreed that cyberbullying causes stress (Anderson and Jiang, "Teens, Social Media").

Recession of 2008–2009 or were born into families still suffering from its aftereffects.[10] More recently, they have witnessed and perhaps participated in large-scale protests. They have suffered from the disappointments, displacements, restrictions, illness, and loss brought on by a global pandemic.

A 2014 survey suggests a related cause for the relatively poor mental health of Gen Z: the tug-of-war between their ambitions for and anxieties about the future. While 67 percent affirmed that a college degree would open the door to their desired careers, 67 percent also worried about paying for their education, and 64 percent were concerned about their ability to land a job.[11] It would seem that many Gen Zers cherish goals of employment and prosperity while harboring fears that those goals lie out of reach.

The new generation of college students is diverse, tech-savvy, and somewhat anxious. They are also interested in spirituality. According to a 2014 survey, 78 percent of Americans in their late teens believed in God, while 21 percent did not. Results of a study conducted in 2015 indicate that 47 percent of undergraduates attended religious services on a weekly basis.[12] It is safe to say, however, that most Gen Zers have never considered the academic study of religion or the Bible.

What is a biblical studies professor to do? In this book, we have compiled research-based and classroom-tested strategies for undergraduate instruction. Contributions are categorized into four parts. First, we turn to the Association of American Colleges and Universities. In 2015, just as Gen Z undergraduates began to matriculate, the Association of American Colleges and Universities published a set of learning outcomes for "Liberal Education and America's Promise." These outcomes, they say, prove "essential for success in life, civil society, and work in the twenty-first century." In part 1 of this volume, therefore, we share some ideas for applying them in the undergraduate biblical studies classroom. Susan E. Haddox describes biblical studies courses that develop critical and creative thinking, written and oral communication, inquiry and analysis, information literacy, and teamwork as part of an integrated core curriculum. Jocelyn McWhirter outlines four ways to get students thinking critically about controversial and sensitive topics concerning gender and

---

10. Corey Seemiller and Meghan Grace, *Generation Z Goes to College* (San Francisco: Jossey-Bass, 2016), 6–7, 11.

11. "Fourth Installment," 1.

12. "Fourth Installment," 8–9.

biblical interpretation. Christopher M. Jones explains how he involves students in inquiry and analysis of the biblical canon with an approach that differentiates a liberal education from authoritarian indoctrination. We end part 1 with two quick tips. George Branch-Trevathan guides students in answering basic historical and literary questions about biblical writings, and Sylvie T. Raquel puts the active learning in the book of Acts.

We devote part 2 to reading and information literacy. Since many Gen Z students lack the advanced reading skills necessary for success in biblical studies and most white-collar careers, Raquel suggests some strategies for strengthening interest, confidence, and comprehension among student readers. Kimberly Bauser McBrien shows how online social annotation promotes out-of-class conversation while fostering exegetical skills. Steve Jung shares eight assignments that improve students' information literacy. In the quick tips segment, Kara J. Lyons-Pardue lays out a strategy for brief student presentations based on Bible dictionary articles, and Timothy A. Gabrielson describes how he helped his class to hear Romans from the perspective of a first-century house church.

In part 3, we focus on addressing Gen Z experiences and learning preferences. Melanie Howard explains how she relates biblical studies to her Latinx students' experiences of translation, identity formation, and family solidarity. Kathleen Gallagher Elkins addresses student mental health, recommending trauma-informed teaching for biblical studies. Lesley DiFransico narrates the development of a relevant, activity-based course called Food, Hunger, and the Bible. John Van Maaren and Hanna Tervanotko present a small-scale study about the effects of course-based experiential learning on student learning, well-being, and retention. The quick tips include Robby Waddell's strategic use of a familiar tale for introducing students to the Synoptic problem, Callie Callon's exercises for helping students realize why each evangelist portrays a different Jesus, and Katherine Low's insights on how a bingo game exposes students to ancient ideas about life, death, and political crisis through the lens of twenty-first-century zombie culture.

Finally, part 4 concerns instruction using online resources and interfaces. Eric A. Seibert explains how brief video clips can command students' interest and prepare them to discuss challenging topics. Seth Heringer demonstrates the power of using digital images of ancient manuscripts to introduce textual criticism. Carl N. Toney evaluates the accessibility and features of nine free e-Bible tools. Timothy Luckritz Marquis promotes the construction of online environments that support the interactive interpretation that takes place in a physical classroom. We end with three quick tips for online instruction: Nicholas A. Elder's ideas for adapting three in-class activities for online use, John Hilton III's advice for aligning teaching and assessments with learning outcomes for each lesson, and McWhirter's plan for creative, collaborative analysis of Luke's parables.

We hope that this volume will help biblical studies professors—whether born in the Baby Boom, Gen X, or Millennial years—hone their instruction for Gen Z students. We are pleased to offer these strategies for teaching them to read, interpret, and learn from the Bible. We value our discipline for the many ways that it forms its practitioners, and we dedicate this book to those in every generation who have instructed us.

Bibliography

Anderson, Monica, and Jingjing Jiang. "Teens, Social Media, and Technology: 2018." Pew Research Center, 31 May 2018. https://tinyurl.com/SBL03108d.

Bethune, Sophie. "Gen Z More Likely to Report Mental Health Concerns." *MP* 50 (2019): 20.

Doyle, Terry, and Todd Zakrajsek. *The New Science of Learning: How to Learn in Harmony with Your Brain*. Sterling, VA: Stylus, 2013.

"Fourth Installment of the Innovation Imperative Polling Series: Portrait of Generation Z." Northeastern University, 18 November 2014.

Frey, William. "Now, More than Half of Americans Are Millennials or Younger." *The Avenue*, 30 July 2020. https://tinyurl.com/SBL03108c.

Parker, Kim, and Ruth Igielnik. "On the Cusp of Adulthood and Facing an Uncertain Future: What We Know about Gen Z So Far." Pew Research Center, 14 May 2020. https://tinyurl.com/SBL03108a.

Seemiller, Corey, and Meghan Grace. *Generation Z Goes to College*. San Francisco: Jossey-Bass, 2016.

Selingo, Jeffrey J. "The New Generation of Students: How Colleges Can Recruit, Teach, and Serve Gen Z." *The Chronicle of Higher Education*. 2018. https://tinyurl.com/SBL03108b.

PART 1
LEARNING OUTCOMES

Taking the LEAP:
Biblical Studies across an Integrative General Education Program

Susan E. Haddox

In the current climate of higher education, administrators, parents, and students alike often question the relevance of biblical studies in preparing students for the fast-paced, ever-changing twenty-first century. Administrators looking only at low numbers of majors often view religious studies departments as easy targets for cuts. In the face of such reductions, the role of biblical studies in the general education program, though always strong, becomes an ever-increasing focus. Articulating the specific contributions our practices and values make toward the educational goals and outcomes of our institutions can help justify our continuing place at the university table. Our courses have long embodied principles that form the core of twenty-first-century educational frameworks. These principles include critical reading and thinking, importance of cultural context, integration of knowledge, communication skills, and social responsibility. Though the texts are ancient, the issues endure. The pedagogy of biblical studies can lead the way within an integrative general education curriculum, such as that championed by the Association of American Colleges and Universities.

In 2005, the Association of American Colleges and Universities began its Liberal Education and America's Promise (LEAP) initiative, an effort that included more than three hundred colleges and universities in an action network "to share best practices in undergraduate education, strengthen educational achievement on their own campuses, and improve their abilities to communicate about the value of a liberal education in today's world."[1] The initiative articulated several "essential learning out-comes" in its *College Learning for the New Global Century* report.[2] The purpose of the learning outcomes is to provide guidelines to prepare students for the challenges and complexities of the twenty-first century. The outcomes center on four major areas: "Knowledge of Human Cultures and the Physical and Natural World," "Intellectual and Practical Skills," "Personal and Social Responsibility," and "Integrative and Applied Learning."[3] What sets these outcomes apart from those of a traditional liberal arts education is the explicit naming of integration and applied learning.

Designing the LEAP-Based Integrative Core

My institution developed a LEAP-based integrative core in 2012. The University of Mount Union is a small comprehensive university in Alliance, Ohio. It enrolls about twenty-three hundred students, of whom approximately 90 percent are undergraduates. The majority of our students come from northeast Ohio and surrounding areas, including a significant number of first-generation college students. Since its founding, Mount Union has sought to combine liberal and professional education. Liberal education is offered primarily through the general education curriculum. Prior to 2012, the university used a distribution model in which students took one or two courses from the traditional range of subject areas (literature, history, philosophy and religious studies, arts, natural and social sciences, math, foreign language, communication). Most students typically finished these requirements in their first two years. Although the curriculum provided students educational breadth, it lacked overall coherence, and its large size fell out of favor as major programs expanded their course requirements.

The new curriculum, called the Integrative Core, uses the LEAP essential learning outcomes as a guideline. The program has four levels comprising eight courses: first-year seminar, Foundations (4), Themes/

---

1. "The LEAP Vision for Learning: Outcomes, Practices, Impact, and Employer's Views," Association of American Colleges and Universities, 2011, https://tinyurl.com/SBL03108e, 1.

2. Association of American Colleges and Universities, *College Learning for the New Global Century: A Report from the National Leadership Council for Liberal Education and America's Promise*, 2007, https://tinyurl.com/SBL03108f, 3.

3. "LEAP Vision for Learning," 7.

Explorations (2), and capstone (see fig. 1). Foundations emphasize knowledge acquisition. Students complete Foundations courses in humanities, fine arts, social sciences, and natural sciences during their first two years. Themes/Explorations and capstone courses focus on social responsibility and integration during the junior and senior years. All of the levels develop intellectual skills. Biblical studies courses thrive at multiple levels in this LEAP-based curriculum. The close reading, analysis, examination of cultural context, and multivalent interpretation central to the discipline align closely with LEAP outcomes.

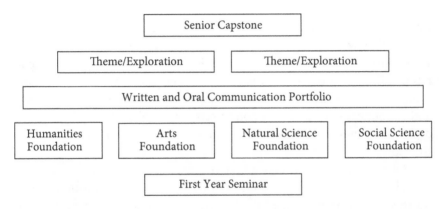

Fig. 1. Mount Union integrative core

As part of the Integrative Core, students complete two e-portfolios. These portfolios are evaluated using modified Association of American Colleges and Universities Valid Assessment of Learning in Undergraduate Education rubrics.[4] These rubrics provide tools to assess the LEAP essential learning outcomes.[5] They emphasize student development. After completing the Foundations level at the end of the sophomore year, each student submits a written and oral communication portfolio with assignments drawn from Integrative Core courses. Faculty members assess these portfolios for sophomore-level competency. Students must pass the written and oral communication portfolio before enrolling in the upper levels

---

4. "VALUE Rubrics," Association of American Colleges and Universities, https://www.aacu.org/value-rubrics.

5. Terrel Rhodes, *Assessing Outcomes and Improving Achievement: Tips and Tools for Using Rubrics* (Washington, DC: Association of American Colleges and Universities, 2010).

of the Integrative Core. In line with the design of the rubrics, the portfolio assesses development at a midpoint across a trajectory of student learning.[6] Students submit a second portfolio as part of the capstone course to demonstrate their further development. In addition to written and oral communication, the capstone portfolio assesses critical and reflective thinking and complex problem solving. The portfolios include materials from upper-level Integrative Core courses and their major field of study.

First-Year Seminar: Genesis

I have developed biblical studies courses for three levels of the Integrative Core: a first-year seminar on Genesis, an introductory Bible course as a Foundations, and multiple upper-level Bible courses for Themes/Explorations. Each of these courses develops written and oral communication skills, engages critical reading and thinking, requires reflective learning, and introduces content with implications for social responsibility. I have designed assignments to assess the outcomes of the LEAP-based Integrative Core.

All entering students take a first-year seminar. It introduces students to college-level academic expectations and helps them transition to the university environment. The LEAP outcomes for first-year seminars focus on the development of intellectual and practical skills. These include critical and creative thinking, written and oral communication, and inquiry and analysis. They also introduce elements of information literacy and teamwork.[7] In addition, first-year seminars incorporate elements of social and personal responsibility by allowing students to reflect on their vision for their education and what they need to achieve that vision.

A study of Genesis facilitates these goals. My course includes three types of assignments to develop critical thinking and writing. First, students write several reflections about their educational journey in conjunction with the journeys portrayed in Genesis. For example, students

---

6. Jennifer Grouling, "The Path to Competency-Based Certification: A Look at the LEAP Challenge and the VALUE Rubric for Written Communication," *JWA* 10 (2017), https://tinyurl.com/SBL03108g, 3.

7. First-year seminars that include the intellectual and practical skills listed are one of the high-impact practices cited by the Association of American Colleges and Universities. See George Kuh, Ken O'Donnell, and Carol Geary Schneider, "HIPs at Ten," *Change* 49.5 (2017): 10.

reflect on temptations and choices they face as new college students in light of Gen 3 and how to overcome obstacles to their success in light of Jacob's story in Gen 25–35. Second, they complete short text exercises focusing on a specified exegetical issue in a passage. For example, they compare and contrast the two creation stories in Gen 1–2 and analyze power dynamics in Gen 16 and 21. Third, the students write a formal research paper about a current issue for which Genesis is relevant. Issues might include evolution and creationism in schools, environmental issues, debates about sexuality, gender roles, and animal rights. The assignment is scaffolded with a topic proposal and preliminary bibliography, outline, draft, and final version. Together, these assignments require the students to engage the texts from multiple angles: personal, analytical, and social. They have many opportunities to practice writing with low-stakes reflections, medium-stakes text responses, and a high-stakes research paper. They develop critical reading skills and information literacy. They also address issues of social responsibility as they study how topics in Genesis, such as slavery and gender roles, have shaped society.

The class also includes two major oral assignments. The more formal assignment is a group presentation, linked with the high-stakes research paper and addressing a contemporary social issue related to Genesis. This assignment enables students to consolidate their research and analysis and present it in two different forms. The second oral presentation is less formal. Students role-play various characters from Genesis in the talk show *Spilling the Beans with Tamar bat Sheba*. As host, I invite my guests, such as Abraham, Sarah, and Hagar, to tell their stories from their perspectives. I then ask them questions. The guests also question each other before I open the floor to the audience. This assignment works well. The students get into their parts and have fun exploring the dynamics of the characters. Some of the students figure out the pun in the talk show title when we get to Gen 38. Together, these assignments develop several oral communication skills. The talk show requires creativity in extemporaneous speaking and impromptu responses to questions. The group presentation requires collaboration, organization, and citation. With multiple opportunities to present in front of the class, students build confidence in oral presentation.

As a final assignment, students complete the M-Source project (where "M" stands for Mount Union). This project requires students to engage critically and creatively with the Bible. Students select a text and provide a creative interpretation. They can rewrite a story from the perspective of a different character, compose a poem or a song, or create a visual interpretation. One student used Legos to create a stop-motion animated film of the Akedah. Another wrote a diary entry for a worker on the Tower of Babel. The project gives them the opportunity to exhibit talents—including artistic, musical, poetic, and literary skill—that may not manifest themselves in traditional classroom work. It can boost the confidence of students who may not excel at the traditional academic tasks of writing and formal speaking but can still engage deeply with the material.

Foundations: Biblical Texts and Contexts

I teach Biblical Texts and Contexts, our introductory Bible course, at the Foundations level. This level addresses the LEAP outcome of "knowledge of human cultures and the physical and natural world, *focused* by engagement with big questions, both contemporary and enduring."[8] At Mount Union, the Foundations are set up to address three major questions in each of four perspectives of human inquiry: humanities, arts, natural sciences, and social sciences. First, what kinds of questions does this perspective ask? Second, how does this perspective go about answering them? And finally, why is this perspective important? Within each area, the faculty has set learning goals related to the respective concepts and methods of the disciplines. In addition, intellectual and practical skills continue to be emphasized.

Biblical Texts and Contexts is a natural fit for Foundations because inquiry and analysis have always formed the basis of the course. Aligning it with the LEAP and Foundations outcomes helped me to improve the course in several ways. First, it encouraged me to make its methodology more explicit. It reminded me to cover the why of approaches, not just the how. For example, when we perform a word study, I spend more time discussing why differences between texts and translations are important, rather than just explaining how to use online concordances and lexicons. Since methodological clarity is an important goal in the Foundations level, I emphasize what each type of exegetical approach (literary, historical, ideological) contributes to understanding a text. Second, alignment with LEAP and Foundations outcomes helped me to improve the assignment design, especially for oral assignments. These assignments now have

---

8. "LEAP Vision for Learning," 7, emphasis original.

clearer links to course outcomes and stronger scaffolding. Finally, the multiple demands of the course required me to think more deliberately about how to focus it. I have reduced the number of texts I cover and concentrate instead on themes. These themes include creation, identity, covenant, slavery, marriage, sexuality, violence, and leadership. I use them to highlight the types of questions the humanities address as well as the relevance of biblical studies in our society.

In-class activities and assignments show students how biblical studies addresses those issues. To develop the necessary critical reading skills, we devote much class time to reading texts closely, comparing and contrasting parallel texts. One exercise I use to illustrate the importance of paying attention to details such as word choice involves comparing Matt 5 (the Sermon on the Mount) with Luke 6 (the Sermon on the Plain). I divide the students into small groups, assign them short parallel pericopes, and ask them to note all the differences between the two versions. One year, a group comparing Matt 5:46–48 and Luke 6:32–36 reported they had not found any differences. I was flabbergasted. "What do you mean you found no differences?" I asked. "There are lots of them! Look again! Whom does Matthew name as the basic example of people whose standard of righteousness believers should exceed? Tax collectors and gentiles. Whom does Luke name? Sinners. In what way does Matthew ask believers to imitate God? By being perfect. What about Luke? By being merciful." The occasion turned into a helpful teaching moment. We discussed how those subtle differences—differences that had not even registered with the students—had a significant effect for analysis. The word choices revealed information about the intended audiences of Matthew and Luke as well as their attitudes toward the law and the prophets. The exercise also exposed a hermeneutical circle. Without a larger context, such as the implied audience, students could not recognize the text-level differences. Yet the context itself emerges from analyzing text-level differences. As the students develop facility in close reading, it inspires them to inquire more deeply into the texts.

The primary writing assignment for Biblical Texts and Contexts builds on those close reading skills and helps students to explore one of the themes of the course in detail. In the "What does the Bible say about ... ?" assignment, students select from a list of social issues on which the Bible is brought to bear. These include marriage, homosexuality, poverty, slavery, women's leadership, political leadership, holy war, sexual violence, and end of the world. Once they select their topic, students research Bible passages that address their topic from a variety of angles. I scaffold the assignment into four exegesis exercises. The first exercise requires students to identify passages relevant to their topic and to start investigating research sources. To help students acquire basic information literacy for biblical studies, we talk about why open, free internet resources are usually inappropriate for academic research, and I orient them to the library databases.[9] The first exercise allows me to help them curate the biblical passages to a manageable number (two or three) and give further resource suggestions.

Exercises 2–4 lead students through various exegetical methods. In the second, students explore literary approaches to the text, including word studies and various literary and narrative features. The third requires them to research historical and socioeconomic approaches. The fourth addresses ideological and theological issues, including reader response, for which they refer to a social-location inventory they completed earlier in the semester. Students do most of their research in the course of completing the exercises.

As they write their paper, students must articulate a clear thesis and support it with at least two of the exegetical approaches from the exercises. Students seem to struggle with the concept of a thesis, so each year I spend time explaining it. For the "What does the Bible say about … ?" project, I encourage them to develop analytical rather than argumentative theses. Instead of arguing a position ("The Bible says homosexuality is wrong"), they should make an analytical claim ("Many of the biblical passages associate same-sex relations with idolatry"). This approach encourages nuance in analysis of some of the hot-button topics and recognition of the diversity of voices in the biblical texts. As students apply various exegetical methods, they begin to perceive complexities in the passages they study. They appreciate the contribution of biblical studies to discussions of social issues in which the Bible is too often made to speak with one voice and without context. The "What does the Bible say about … ?" project constitutes a major proportion of the course, helping students address the Foundations questions and improve their communication skills. The written assignment is highly scaffolded, with professor feedback on four exegesis exercises and a draft. Students writing on the same topic also review each other's drafts. Finally, they submit a revised version. The feedback helps students navigate the exegetical approaches, which requires

---

9. See Steve Jung's essay in this volume.

most of them to read the texts in new ways. It also improves their writing, especially in terms of crafting a thesis and organizing an argument. Recently one of our majors said that the exegesis papers he wrote with me were the hardest research papers he had written at the university, but that they really helped him be a better writer in all his classes. The student's testimony underscores research suggesting that well-designed, challenging assignments that require a significant student investment result in improved student learning.[10]

The oral assignments in Biblical Texts and Contexts serve the dual purpose of helping students to interact with questions of the discipline and to improve their public speaking. Formal and informal assignments give students multiple opportunities to practice speaking. The formal assignment is part of the "What does the Bible say about … ?" project. The students present the thesis and research from their paper with introductions and structure to engage a listening audience. Their presentations are recorded for potential use in the written and oral communication portfolio. They may use visual aids to support their presentation, but it is not mandatory. They must cite their sources orally, however, as required for the written and oral communication portfolios. Because of the significant scaffolding that underlies the project as a whole, the oral presentations are generally of high quality. The topical focus of the project helps students to develop a clear central point, and writing the paper helps them to consider the organization of the argument.

Informal oral communication assignments include short presentations about articles found on the Society of Biblical Literature's Bible Odyssey website.[11] Each two-minute presentation must contain an introduction, a conclusion, and five major points from the article. Students present four articles over the course of several weeks. The assignment effectively builds skills in several ways. First, since the Bible Odyssey articles are geared toward a general audience, students can easily understand and explain the content. Second, the tight structure and time limit keep students focused. Third, the multiple opportunities to present give them practice at oral presentations. Instructor feedback and repeated attempts lead to noticeable improvement from the first to the fourth presentation. Finally, the exercise

---

10. Daniel F. Sullivan and Kate Drezek McConnell, "It's the Assignments—A Ubiquitous and Inexpensive Strategy to Significantly Improve Higher-Order Learning," *Change* 50.5 (2018): 17–18.

11. Bible Odyssey, Society of Biblical Literature, http://bibleodyssey.org/.

introduces students to a high-quality, accessible resource that they can continue to consult after the course.

The final assignment addresses the LEAP goal of creative thinking. In lieu of a final exam, students complete a Midrash project. As in the M-source first-year seminar project, students select a passage and provide a creative interpretation, which they then present to the class during the final exam period. In one of the best projects, a student choreographed a dance depicting the woman who washed Jesus's feet and dried them with her hair. Students have written and performed songs. Another used Minecraft to create a model of the tabernacle. Students are able to display the analytical skills developed over the course of the semester in a creative medium, making the Midrash project an effective final assignment for a Foundations course.

Themes/Explorations:
Paul and the Epistles, Old Testament Interpretation, and Jesus and the Gospels

In the junior year, the emphasis shifts to integrating knowledge across the curriculum. The Integrative Core has seen two iterations of this level: Themes and Explorations. For Themes, students took two courses on the same theme in different disciplines. The courses continued to build disciplinary knowledge while leading students toward integration between disciplines around a common topic. Explorations courses focus on values and reasoning or diversity and global learning. Students take one course from each category. Although the courses are not linked, each still emphasizes integration. Values-and-reasoning courses explore how belief systems shape the construction and perception of knowledge. They also address ethical perspectives. Explorations courses (as did Themes courses) continue to develop communication and critical thinking while emphasizing collaboration.[12] They also address the LEAP outcome of personal and social responsibility.

I have taught my three upper-level Bible courses—Paul and the Epistles, Old Testament Interpretation, and Jesus and the Gospels—at the

---

12. The option to use a study-abroad experience to fulfill one of the theme or explorations courses incorporates another high-impact practice (Kuh, O'Donnell, and Schneider, "HIPs at Ten," 10).

Themes/Exploration level. Paul and the Epistles fits with the theme "Personhood and the State," and Old Testament Interpretation (focused on Deuteronomistic History) fits with the theme "War and Peace." All three courses now function as values-and-reasoning Explorations with very similar goals and assignments.

The Themes/Explorations level builds on the Foundations level to help students improve their written and oral communication and critical thinking skills. In each of the upper-level Bible classes, students write an exegesis paper. Since few students have any familiarity with this form of close text analysis, I provide a curated list of passages that are amenable to the approaches I assign. These passages range from ten verses to a whole chapter. The paper is scaffolded with four exegesis exercises similar to those for the "What does the Bible say about … ?" project. In the first, the students identify their pericope, develop some preliminary questions they would like to explore, and compile a preliminary bibliography. I help students focus on questions appropriate for exegetical research and provide additional source suggestions. The other three exercises lead them through various approaches: literary, historical, socioeconomic, ideological, and reader response. Students write a draft and final version of the exegesis paper. I provide feedback at each stage on both content and writing with a focus on thesis development and organization. The paper is challenging, especially for students from majors that require little writing, but the multiple stages help them succeed.

Students sharpen their oral communication skills with informal and formal speaking opportunities. In a less formal assignment, they present scholarly articles in the context of class discussion. Students provide a summary and critique of an article and raise questions for discussion. Because they have more than one opportunity to present, they can incorporate feedback from the first presentation to improve the next. Each course also has a major collaborative presentation that requires analysis and application. For Paul, the students present about one of the epistles. They provide historical context about the community to which it was written, an analysis of the major themes in the letter, and at least one example of how those themes connect to contemporary issues. In the Old Testament Interpretation class, students present a modern case of holy war, such as the Troubles in Northern Ireland, the Boko Haram insurgency in Nigeria, or conflicts in Myanmar and Sri Lanka. They compare and contrast these conflicts with holy wars described in the Deuteronomistic History. In Jesus and the Gospels, they present a visual representation of one gospel's passion narrative. Students have created a video news-cast reporting on the passion events, dramatized a reading, and crafted a series of images. Translation of a gospel's perspective into a different medium requires both close reading of the text and the ability to adapt and apply the material.

Other assignments focus on Themes/Explorations goals of critical and creative thinking and ethical reasoning. Students in the Paul class write their own epistles. They must include quotations from four of Paul's letters. They can write either as Paul to one of their own contemporary communities or as if from one of Paul's communities in reply to Paul. Most of them opt for the former, which allows them to integrate and apply Paul's writings to communities such as their fraternity, their home church, or the university. They address such issues as conflict, discrimination, and selfishness. Similarly, Jesus and the Gospels students write their own gospels. They identify an intended audience and include quotations from at least three canonical gospels and one noncanonical gospel. Some students opt to create a children's gospel with illustrations. Others address their gospel to their peers. They decide how they want to represent Jesus to that audience and identify relevant aspects of the story to include. For both the epistle and the gospel, students write a reflection explaining their intended audience, their purposes in writing, and how they tailored their content and style for effective communication. The assignments require careful analysis and creative adaptation of the biblical texts. Students often comment on how much it means to be able to connect personally with the text.

A final assignment type focuses on integration, a significant out-come for the Theme classes. Integration of disciplinary perspectives in the Themes prepares students to work collaboratively on complex problems at the fourth-year capstone level. Students in Old Testament Interpreta-tion write a reflective essay about war and peace, integrating ideas from the class. In their exegesis papers, they use multiple interpretive approaches to biblical texts. In their group presentations, they apply these approaches to modern situations of holy war. In the reflective essay, they discuss the concepts of war and peace more broadly. If they have taken another course in the Theme, they also discuss how the different perspectives of the two disciplines contribute to their understanding of the issues. In Paul and the Epistles, the integrative assignment is a creative collaborative project that addresses some aspect of the state or personhood, such as power, gender, sexuality, ethnicity, and slavery. One group of students had taken Literature and Human Rights as the other course in the Theme. For their project, they integrated the two disciplines by writing a set of diaries from people in different situations of empire or oppression. One was from the time of Paul in the Roman Empire. Another was set in the Japanese Empire. A third was a contemporary person who read Paul's epistles while facing abuse. The diaries connected common themes from both courses. In an Explorations class, I encourage students to create projects that integrate skills and perspectives from their majors. A group of religious studies majors created a Paulbook page, on which Paul responded to questions and comments from individual Corinthians, Philippians, and Thessalonians. They used this creative project to address serious concerns about inclusion and community cohesion with a touch of humor. Another group of communication majors developed public-service announcement podcasts on issues of diversity and inclusion, basing them on Paul's epistles. Political science majors designed a campaign strategy for Paul. All of these assignments help students to connect biblical studies with other aspects of their education. They not only serve the LEAP outcomes for integration, but they also emphasize the relevance of biblical studies to other academic disciplines.

Conclusion

Biblical studies courses fit perfectly into a LEAP-based curriculum. The discipline's core competencies of close reading, analysis, cultural context, and multivalent interpretation align closely with LEAP Essential Learning Outcome goals. Biblical studies promotes knowledge of human cultures using texts that raise big questions about human experience and the world. The text-based nature of the field fosters development of intellectual skills, such as critical thinking, inquiry and analysis, and written and oral communication. Creative interpretation engages students in inquiry and increases their facility with analysis. Understanding the Bible and its contexts, ancient and modern, helps students develop ethical reasoning and intercultural knowledge, and biblical studies regularly integrates perspectives across disciplines to address complex issues. As part of my institution's LEAP-based Integrative Core, my courses foster LEAP outcomes while involving students in academic study of the Bible. My students develop lasting values, attitudes, and skills, and I demonstrate the relevance of biblical studies for undergraduate education in the twenty-first century.

Bibliography

Association of American Colleges and Universities. *College Learning for the New Global Century: A Report from the National Leadership Council for Liberal Education and America's Promise.* 2007. https://tinyurl.com/SBL03108f.

Bible Odyssey. Society of Biblical Literature. http://bibleodyssey.org/.

Grouling, Jennifer. "The Path to Competency-Based Certification: A Look at the LEAP Challenge and the VALUE Rubric for Written Communication." *JWA* 10 (2017). https://tinyurl.com/SBL03108g.

Kuh, George, Ken O'Donnell, and Carol Geary Schneider. "HIPs at Ten." *Change* 49.5 (2017): 8–16.

"The LEAP Vision for Learning: Outcomes, Practices, Impact, and Employer's Views." American Association of Colleges and Universities, 2011. https://tinyurl.com/SBL03108e.

Rhodes, Terrel. *Assessing Outcomes and Improving Achievement: Tips and Tools for Using Rubrics.* Washington, DC: Association of American Colleges and Universities, 2010.

Sullivan, Daniel F., and Kate Drezek McConnell. "It's the Assignments—A Ubiquitous and Inexpensive Strategy to Significantly Improve Higher-Order Learning." *Change* 50.5 (2018): 16–23.

"VALUE Rubrics." Association of American Colleges and Universities. https://www.aacu.org/value-rubrics.

Thinking Critically about Gender and Biblical Interpretation

Jocelyn McWhirter

Teaching biblical studies is hard. Not many people view the Bible from a scholar's perspective, and undergraduates are no exception.[1] When instructors add gender to the course topic, teaching the Bible gets even harder. It personally affects those students who happily adhere to traditional sex and gender norms as well as others who have broken with customs that they consider outmoded, restrictive, and unjust. It even affects those who publicly acknowledge their family's values while privately flouting them. Nobody comes to an upper-level course on gender and biblical interpretation without some predisposition.

When I agreed to teach an already-existing course titled Gender and Biblical Interpretation, therefore, I resolved not to let any particular predisposition dominate the agenda. I did not want to make the course into an advocacy platform for progressive, traditionalist, feminist, or any other kind of argument. I wanted to expose students to all kinds of interpretations along with the commitments that generate them, the arguments that support them, and their implications for the lived experience of Jews and Christians who look to the Scriptures for guidance. I also wanted to recognize their implications for my students' experiences as they interacted with the biblical texts, the arguments of scholars and religious specialists, and the discourse of their peers. In this chapter, I will explain how I have taught my students to think critically about gender and biblical interpretation within an undergraduate liberal arts context and the discipline of biblical studies. I will explain my critical approach to biblical texts that

---

1. John Van Maaren addresses this issue in his article "Transformative Concepts and Troublesome Knowledge: Toward a Threshold Concept Framework for Biblical Studies," *WabJT* 1 (2020): 61–78, https://tinyurl.com/SBL03108h.

raise issues about sex and gender, and I will present techniques for analyzing the perspectives of interpreters from various social locations and advocacy positions. By introducing students to the concept of discourse as advocacy and then inviting them to analyze and evaluate the discourse of the Bible and its interpreters, I effectively engage them in thinking critically about sex, gender, and biblical interpretation.

Institutional Context

I teach at a small, residential, undergraduate liberal arts college. Our purpose statement speaks eloquently of our values, especially of "thinking logically, imaginatively, and humanely ... in a residential setting; a supportive, intellectually stimulating community which exhibits and prizes curiosity, creativity, dissent and diversity." Students learn from "Western and other intellectual and spiritual traditions" while being encouraged "to question and challenge them, to evaluate ethically the social uses they serve and the ends they advocate." "The primary responsibility of students ... is to develop mastery in the methods by which knowledge is acquired, critically evaluated, and appropriately applied."[2]

These purposes, articulated in 1993, cohere with the American Association of Colleges and Universities LEAP Essential Learning Outcomes generated fifteen years later. LEAP is a "national public advocacy and campus action initiative" that "champions the importance of a liberal education—for individual students and for a nation dependent on economic creativity and democratic vitality."[3] According to LEAP's founding documents, one of the "Essential Learning Outcomes" of a liberal arts education is "critical and creative thinking."[4] To think critically about a position is, in part, to analyze one's "own and others' assumptions" and to evaluate "the relevance of contexts," whether "historical, ethical, political, cultural, environmental, or circumstantial."[5] This is what I envisioned for Gender and Biblical Interpretation—that students would analyze various and often

---

2. "The Purpose of the College," Albion College, https://tinyurl.com/SBL03108i.

3. "Liberal Education and America's Promise," American Association of Colleges and Universities, https://tinyurl.com/SBL03108j.

4. "Essential Learning Outcomes," American Association of Colleges and Universities, https://tinyurl.com/SBL03108k.

5. "Critical Thinking VALUE Rubric," American Association of Colleges and Universities, https://tinyurl.com/SBL03108l.

prescriptive Bible interpretations around sex, sexuality, and gender while evaluating the contexts that have generated them, applied them, and often struggled with them.

Having established this goal, I needed to examine the course's constraints. Gender and Biblical Interpretation had to answer this catalog description: "Methods of biblical interpretation and their relation to gender construct in society and biblical authority."[6] This description was broad enough to accommodate my intention to address hermeneutics, assumptions and biases, and the prescriptive use of the Bible in religious communities.

Less flexible were the constraints imposed by the college's gender studies core requirement. Courses that fulfill this requirement, as does Gender and Biblical Interpretation, must

1.   foster inquiry into the cultural construction of gender;
2.   focus on the perspectives that gender brings to the discipline;
3.   place the issues of gender in their historical context.[7]

As restrictive as they are, these criteria still fit my hermeneutical and philosophical agenda. They did not ask me to advocate any political position or indeed any values other than critical inquiry into gender constructs and biblical interpretation with attention to historical and cultural location.

Other course constraints devolved from our department's mission, its curriculum, the college's scheduling system, and classroom options. I did not have much choice about the department's mission, although I was comfortable with it. In brief, we operate within a historically Methodist institution yet "are concerned with the academic study of religion." "Our department does not promote any particular 'brand' of theology or spirituality.... We encourage our students to explore religion using various modes of analysis including historical-critical, philosophical, and comparative approaches that keep the life of the mind and the life of the soul in creative tension."[8] Since I was charged with engaging a religiously diverse group of students in the academic study of gender and biblical interpre-

---

6. "RS 320: Gender and Biblical Interpretation," Albion College, https://tinyurl.com/SBL03108m.

7. "Academics at Albion College," Albion College, https://tinyurl.com/SBL03108n.

8. "Academics at Albion College."

tation, I decided that we would read representative interpretations from Jewish, Roman Catholic, and Protestant traditions.

I did not have much choice about the department curriculum, either. Because we are largely a service department, we shun prerequisites. I knew that, in a 300-level course, I could expect mostly upper-class students with varying degrees of biblical literacy and exposure to the academic study of religion. Many would enroll solely to fulfill their gender studies requirement. As with any other course I teach, I could assume nothing about students' backgrounds or their interest in the topic at hand.

When it came to the course schedule and classroom assignment, I was able to negotiate. I opted for biweekly two-hour meetings over the course of the semester. This schedule would allow us to devote ample time to each topic. I also planned to end the first hour with a ten-minute break—an opportunity to stretch, recharge with caffeine, eat a snack, and enjoy each other's company (for those of us who could break away from our infernal electronic devices). I always try to schedule my classes in a room with movable desks so that we can sit in a large circle and easily break into small groups. The blackboard, where we construct knowledge, is the center of attention; the video screen, where we view images, is off to one side.

Once I had articulated my vision, surveyed the course constraints, and considered the student demographics and classroom environment, I settled on four learning outcomes. By the end of the semester, students would be able to

1. interpret biblical texts in light of their historical contexts;
2. analyze arguments that appeal to these texts;
3. evaluate the ethical implications of these arguments; and
4. apply their conclusions to their own lives.

These student learning outcomes reflected my intended focus on critical thinking about interpretation, its contexts, its warrants, its ends, and its personal and social implications. I was now ready to design a course that would engage students with the discipline of biblical studies, biblical texts that raise issues about sex and gender, and the Bible interpreters who address those issues.

Gender and Biblical Studies

My perspective on the relationship between gender and biblical studies has been influenced primarily by the Christian scholars Andrew K. M. Adam, Donald Juel, and Mary Ann Tolbert. Adam was one of my graduate school instructors. I came to agree with him that "the inherent ambiguity of human perception and communication renders them unfit elements for anything so rigid as a foundation." "Science and reason are inevitably constituted by the intellectual traditions in which they stand, are implicated in (personal and) political struggles, and are inevitably subject to 'subjective' biases in countless ways." The biblical text, the world behind the text, the author, the reader: all are constructs. We have no truths, no realities; only arguments. Therefore, we cannot propound correct interpretations. "At most," says Adam, "we can hope to devise a theory that clarifies why some interpretations seem more persuasive than others, and how we can learn to generate and adopt these more convincing interpretations."[9] For Adam, a "more convincing" interpretation is aesthetically pleasing: "rich in detail and nuance"; "illuminating and evocative"; ethically "commendable."[10]

Juel was my dissertation director. In his inaugural address at Princeton Theological Seminary, he questioned the value of biblical criticism for establishing the absolute truth about God's will and ways. "I am suspicious of foundational language," he said,

> as though our reading of the Bible will yield solid, immovable rocks on which to locate our edifices. Living with the Scriptures is more like sailing than like building cathedrals. We don't have control over the elements—just enough to navigate in the face of surprising shifts of wind and changed water conditions. Some would perhaps hope for more stability, but for sailors bedrock is where sunken ships lie.

This hermeneutic guided his exegetical practice, informed as it was by his familiarity with Greek, Israel's Scriptures, and first-century Jewish tradition. "We have … our wits," he said, "some suggestions offered by the host of witnesses that surrounds us, and the promise that the Spirit of truth will

---

9. Andrew K. M. Adam, *What Is Postmodern Biblical Criticism?*, GBS (Minneapolis: Fortress, 1995), 7, 15, 23.

10. Andrew K. M. Adam, *Making Sense of New Testament Theology: "Modern" Problems and Prospects*, StABH 11 (Macon, GA: Mercer University Press, 1995), 184, 186.

lead us into the truth."[11] He was known for interpretations "rich in detail and nuance," "illuminating and evocative," and ethically "commendable."

I have never met Tolbert. Having been trained by Adam and Juel, however, I was ready to accept her application of their hermeneutical principles to feminist hermeneutics. "*All* interpretations are 'subjective,'" writes Tolbert. "All readings are influenced by the vested interests and concerns of the interpreter." "All scholarship is advocacy." "It is only those whose very being (e.g., black, female, Native American) prevents them from fully participating in the dominant cultural structure ... who experience the *aporia* of life and who consequently understand 'reality' to be ideologically formulated."[12]

The hermeneutical principles articulated by Adam, Juel, and Tolbert open up the possibility for critical thinking; that is, attention to vested interests and concerns (our own and those of others) and the contexts for the production and interpretation of the Bible. In the second week of class, therefore, I introduce students to these principles by having them read Tolbert's essay, "Defining the Problem: The Bible and Feminist Hermeneutics."[13] I find that most students agree with Tolbert about unavoidable subjectivity. The idea is not a "disorienting dilemma" for them as it would have been for me at their age.[14] Most students tend to believe that we all have our own opinions and that we should not dictate the opinions of others.[15]

More disorienting for students is the idea that all scholarship is advocacy. In class, therefore, I argue for critical thinking. If we are not in college to learn the truth, then we are there to be persuaded and to persuade. It follows that we might want to train ourselves to examine assumptions—our

---

11. Donald H. Juel, "Your Word Is Truth: Some Reflections on a Hard Saying," in *Shaping the Scriptural Imagination*, ed. Shane Berg and Matthew L. Skinner (Waco: Baylor University Press, 2011), 30–31.

12. Mary Ann Tolbert, "Defining the Problem: The Bible and Feminist Hermeneutics," *Semeia* 28 (1983): 117–20.

13. Tolbert, "Defining the Problem," 113–26.

14. For the expression "disorienting dilemma," see Stephen Brookfield, *Teaching for Critical Thinking: Tools and Techniques to Help Students Question Their Assumptions* (San Francisco: Jossey-Bass, 2012), 71–73.

15. This claim is borne out in a 2014 social-scientific study of American college students, 70 percent of whom described themselves as open-minded. See Corey Seemiller and Meghan Grace, *Generation Z Goes to College* (San Francisco: Jossey-Bass, 2016), 10.

own and those of others—and to pay attention to contexts, whether historical, political, cultural, or circumstantial. We might want to learn what constitutes convincing evidence, how to draw convincing conclusions from that evidence, how to evaluate our conclusions for ethical integrity, and how to express ourselves clearly and persuasively. If we do, we may be able to avoid not only adopting other people's advocacy positions as received truth but also positing our own advocacy positions without careful consideration and compelling rhetoric.

Thinking Critically about Gender and Biblical Interpretation

Critical thinking must be learned, especially in the field of biblical studies. Most of us enter the discipline taking so much for granted: our beliefs, our understanding of religious tradition, and how our beliefs and traditions dictate our personal and political commitments. We are not used to analyzing assumptions, either our own or those of our families, teachers, and faith communities. We see our beliefs and commitments as matters of personal choice without recognizing the influences of history, culture, politics, and circumstances. Especially personal are our beliefs about God, the Bible, sex, sexuality, and gender. It takes courage for us to recognize and analyze our assumptions, to be open to alternative perspectives, and to contemplate changes in faith and practice.[16]

In Gender and Biblical Interpretation, then, we start with our assumptions about whether sexual identity and gender expression are biologically or socially determined. Most students are open to examining arguments from sociology and cognitive psychology. They easily recognize that the gender norms in our society have changed drastically within the last seventy years. This leads to the realization that the Bible reflects norms that are two to three thousand years old. Religious communities that believe in the Bible as the word of God are thus faced with the challenge of interpreting an ancient document and applying its precepts in a modern world.

Since that challenge opens up the topic of biblical hermeneutics, we turn to the contexts in which the Bible has been written and interpreted. In our three-day unit on hermeneutics, we outline the authoritative texts for Jews (Tanak and Talmud), Roman Catholics (Old and New Testaments, Deuterocanonical books, and official church doctrine), and Protestants

---

16. Brookfield, *Teaching for Critical Thinking*, 225.

(Old and New Testaments). We review the histories of these texts. We also generalize about conservative and liberal assumptions concerning their authority: that theological conservatives tend to regard their sacred texts as the revealed word of God, while theological liberals tend to regard them as, in the words of Marcus Borg, "a human product," "generated in response to God."[17] We pay attention to feminist hermeneutics, defined by Tolbert as "a reading of a text ... in light of the oppressive structures of patriarchal society" according to a biblical tradition that "has informed liberation, the infinite worth of the individual, and the call to fight against evil."[18] It becomes obvious that these various assumptions will generate differing interpretations of the Bible and understandings of how Christians or Jews ought to appropriate it.

As we begin thinking critically about gender and biblical interpretation, I use a number of techniques to promote classroom learning. These include interactive lectures, diagrams and drawings on the board, out-loud reading of assigned biblical texts and scholarly interpretations, viewing and listening to interpretations by visual and musical artists, small group discussions, and individual reflections in weekly journal entries. In a course with topics that include various kinds of sexual violence, I issue trigger warnings as appropriate. I also practice devil's advocacy as described by Stephen Brookfield in his book *Teaching for Critical Thinking*. According to Brookfield, "Devil's Advocacy deliberately articulates a different perspective on what [someone] has just said or opens up questions about it."[19] I consistently push students to examine all claims from a variety of perspectives, including the perspectives of the Jewish, Catholic, and Protestant interpreters whose work they have read.

Other techniques come into play as we move on to units concerning gender roles in the family, gender roles in the public sphere, sex and sexuality, and gender and God. For example, one of the first cultural contexts we encounter in the Bible is the patrilineal descent organization reflected in the stories of Israel's patriarchs and matriarchs. Patrilineal descent organization was designed to help propertied families prosper in a primitive agrarian society in which one's sex determined one's role

---

17. Marcus Borg, *Reading the Bible Again for the First Time: Taking the Bible Seriously but Not Literally* (New York: HarperCollins, 2001), 27.

18. Tolbert, "Defining the Problem," 119–20.

19. Brookfield, *Teaching for Critical Thinking*, 66–67.

in the household economy. Men tended flocks and cultivated fields; women cared for the needs of the family, bearing and nurturing its children. Of those children, the sons would inherit their father's property. The oldest son would receive most of it while the younger sons would gain equal shares of the remainder. Daughters were married into other families.[20] These social norms increased the chances that at least the oldest son would possess adequate resources to support his offspring.

Patrilineal descent organization is ripe for the kind of ideology critique advocated by Brookfield. In an ideology critique, says Brookfield, "learners are presented with a typical organizational or community practice. [They] are asked to identify what the practice is intended to accomplish, who benefits from it, who is harmed by it, what inconsistencies [and] contradictions are embedded in the practice, why these are ignored, and how it could be reconfigured to be more socially just."[21] Keeping in mind that patrilineal descent organization is meant to assure that a man's property stays within his family, students perform ideology critique when they contemplate the privileges of the patriarchs Abraham, Isaac, Jacob, and Judah along with the expectations of their senior wives Sarah, Rebekah, and Leah together with their oldest sons Isaac, Esau, Reuben, and Er. Students also turn ideology critique on the compromised status of the Egyptian slave Hagar, the second son and then son-in-law Jacob, and Er's childless widow, Tamar. They come to appreciate how Hagar, Jacob, and Tamar attempt to improve their status.

Students then add to the critique by evaluating various interpretations of the Genesis stories. Why, for example, does twentieth-century German man Gerhard von Rad regard Hagar as "wild," "colorful," "raw-boned," "rebellious," and "proud"? Why does he argue that her flight from Sarah "offends against right and custom," that God instructs her to return in order to rectify the irregularity, and that God saves Ishmael because of God's promises to Abraham?[22] Why does Renita Weems, an African American woman writing later in the century, view Sarah and Hagar through a

---

20. Gale A. Yee, "Hosea," in *Women's Bible Commentary*, ed. Carol A. Newsom, Sharon H. Ringe, and Jacqueline E. Lapsley, 3rd ed. (Louisville: Westminster John Knox, 2012), 301.

21. Stephen Brookfield, "Developing Critical Thinkers," 2012, https://tinyurl.com/SBL03108a1, 18.

22. Gerhard von Rad, *Genesis: A Commentary*, OTL (Philadelphia: Westminster, 1961), 189, 191–92.

lens of race and social class, asserting that Hagar returns to Sarah because she has learned to define herself as a slave and that God saves Ishmael because God hears the cry of oppressed children?[23] And why does Susan Niditch, an American Reform Jewish woman writing in 1998, emphasize God's care for the woman and her child who struggle "on the fringes"?[24] To what extent can we judge these arguments as right or wrong? How does each argument comment on the strengths and weaknesses of a system that favors propertied fathers and their oldest sons?

From gender roles in the family, we move on to gender roles in the public sphere: prophet, judge, king, queen, disciple, and leader in the early church. This last topic lends itself to a critical-thinking exercise that Brookfield calls critical debate. "Here," he says, "the teacher chooses a contentious issue within the field of study on which opinion is divided among scholars or practitioners, and then she frames this issue as a debate motion."[25] In Gender and Biblical Interpretation, we debate the following motion: "Protestant churches should not ordain female ministers." (The debate is restricted to Protestant Christians since in other branches of the church the topic is not officially a matter for debate.)

In class, I randomly assign a position to each student. The student may or may not agree with that position. Either way, they must follow individualized instructions to research a particular Bible passage used to defend it. They read not only the passage itself but also the work of various interpreters who argue one or both sides of the position based on that passage. They then construct a thirty-second argument either defending their assigned position or rebutting the opposite position.

Next, they organize themselves into teams: one in support of women's ordination, the other against. Within each team, they sort themselves by three types of arguments:

1. This is what God intended when God created men and women.
2. This is how the early church actually operated.
3. These were the instructions given by Paul.

---

23. Renita J. Weems, *Just a Sister Away: A Womanist Vision of Women's Relationships in the Bible* (San Diego: LuraMedia, 1988), 2–6, 13, 18–19.

24. Susan Niditch, "Genesis," in Newsom, Ringe, and Lapsley, *Women's Bible Commentary*, 36.

25. Brookfield, *Teaching for Critical Thinking*, 110–11.

This typology gives them some idea of the kinds of arguments that will govern the debate as a whole as well as where they should insert their own argument. Once the teams are ready, the side arguing against women's ordination leads off, with its first point based on the creation story. The debate unfolds from there, with students from alternating teams each laying out one argument for or against, either introducing new points or rebutting previous points with evidence from the Bible and its interpreters. With thirty arguments in all, I find that the debate takes about fifteen minutes.

In Brookfield's exercise, students end a critical debate by voting on the motion and sharing what they learned. In my class, we end by discussing how the biblical authors' agendas (political and theological) and social contexts seem to drive their portrayals of male and female authority, how exegetes' agendas and social contexts seem to drive their interpretation of those portrayals, and how (if at all) we can make convincing arguments from the Bible about women's ordination. Students generally use their weekly journal entries to reflect on how they experienced the debate.

After mid-term, we turn to the unit on sex and sexuality. Topics include purity regulations, the Song of Songs, extramarital sex, adultery, rape, incest, and homosexuality. The session devoted to adultery, rape, and incest includes my favorite exercise of the semester (and perhaps of my entire teaching repertoire): *The Dr. Pill Show*.

The Dr. Pill Show is a form of scenario analysis. In order to conduct a scenario analysis, says Brookfield, "you take a piece of material you are trying to teach and rewrite it as a description of an imagined event in which a fictional character is making a choice. Students are then asked to put themselves in the head of the character and try to identify the assumptions that character might be operating under."[26] In Gender and Biblical Interpretation, we do not have to construct a scenario for adultery, rape, and incest. We have one ready-made in 2 Sam 11–18. We can analyze the characters' choices by hosting the David family on *The Dr. Pill Show*.

Students prepare for the show in class. I divide them into seven small groups. Six groups familiarize themselves with the experience of a member of David's family, focusing on the motivations, choices, and outcomes for David, Bathsheba, Amnon, Absalom, Tamar, or Connie, David's "number-nine concubine." If they wish, they can draw on various theories about ancient customs reflected in the text. They have learned

---

26. Brookfield, *Teaching for Critical Thinking*, 86–87.

that laws about adultery and rape seem to protect the interests of fathers and husbands (such as David and Uriah) in the reproductive potential of their daughters and wives (such as Tamar, Bathsheba, and Connie). Stories about childless women (Tamar becomes one of them) seem to indicate that a woman's status depended on the status of her husband as well as her ability to bear his sons. Rape and adultery laws also seem to presume that the violation of a daughter or a wife (Bathsheba, Tamar, and Connie) amounted to the violation of her father or husband (David and Uriah), that a man (Amnon) who raped a virgin (Tamar) must marry her, and that it was up to a raped woman's male relatives (David and Absalom) to restore the family's honor.[27]

Each of the six groups chooses a representative to play the part of its character on *The Dr. Pill Show*. The rest of the group joins the audience to support their character and heckle the others (all in good fun). I play the role of Dr. Pill McWhirter, seated center stage with the members of the David family arrayed on either side of me. Starting with David and Bathsheba, I interview them all. I let them tell their stories, explain their choices, and hear from the family members affected by those choices. The interviews are interrupted three times by the antics of the seventh group, which has prepared sixty-second spots advertising products that might appeal to tenth-century BCE Judeans. Needless to say, these commercials have the audience (and sometimes Dr. Pill) falling off their chairs.

The comic scenario creates an emotional atmosphere where students can express their feelings about the audacity and impunity of David and his sons. They can question Bathsheba's motives—and their assumptions about those motives—whether she says, "I loved my husband Uriah, but I thought I would be better off with David," or, "How could I refuse the king?" Nobody questions the obvious distress of Tamar and Connie (the number-nine concubine), whose bodies have been violated and whose prospects have been ruined. Everyone learns something—even Dr. Pill, when Bathsheba, questioned about her prospects, once answered, "I have plans for my son Solomon." It dawned on me that the only woman with a "happy" ending is the one whose seducer married her and fathered her son, who then succeeded him as king.

---

27. Yee, "Hosea," 302.

Toward the end of the semester, students have gained a certain level of comfort with thinking critically about gender and biblical interpretation. They have faced some sensitive issues concerning family politics, religious leadership, sex, and sexuality. Now they face what for some is the most sensitive issue of all: language about God. By this point, most students are prepared. They are ready to examine the contexts and assumptions behind titles such as *Lord* and *Father* and metaphors such as warrior, as well as Judith Plaskow's preference for gender-neutral metaphors such as lover, friend, rock, and source.[28] They confront the New Testament portrayal of Jesus as the (masculine) Son of God and Elizabeth A. Johnson's argument that Jesus is (feminine) Sophia personified.[29] They also analyze various views of Mary, the mother of Jesus. She is "retiring," "unobtrusive," and "reticent," "a significant model of ideal Christian womanhood," says Baptist theologian Charles Ryrie.[30] As "the attentive Virgin," "the Virgin in prayer," "the Virgin-Mother," and "the Virgin presenting offerings," Mary is a model for the Church, says Pope Paul VI.[31] "As Mother of the divine Christ," she is Heaven's Queen, says Pope Pius XII.[32] Despite her social compliance with her patriarchal culture, she is called God's "servant" (Luke 1:38), "the spiritual equal of Moses, Abraham, David, and even Jesus himself," says feminist theologian Jane Schaberg.[33]

As students discuss these issues in large and small groups, they address critical questions. What do religious communities gain by adopting either biblical language or alternative language for God? What do they lose? How might we evaluate various views of Mary? Since Mary is primarily portrayed as a mother, how do we assess Susan Garrett's conclusion that "feminine imagery [associated with Mary] is dangerous because (whether intentionally or not) it promotes an ethos in which women are not allowed

---

28. Judith Plaskow, *Standing Again at Sinai: Judaism from a Feminist Perspective* (San Francisco: Harper & Row, 1990), 161, 165.

29. Elizabeth A. Johnson, *She Who Is: The Mystery of God in Feminist Theological Discourse* (New York: Crossroad, 1992), 91.

30. Charles Caldwell Ryrie, *The Role of Women in the Church* (Chicago: Moody, 1970), 23.

31. Paul VI, *Marialis Cultus, Apostolic Exhortation*, 1974, https://tinyurl.com/SBL03108o.

32. Pius XII, *Ad caeli Reginam, Encyclical Letter*, 1954, https://tinyurl.com/SBL03108p.

33. Jane Schaberg, "Luke," in *Women's Bible Commentary*, ed. Carol A. Newsom and Sharon H. Ringe, expanded ed. (Louisville: Westminster John Knox, 1998), 372.

to control their own bodies and their own destinies"?[34] As always, I play
devil's advocate. If students do not jump in with opposing views or challenging questions, I do.

At every stage of the course—from gender roles in the family to
gender roles in the public sphere, sex and sexuality, and gender and
God—students think critically about gender and biblical interpretation.
They examine biblical interpretation in context, whether that context is
a biblical author's, an interpreter's, or their own. I consistently challenge
them to evaluate their conclusions from theological and ethical stand-
points. In the end, students invariably recognize the inherent subjectivity
of interpretation. Most of them have learned to identify "their own and
other's assumptions and several relevant contexts when presenting a position" on gender and biblical interpretation.[35] They have achieved one of
the American Association of Colleges and Universities's Essential Learning Outcomes of a liberal arts education.

Bibliography

"Academics at Albion College." Albion College. https://tinyurl.com/
SBL03108n.
Adam, Andrew K. M. *Making Sense of New Testament Theology: "Modern"
Problems and Prospects.* StABH 11. Macon, GA: Mercer University
Press, 1995.
———. *What Is Postmodern Biblical Criticism?* GBS. Minneapolis: Fortress,
1995.
Borg, Marcus. *Reading the Bible Again for the First Time: Taking the Bible
Seriously but Not Literally.* New York: HarperCollins, 2001.
Brookfield, Stephen. "Developing Critical Thinkers." 2012. https://tinyurl.
com/SBL03108a1.
———. *Teaching for Critical Thinking: Tools and Techniques to Help Stu-
dents Question Their Assumptions.* San Francisco: Jossey-Bass, 2012.
"Critical Thinking VALUE Rubric." American Association of Colleges and
Universities. https://tinyurl.com/SBL03108l.

---

34. Susan R. Garrett, "Revelation," in Newsom and Ringe, *Women's Bible Commentary,* 471.
35. "Critical Thinking VALUE Rubric."

"Essential Learning Outcomes." American Association of Colleges and Universities. https://tinyurl.com/SBL03108k.

Garrett, Susan R. "Revelation." Pages 469–74 in *Women's Bible Commentary*. Expanded ed. Edited by Carol A. Newsom and Sharon H. Ringe. Louisville: Westminster John Knox, 1998.

Johnson, Elizabeth A. *She Who Is: The Mystery of God in Feminist Theological Discourse*. New York: Crossroad, 1992.

Juel, Donald H. "Your Word Is Truth: Some Reflections on a Hard Saying." Pages 13–31 in *Shaping the Scriptural Imagination*. Edited by Shane Berg and Matthew L. Skinner. Waco: Baylor University Press, 2011.

"Liberal Education and America's Promise." American Association of Colleges and Universities. https://tinyurl.com/SBL03108j.

Niditch, Susan. "Genesis." Pages 27–45 in *Women's Bible Commentary*. Edited by Carol A. Newsom, Sharon H. Ringe, and Jacqueline E. Lapsley. 3rd ed. Louisville: Westminster John Knox, 2012.

Paul VI. *Marialis Cultus, Apostolic Exhortation*. 1974. https://tinyurl.com/SBL03108o.

Pius XII. *Ad caeli Reginam, Encyclical Letter*. 1954. https://tinyurl.com/SBL03108p.

Plaskow, Judith. *Standing Again at Sinai: Judaism from a Feminist Perspective*. San Francisco: Harper & Row, 1990.

"The Purpose of the College." Albion College. https://tinyurl.com/SBL03108i.

Rad, Gerhard von. *Genesis: A Commentary*. OTL. Philadelphia: Westminster, 1961.

"RS 320: Gender and Biblical Interpretation." Albion College. https://tinyurl.com/SBL03108m.

Ryrie, Charles Caldwell. *The Role of Women in the Church*. Chicago: Moody, 1970.

Schaberg, Jane. "Luke." Pages 363–80 in *Women's Bible Commentary*. Edited by Carol A. Newsom and Sharon H. Ringe. Expanded ed. Louisville: Westminster John Knox, 1998.

Seemiller, Corey, and Meghan Grace. *Generation Z Goes to College*. San Francisco: Jossey-Bass, 2016.

Tolbert, Mary Ann. "Defining the Problem: The Bible and Feminist Hermeneutics." *Semeia* 28 (1983): 113–26.

Van Maaren, John. "Transformative Concepts and Troublesome Knowledge: Toward a Threshold Concept Framework for Biblical Studies." *WabJT* 1 (2020): 61–78. https://tinyurl.com/SBL03108h.

Weems, Renita J. *Just a Sister Away: A Womanist Vision of Women's Relationships in the Bible*. San Diego: LuraMedia, 1988.

Yee, Gale A. "Hosea." Pages 299–308 in *Women's Bible Commentary*. Edited by Carol A. Newsom, Sharon H. Ringe, and Jacqueline E. Lapsley. 3rd ed. Louisville: Westminster John Knox, 2012.

Bring Back the Trivium!
Rhetoric and Antiauthoritarianism
in Biblical Studies

Christopher M. Jones

In this essay, I explain how I made my undergraduate biblical studies classes more explicitly antiauthoritarian in the wake of Donald Trump's political ascendancy. I began writing it shortly after he was elected president of the United States in 2016. I am now completing it following the 2020 election, and Donald Trump will no longer be president when it is published. Authoritarian tendencies may continue to shape US politics, however, and thus the practices that I have adopted will remain relevant for undergraduate biblical studies pedagogy. Authoritarianism is a perpetual threat to liberal democracy, and US democracy is particularly vulnerable as the country's demographics transition from white majority to majority-minority status.[1] Public liberal arts education, meanwhile, serves as a bulwark of liberal democracy because it promotes broadly liberal values such as free inquiry, epistemic humility, and a shared commitment to truth.

In what follows, I will recount the changes that I made in my approach to teaching and the reasons that I made them. I agree with pedagogical constructivists that people learn by reorienting their deep-level schemata about the world and reintegrating data (old and new) into those schemata. I am also persuaded that prior schemata are most persistent when they are closely connected to a person's identity, and that any attempt to confront such schemata with logic and evidence is unlikely to succeed if students feel that their identity is threatened by course content. So rather than

---

1. Jonathan Knuckey and Komysha Hassan, "Authoritarianism and Support for Trump in the 2016 Presidential Election," *SSJ* 57 (2020): 1–14.

directly confront students' deeply held convictions about the literal truth of the Bible or the nature of political authority, I take an indirect approach that lets them discover for themselves the contingent and contentious processes behind the creation of biblical canons as well as the implications for their own political worldviews. In this way, I hope to create a learning environment that includes students who feel threatened by Trump's politics as well as those who support them, a learning environment in which all students can develop their own rational and evidence-based positions on issues that are important to understanding the Bible and to participating in liberal democracy.

Authoritarian Epistemologies and the Liberal Arts

I begin with a simple premise, one that I have always accepted: biblical studies should be taught as part of a liberal arts education in the United States. Let me now unpack that premise, starting with *biblical studies*. Biblical studies is not the study of the Bible. Biblical studies is, rather, the study of the sociohistorical processes by which various streams of tradition (oral and literary) coalesced into a particular reified category (Scripture), took on particular semifixed forms (canon), and became an ostensibly single and authoritative bound volume (the Bible). I therefore teach Bible courses while interrogating the very concept of Bible.[2] Students who walk into my biblical studies classroom with a Bible in their hands should walk out of it holding a vast network of contingent and contested processes in their minds.

It is this sense of contingency and complexity that makes biblical studies part of the liberal arts. The United States of America is, in theory, a liberal democracy, and the goal of a liberal education should be to prepare students for a lifetime of engaged citizenship.[3] Democratic citizenship, in

---

2. On the distinction between "Bible" and "the Bible," see Timothy Beal, "Cultural-Historical Criticism of the Bible," in *New Meanings from Ancient Texts: Recent Approaches to Biblical Criticisms and Their Applications*, ed. Steven L. McKenzie and John Kaltner (Louisville: Westminster John Knox, 2013), 1–20.

3. William Cronon, "'Only Connect ...' The Goals of a Liberal Education," *AmSchol* 67.4 (1998): 1–6. Etymologically, the idea of liberal arts goes back to classical antiquity, and it refers quite literally to those skills (Latin: *ars*) befitting of a free (Latin: *liberalis*) person. A liberal education was part of what distinguished a free person from a serf or a slave. In this sense, liberal education is a poor fit for an ostensibly egalitarian democratic

turn, depends on our capacity to distinguish opponents from enemies and to recognize that people who disagree with us may still be striving toward a common good. This kind of epistemic humility is one of the factors that distinguishes liberal democracy from authoritarianism, a system in which the highest good is embodied by a leader or a party and is thus enacted through loyalty and obedience.[4] In a liberal society, by contrast, free citizens may believe that they are right in their ideals, their core beliefs, and their policy positions, but they also recognize that all political realities, even those enacted by their party, are by nature incomplete and in process. Liberal democracy is always in process. A public liberal arts or general-education curriculum, then, should prepare citizens to participate together in this process. It should instill epistemic humility and a commitment to disciplined, evidence-based thinking.

Epistemic humility and evidence-based thinking, because they entail a willingness to change our ideological commitments, require that all participants feel some measure of safety and security in expressing their identities. Trumpism has had the opposite effect on students. It divides them and heightens their sense of vulnerability. This is especially true for students from minoritized backgrounds. The Trump administration

---

society that strives for inclusive citizenship. Moreover, the reality of higher education in the United States is that people from socially, economically, and racially privileged groups will have more access to a liberal education and will stand to benefit more from the status that it conveys. Nevertheless, I find that the liberal arts provide a model for what education should look like in a free society. The ideal of inclusive, egalitarian citizenship will only be achieved dialectically. On this point, see Paolo Freire, *Education for Critical Consciousness*, trans. Myra Bergman Ramos (New York: Continuum, 1994), 41–58; Kevin Gannon, *Radical Hope: A Teaching Manifesto*, TLH (Charleston: West Virginia University Press, 2020), 4–7. We start with the tools that we have, and we use them to instill critical consciousness in the people who are statistically most likely to be tomorrow's leaders. On this point, see Katy Swalwell, *Educating Activist Allies: Social Justice Pedagogy with the Suburban and Urban Elite*, CSTS (New York: Routledge, 2013), 12–14. For an overview of the role of the liberal arts in contemporary college education, see "Advocacy for Liberal Education," American Association of Colleges and Universities, https://tinyurl.com/SBL03108q.

4. Since this essay is about the relationship between liberal democracy and the liberal arts, I want to be clear at the outset that I will be using the term *liberal* as it is used in comparative politics, where it refers to political ideologies that support freedom, the consent of the governed, due process, and electoral fair play. It is a distinctly North American convention to use *liberal* to refer to people on the left of the political spectrum.

engaged in a campaign to roll back the rights of minoritized people.[5] Trump's rhetoric concerning race often intimidates minoritized Americans and stokes the fears of white Americans.[6] His presidency emboldened white nationalists, with a corresponding uptick in hate crimes against minoritized Americans.[7] Minoritized students have objective reasons to be more fearful and on edge in an era defined by the Trump presidency and its aftereffects.

Trump's rhetoric has also heightened the sense of vulnerability among students who support him. His is unmistakably the rhetoric of a populist-nationalist demagogue.[8] It has inflamed partisan loyalties by

---

5. This campaign affected a number of groups. For example, Trump claimed that he had done more for black Americans than any other president except Abraham Lincoln, but this claim has met with widespread rebuke. See Rashawn Ray and Keon L. Gilbert, "Has Trump Failed Black Americans?," Brookings Institution, 15 October 2020, https://tinyurl.com/SBL03108r. His administration expedited the deportation of undocumented migrant laborers, eliminating due process in ways that could threaten the status of legal immigrants as well. See Maria Sacchetti, "Trump Administration to Expand Its Power to Deport Undocumented Immigrants," *Washington Post*, 22 July 2019, https://tinyurl.com/SBL03108s. It sought to reverse the Obama-era Deferred Action for Childhood Arrivals (DACA) initiative, which protected roughly 700,000 undocumented people brought to the United States as children. See Brent Kendall, Jess Bravin, and Michelle Hackman, "Trump's Bid to End DACA Blocked by Supreme Court," *Wall Street Journal*, 18 June 2020, https://tinyurl.com/SBL03108t. It attempted to narrow the legal definition of sex discrimination to exclude transgender people from protection. See Stephanie Armour, "Trump Administration Issues Rule to Roll Back Transgender Protections in the Affordable Care Act," *Wall Street Journal*, 12 June 2020, https://tinyurl.com/SBL03108u; Lola Fadulu, "Trump's Rollback of Transgender Rights Extends through Entire Government," *New York Times*, 6 December 2019, https://tinyurl.com/SBL03108v.

6. David Leonhardt and Ian Prasad Philbrick, "Donald Trump's Racism: The Definitive List, Updated," *New York Times*, 15 January 2018, https://tinyurl.com/SBL03108w.

7. Griffin Sims Edwards and Stephen Rushin, "The Effects of President Trump's Election on Hate Crimes," 14 January 2018, https://dx.doi.org/10.2139/ssrn.3102652; Benjamin Newman et al., "The Trump Effect: An Experimental Investigation of the Emboldening Effect of Racially Inflammatory Elite Communication," *BJPS* 50 (2020): 1–22; Adeel Hassan, "Hate-Crime Violence Hits 16-Year High, F.B.I. Reports," *New York Times*, 12 November 2019, https://tinyurl.com/SBL03108x.

8. Robert Rowland, "The Populist and Nationalist Roots of Trump's Rhetoric," *RPA* 22 (2019): 343–88; Lars J. Kristiansen and Bernd Kaussler, "The B——t Doctrine: Fabrications, Lies, and Nonsense in the Age of Trump," *IL* 38 (2018): 15.

othering and scapegoating people outside the core group, particularly by trafficking in the rhetoric of white grievance.[9] Trump's political career began with a baseless denial of the legitimacy of the first black American president. Since that time, his rhetoric has implied that nonwhite people are un-American.[10] Its influence on white nationalist groups has underscored those implications.[11] Trump's rhetoric works by heightening the sense of vulnerability among white Americans and then presenting Trump himself as the only one who can protect them. It has the same impact on our students as it has on the populace at large. It makes many of them feel more vulnerable, more suspicious of those who disagree

---

9. Matthew MacWilliams, "Who Decides When the Party Doesn't? Authoritarian Voters and the Rise of Donald Trump," *PSP* 49 (2016): 716–21.

10. On President Trump's birtherism, see Michael Barbaro, "Donald Trump Clung to 'Birther' Lie for Years, and Still Isn't Apologetic," *New York Times*, 16 September 2016, https://tinyurl.com/SBL03108y. President Trump told four first-year members of Congress (Ilhan Omar, Rashida Tlaib, Alexandria Ocasio-Cortez, and Ayanna S. Pressley) to "go back and help fix the totally broken and crime infested places from which they came." Of the four, all are American citizens and all but one was born in the United States. See Katie Rogers and Nicholas Fandos, "Trump Tells Congresswomen to 'Go Back' to the Countries They Came From," *New York Times*, 14 July 2019, https://tinyurl.com/SBL03108z. As a candidate, Trump called for a "total and complete shutdown" of Muslims traveling to the United States, and his campaign clarified that this would apply to immigrants, tourists, and American Muslims currently abroad. See "Donald Trump: Ban All Muslims Entering US," *The Guardian*, 7 December 2015, https://tinyurl.com/SBL03108aa. He argued that Gonzalo Curiel, a US-born judge of Mexican descent, could not be unbiased toward his case because of his campaign's agenda to build a border wall. See Daniel White, "Donald Trump Ramps Up Attacks against Judge in Trump University Case," *Time*, 2 June 2016, https://tinyurl.com/SBL03108ab.

11. Following the "Unite the Right" rally in Charlottesville, in which a white nationalist murdered counterprotester Heather Heyer, the president decried violence and proclaimed that there were "very fine people" on both sides. See Glenn Thrush and Rebecca R. Ruiz, "White House Acts to Stem Fallout from Trump's First Charlottesville Remarks," *New York Times*, 13 August 2017, https://tinyurl.com/SBL03108ac. He appointed a white nationalist, Stephen Miller, as his senior policy adviser. See Michael Edison Hayden, "Stephen Miller's Affinity for White Nationalism Revealed in Leaked Emails," Southern Poverty Law Center, 11 November 2019, https://tinyurl.com/SBL03108ad. For a more in-depth analysis of Trump's relationship with whiteness, see Ibram X. Kendi, "Is This the Beginning of the End of American Racism?," *The Atlantic*, September 2020, https://tinyurl.com/SBL03108ae; Ta-Nehisi Coates, "The First White President," *The Atlantic*, October 2017, https://tinyurl.com/SBL03108af.

with them, and thus less likely to attempt to communicate honestly and openly with one another.

Trump's rhetoric undermines epistemic humility and evidence-based thinking in another way as well: he routinely makes assertions that have no basis in fact. Harry Frankfurt, a philosopher of language, uses the term "b——t" to refer to discourse that has no regard for the truth and that only serves to bolster the speaker's influence.[12] It is not the same thing as lying. A liar knows the truth and attempts to hide it. A person who engages in b——t (in the manner articulated by Frankfurt), by contrast, does not care what is true and says whatever will be beneficial to them at any particular moment. President Trump's penchant for this sort of rhetoric is well documented and has been subject to considerable analysis, both scholarly and journalistic.[13] It is different in both kind and degree from the lies routinely told by past presidents.[14] It is, moreover, an expression of his authoritarian tendencies. B——t is a common tactic in authoritarian states because it serves two purposes: it undermines anybody's claim to know the truth and it serves as a test of loyalty. Authoritarian leaders invent realities not because they expect people to believe them but because it allows them to see who is willing to spread such claims without question.[15] It is no coincidence that, from the start of his campaign, Trump's most significant base of support has come from voters with marked authoritarian tendencies. A study by Matthew MacWilliams showed that people who value hierarchy over justice and obedience over independent judgment are more likely

---

12. Harry Frankfurt, *On B——t* (Princeton: Princeton University Press, 2005), 33. Frankfurt is on record arguing that Trump's rhetoric is indeed b——t. See Harry G. Frankfurt, "Donald Trump Is BS, Says Expert in BS," *Time*, 16 May 2016, https://tinyurl.com/SBL03108ag.

13. Scholarly articles include Alison MacKenzie and Ibrar Bhatt, "Lies, B——t, and Fake News: Some Epistemological Concerns," *PSE* 2 (2020): 9–13; Chris Gavaler and Nathaniel Goldberg, "Beyond B——t: Donald Trump's Philosophy of Language," *PN* 121 (2017): 22–23; Kristiansen and Kaussler, "B——t Doctrine," 13–52. Journalistic accounts include Matthew Yglesias, "The B——tter in Chief," *Vox*, 30 May 2017, https://tinyurl.com/SBL03108ah; Eric Alterman, "During a Pandemic, Trump's 'B——t' Will Be Deadly," *The Nation*, 12 March 2020, https://tinyurl.com/SBL03108ai; David A. Graham, "On Trump's B——t," *The Atlantic*, 1 July 2019, https://tinyurl.com/SBL03108cv.

14. Kristiansen and Kaussler, "B——t Doctrine," 27–28.

15. Yglesias, "B——tter in Chief."

than average voters to support Trump.[16] These studies do not imply that each of the seventy-one million Americans who voted to reelect Donald Trump in 2020 is an authoritarian. There is a significant overlap, however, between Trump's authoritarian tendencies and the makeup of his coalition—and many college students are part of that coalition.

It would be inappropriate for a public liberal arts instructor to engage in partisan politics or to support one party over another in their curriculum. As a liberal arts teacher, I have embraced an obligation to promote the liberal values that befit citizenship in a democratic society. In particular, I model epistemic humility and a commitment to evidence-based argumentation. In biblical studies, that means confronting the evidence and thinking carefully about it, regardless of whether it supports our prior convictions. Our students rarely enter our classrooms, however, with neutral perspectives on the truth claims that we evaluate or the narratives that we aim to disrupt. For many of our students, the idea that the Bible is multiform and subject to historical contingency poses a direct threat to their core ideals. How do we avoid alienating them? How do we keep them from retreating to the comforting safety of an authoritarian epistemology?

Keeping Students in the Conversation

I will begin answering these questions by addressing how not to use biblical studies classes to resist authoritarianism and promote liberalism. First, professors cannot let partisan political affiliations intrude on pedagogy. As a private citizen, I have all sorts of principled positions on political issues, some of which correspond with a partisan perspective. I do not, however, teach as a private citizen, and I cannot teach students my personal biases. Neither can I circumscribe my students' speech on the basis of partisan political positions. The field we are studying, not partisan political alignments, must define the ideological boundaries of the classroom.[17]

Another approach that I reject is one that focuses on simply confronting students with evidence that runs counter to their prior

---

16. MacWilliams, "Who Decides," 716–21.

17. This epistemic foundation allows me, as professor, to quickly move past (and when necessary even shut down) conversations rooted in racist science, ancient-aliens theories, and other positions that are not taken seriously within the guild of biblical scholarship.

assumptions. We might, for example, integrate a number of interpretations posed by Trump and his supporters into our biblical studies curriculum, and we might devote class time (and graded assignments) to evaluating these interpretations on their merits from the perspective of biblical scholarship. We might also subject the interpretations of Trump's critics (on the right and on the left) to the same standard of critical evaluation. Using such an approach, we might then help all students learn to use their critical-thinking skills to make up their own minds about whether to support or reject the politicians who advance these claims.

I reject this approach for reasons that will be central to my argument in the rest of this essay. Directly confronting our students' ideological biases and partisan commitments is not an effective use of our class time. Far more information flows around us than we have time to process, and partisanship and group affiliation serve as fundamental strategies for information aggregation and filtering. Regina Rini argues that partisan epistemology (by which we attribute greater weight to information shared by people who also share our normative commitments) is a reasonable adaptation in an epistemically nonideal world.[18] It will require institutional reform, particularly in the ways that social media platforms treat the dissemination of demonstrably false claims, to make a substantive impact on the spread of fake news.[19] It is not reasonable to expect a single introductory college class to transform our students into savvy and discerning consumers of information; neither is it desirable to try to convince them not to give priority to information that originates within their ideological bubble.[20] What we can do, as biblical studies teachers, is help our students become more reflective consumers of information. We can model for them the epistemic

---

18. Regina Rini, "Fake News and Partisan Epistemology," *KIEJ* 27.2 supplement (2017): E-43–E-64. Rini argues that the spread of fake news (i.e., information that mimics the form of traditional media but is known by its creators to be substantially false) relies on essentially virtuous epistemic practices on the part of consumers, such as trust in individual testimony and a reasonable preference for partisanship. Rini claims that partisan epistemology is reasonable because the human brain cannot possibly evaluate every truth claim that it encounters, and copartisans who (we assume) share many of our own core values seem more likely to be reliable.

19. Rini, "Fake News and Partisan Epistemology," E-55–E-58.

20. Sarah McGrew et al., "The Challenge That's Bigger Than Fake News: Civic Reasoning in a Social Media Environment," *AE* (Fall 2017), https://tinyurl.com/SBL03108aj.

humility that allows a person to explore the full complexity of an issue in ways that transcend its partisan framing.[21]

What does this sort of teaching look like in practice? First of all, it involves creating a truly constructivist classroom, one in which knowledge production is a shared and decentered endeavor. A constructivist approach assumes that students learn by developing new deep-level cognitive frameworks for understanding course content.[22] In order to develop those new frameworks, students need space to recognize the inadequacy of their prior frameworks. We must resist the urge, common among subject-area experts, to correct our students' factual and logical errors while they are in the process of constructing their own interpretations of the content that they are learning. My point is not that facts do not matter. It is that facts only matter to learners when those facts are integrated into holistic cognitive frameworks, and that students need space to develop those frameworks on their own terms.

To push the analogy of cognitive framework, we must imagine learning as a process like that of building a house. Our students' prior understanding of our subject is not an empty lot, and we cannot imagine ourselves simply arriving on the scene and building a house for them. Rather, we must imagine that our students already have existing structures on those lots and that our job is to work with them to inspect their epistemic foundations and retrofit their prior structures to accommodate the new content that we are teaching them.[23] We have to imagine the class as a neighborhood in which each student works in collaboration with their neighbors. If the class is successful, the end result will reflect the same new knowledge for each student, but it will look different because each student has a different preexisting framework.

In order to work with our students as co-architects of their own cognitive frameworks, we have to be welcome on the property. Students have to trust us, and they have to trust their peers. The challenge is that the houses

---

21. There is significant evidence that liberal arts classes are successful in promoting liberal attitudes and discouraging authoritarian attitudes. See Anthony P. Carnevale et al., *The Role of Education in Taming Authoritarian Attitudes* (Washington, DC: Georgetown University McCourt School of Public Policy, 2020).

22. Grant Wiggins and Jay McTighe, *Understanding by Design*, 2nd ed., MEACTS (Upper Saddle River, NJ: Pearson), 91–92.

23. The language about inspecting epistemic foundations was suggested by Jocelyn McWhirter in her editorial feedback to this essay.

we are building in biblical studies classes are particularly important to students' own sense of who they are in relation to the world around them. The Bible and religion are core loci of meaning making for many students. In addition, the content intersects (directly or indirectly) with other aspects of students' identity—aspects such as race, class, gender, nationality, and ability.[24] Any changes to this framework will trigger countless other changes to other webs of significance that they build into their houses—and they know it. Students will not willingly allow just anybody to walk into their sacred houses and start knocking down walls. If they are afraid that someone might start doing it without their consent, they are apt to nail shut the front door and sit by the window with a shotgun.[25]

Antiauthoritarian Epistemologies
in Biblical Studies Classrooms

Students arrive in our classes with strong biases about the content that we teach, and these biases sometimes map onto authoritarian epistemologies. A former president of the United States promotes authoritarian epistemologies, as do minoritized and marginalized people at times in their struggle for liberation. In order to facilitate a shared conversation among all of our students, one in which we can reduce harms to vulnerable students without sacrificing inclusivity and depth, I sought a pedagogy that can create space for evidence-based argument without directly threatening students' sense of identity.

The approach that I now use in my Introduction to Bible course relies heavily on asking open-ended questions and allowing students to draw their own conclusions.[26] What I want students to be able to do, by the end of the course, is to offer an account of biblical canon formation that can attend to the contingent historical processes at play. I want students to be

---

24. Zaretta Hammond, *Culturally Responsive Pedagogy and the Brain: Promoting Authentic Engagement and Rigor among Culturally and Linguistically Diverse Students* (Thousand Oaks, CA: Corwin, 2015), 21–34.

25. Dyan Watson, "Staying in the Conversation: Having Difficult Conversations about Race in Teacher Education," in *Exploring Race in Predominantly White Classrooms*, ed. George Yancy and Maria del Guadalupe Davidson (New York: Routledge, 2014), 40–49.

26. The course is called Introduction to Bible because it covers multiple biblical canons and the process by which those canons emerged.

able to integrate specific textual evidence with specific historical evidence in such a way that they can make an argument for one particular process over another. I do not care whether the story that they tell is likely to be objectively true.

I understand that the previous sentence may seem scandalous or reductively postmodern. My goal here is not to promote radical relativism but to prioritize conceptual depth over surface-level proficiency. We can only teach students a limited amount about traditional philological methods in an introductory course, particularly when the students have no training in ancient languages. We will rarely move very far past asking them to recite classic arguments such as those for or against JEDP, the Deuteronomic redaction of Samuel–Kings, and Markan priority. Students have little capacity for intuitive grasp of arguments rooted in the grammar of unfamiliar languagesm so our arguments have little chance of penetrating into their deep-level conceptual frameworks. They dutifully recite our arguments, or they martyr themselves for Mosaic authorship. Perhaps we encourage them to form their own arguments, but with such a vast disparity in prior knowledge and skill they have little chance of beating us at our own game, especially when we get to set the rules and pick the battlefield.

Rather than forefront classic philological arguments for the contingent composition of Scripture, I begin with a series of exercises designed to help students learn to attend carefully to the text as they have it. My approach depends rather heavily on Paul de Man's classic essay "The Return to Philology."[27] De Man argues that philology is essential to literature, not on the level of grammar but on the level of poetics. De Man reverses the order of the classical liberal arts trivium, placing rhetoric before grammar and logic. Rhetoric deserves primacy, de Man argues, because the structures that shape our own subjectivities are already at work on us before we begin to read. Our grammar and our logic (two ostensibly objective enterprises) are conditioned by our prior commitments. That is true for all of us, whether we are taking our first introductory Bible course or teaching our fiftieth. The most transformative pedagogy we can adopt, says de Man, is simply to invite students to attend carefully to the text as they have it before them and to reflect on the ways that it generates meaning for them.[28]

---

27. Paul de Man, "The Return to Philology," in *The Resistance to Theory*, THL 33 (Minneapolis: University of Minnesota Press, 1986), 21–26.

28. De Man, "Return to Philology," 23–24.

My course covers the production of biblical literatures from the historical origins of Israel (roughly the twelfth century BCE) through the church councils and talmudic disputes of late antiquity. I choose these points because they include everything that eventually ended up in most canons, not because they are fixed beginning and end points in the process. The course begins by emphasizing process, since our first topic of discussion is ancient Near Eastern scribalism. I distinguish between three approaches to textuality: print, manuscript, and oral.[29] I emphasize that orality remains dominant in the production of ancient literature throughout the period that the course covers, even though (by necessity) our course focuses on written evidence.[30] The written texts that are now so precious to us functioned primarily as memory aids for ancient scribes, and their ontology was fundamentally oral (and thus fluid).[31] Consequently, ancient texts had no "original" forms against which manuscripts should be measured. We should speak not of variants but of variance itself.[32]

Many students of course will be skeptical at this point, but I try to circumvent that skepticism by avoiding any specific references to biblical texts. At this point, we are studying ancient Near Eastern scribalism, not the Bible in particular. I do not come right out and say it, but I leave the door open for students to think that maybe, in the Bible's case, the process was different. This is not because I believe it could be so but because I want my students to feel safe staying in the conversation.

Our first direct engagement with biblical literature is with the creation narrative of Gen 1–3. We do two related exercises. First, as do many biblical studies instructors, I break students into groups, point them to Gen

---

29. Eva Mroczek, *The Literary Imagination in Jewish Antiquity* (Oxford: Oxford University Press, 2016), 38–50.

30. Susan Niditch, *Oral World and Written Word: Ancient Israelite Literature*, LAI (Louisville: Westminster John Knox, 1996), 1–8, 39–71; Cynthia Edenburg, "Intertextuality, Literary Competence, and the Question of Readership: Some Preliminary Observations," *JSOT* 35 (2010): 131–33.

31. David M. Carr, "Orality, Textuality, *and* Memory: The State of Biblical Studies," in *Contextualizing Israel's Sacred Writings: Ancient Literacy, Orality, and Literary Production*, ed. Brian B. Schmidt, AIL 22 (Atlanta: SBL Press, 2015), 161–73; Carr, *The Formation of the Hebrew Bible: A New Reconstruction* (New York: Oxford University Press, 2011), 4–36; Carr, *Writing on the Tablet of the Heart: Origins of Scripture and Literature* (New York: Oxford University Press, 2005).

32. Bernard Cerquiglini, *Éloge de la Variante: Histoire Critique de la Philologie* (Paris: Éditions du Seuil, 1989), 111.

1:1–2:4a and 2:4b–25, and invite them to place the following four creative acts of God in chronological order: male humans, female humans, animals, and plants. Of course, the order is different in the two narratives, and students readily discover this. Rather than using this as a gotcha moment and telling them that the variation reflects two different sources, I invite them to develop their own explanations, and I give them space to explore the implications. Many insist on harmonistic explanations, and I do not challenge them directly.

Our next exercise also involves philological close reading. I ask students to carefully examine the garden of Eden narrative in Gen 2–3 and to rank the four main characters in order from most to least truthful. I let them decide what constitutes truthfulness, but I deliberately do not use the word *honest*. Students quickly remark that Adam and Eve are dishonest. The debate centers on God and the serpent. Most students can see that everything that the serpent says is quite literally true. The man and the woman do not die when they eat the fruit, and their eyes are opened so that they become like God, as God himself later confirms. God, meanwhile, forecasts one thing in particular that does not happen: the man and the woman do not die on the day that they eat the fruit. Students debate the particular meanings of various phrases, and I supply them with some Hebrew as it becomes relevant. Does "on the day that you eat" refer to when they will die or to when they start to die? Is the serpent's question intentionally misleading, and thus not truthful? That is the whole point. Students debate, using evidence, and make arguments for their various interpretations. I withhold, as much as I can, any resolution. I want students to live with the reality that we are not certain about the meaning of this text.

This game continues throughout the semester. I remain stingy with any overt act of interpretation. I ask a lot of questions. I do not fret if students draw conclusions that I think are almost certainly not true. What I find is that, as the semester progresses, and as students continue to read the texts, openly and honestly, they begin to question their assumptions. They find that outside frameworks (whether they are pious and harmonistic or dismissive and self-satisfied) rarely produce satisfactory or fun readings of the texts in question. In the process, they are invited to consider all sorts of questions about process and contingency. Were the Jacob and Moses stories originally distinct and competing national myths? Were the tales of King David written as royalist propaganda? Was Hezekiah a great king or a total disaster? Is Deuteronomism an attempt to borrow Mosaic imprimatur for the Josianic reforms, and were these reforms themselves undertaken for reasons of statecraft? Was Enoch a patriarch on the level of Moses for some ancient Judeans and early Christians? Was Paul ever a Christian?

Naturally, I have my own scholarly positions on all of these questions, and of course I would be pleased if my students arrived at the same conclusions after a careful examination of the evidence. But that is not the point of the course. In fact, I care rather little whether students finish the course with any ideas that reflect points of consensus within the discipline of biblical studies. The point is not what they believe after one semester of biblical studies. I probably do not currently agree with a single thing that I would have said after my first semester of biblical studies. The point is that they have confronted a vast body of evidence and have learned how to string it together into persuasive arguments for their own positions. In the process, they have also seen how the same evidence can be used to support a variety of other positions, different from their own, that people arguing in good faith might come to support. My hope is that they come to see patient, generous, evidence-based thinking as a positive thing.

On the surface, it might seem as if this kind of constructivist relativism would support authoritarian epistemologies. One might think that students, when they see that no position necessarily prevails, just conclude that "it's all rhetoric." That has not been my experience. On the contrary, the persistent emphasis on evidence and logic reinforces that there is in fact truth out there. It creates a hard check on authoritarian epistemologies. The lack of closure, meanwhile, reinforces epistemic humility. Truth matters. It is available to us, but never in full, and never with certainty. We must always act as if we could be wrong, and we must always attempt to engage with other people in good faith, not to defend our prior conclusions but to become more sensitive to what might be possible.

Conclusion

This essay describes my best attempt at redesigning a biblical studies curriculum that promotes liberal, democratic values in a world that seems to be moving toward authoritarianism. Authoritarianism, I have argued, rests on a foundation of epistemic prevarication, one for which the only truth that matters is mediated by the person with the most power. Liberal democracy, by contrast, rests on epistemic humility and the divorce of truth from power, in theory if rarely in practice. Any liberal arts course can and should promote liberal values and habits in students, and it should prepare them for citizenship in a liberal democratic society. All real education is utopian, in the truest sense of the word. Liberal arts classes are "impractical" because they prepare students for a society that does not exist yet and will never exist. The mere fact that we still have a place in which to do it is sufficient cause to continue the work for as long as we can. In biblical studies classes, future citizen-leaders can develop their own provisional ideas, in conversation with their peers, about some of the foundational discourses of Euro-American cultures. There is hardly any better training for a life of democratic citizenship.

Bibliography

"Advocacy for Liberal Education." American Association of Colleges and Universities. https://tinyurl.com/03108q.

Alterman, Eric. "During a Pandemic, Trump's 'B——t' Will Be Deadly." *The Nation*, 12 March 2020. https://tinyurl.com/SBL03108ai.

Armour, Stephanie. "Trump Administration Issues Rule to Roll Back Transgender Protections in the Affordable Care Act." *Wall Street Journal*, 12 June 2020. https://tinyurl.com/SBL03108u.

Barbaro, Michael. "Donald Trump Clung to 'Birther' Lie for Years, and Still Isn't Apologetic." *New York Times*, 16 September 2016. https://tinyurl.com/SBL03108y.

Beal, Timothy. "Cultural-Historical Criticism of the Bible." Pages 1–20 in *New Meanings from Ancient Texts: Recent Approaches to Biblical Criticisms and Their Applications*. Edited by Steven L. McKenzie and John Kaltner. Louisville: Westminster John Knox, 2013.

Carnevale, Anthony P., Nicole Smith, Lenka Dražanová, Artem Gulish, and Kathryn Peltier Campbell. *The Role of Education in Taming Authoritarian Attitudes*. Washington, DC: Georgetown University McCourt School of Public Policy, 2020.

Carr, David M. *The Formation of the Hebrew Bible: A New Reconstruction*. New York: Oxford University Press, 2011.

———. "Orality, Textuality, *and* Memory: The State of Biblical Studies." Pages 161–73 in *Contextualizing Israel's Sacred Writings: Ancient Literacy, Orality, and Literary Production*. Edited by Brian B. Schmidt. AIL 22. Atlanta: SBL Press, 2015.

———. *Writing on the Tablet of the Heart: Origins of Scripture and Literature*. New York: Oxford University Press, 2005.

Cerquiglini, Bernard. *Éloge de la Variante: Histoire Critique de la Philologie*. Paris: Éditions du Seuil, 1989.

Coates, Ta-Nehisi. "The First White President." *The Atlantic*, October 2017. https://tinyurl.com/SBL03108af.

Cronon, William. "'Only Connect ...' The Goals of a Liberal Education." *AmSchol* 67.4 (1998): 1–6.

"Donald Trump: Ban All Muslims Entering US." *The Guardian*, 7 December 2015. https://tinyurl.com/SBL03108aa.

Edenburg, Cynthia. "Intertextuality, Literary Competence, and the Question of Readership: Some Preliminary Observations." *JSOT* 35 (2010): 131–48.

Edwards, Griffin Sims, and Stephen Rushin. "The Effects of President Trump's Election on Hate Crimes." 14 January 2018. https://dx.doi.org/10.2139/ssrn.3102652.

Fadulu, Lola. "Trump's Rollback of Transgender Rights Extends through Entire Government." *New York Times*, 6 December 2019. https://tinyurl.com/SBL03108v.

Frankfurt, Harry. "Donald Trump Is BS, Says Expert in BS." *Time*, 16 May 2016. https://tinyurl.com/SBL03108ag.

———. *On B——t*. Princeton: Princeton University Press, 2005.

Freire, Paolo. *Education for Critical Consciousness*. Translated by Myra Bergman Ramos. New York: Continuum, 1994.

Gannon, Kevin. *Radical Hope: A Teaching Manifesto*. TLH. Charleston: West Virginia University Press, 2020.

Gavaler, Chris, and Nathaniel Goldberg. "Beyond B——t: Donald Trump's Philosophy of Language." *PN* 121 (2017): 22–23.

Graham, David A. "On Trump's B——t." *The Atlantic*, 1 July 2019. https://tinyurl.com/SBL03108cv.

Hammond, Zaretta. *Culturally Responsive Pedagogy and the Brain: Promoting Authentic Engagement and Rigor among Culturally and Linguistically Diverse Students*. Thousand Oaks, CA: Corwin, 2015.

Hassan, Adeel. "Hate-Crime Violence Hits 16-Year High, F.B.I. Reports." *New York Times*, 12 November 2019. https://tinyurl.com/SBL03108x.

Hayden, Michael Edison. "Stephen Miller's Affinity for White Nationalism Revealed in Leaked Emails." Southern Poverty Law Center, 11 November 2019. https://tinyurl.com/SBL03108ad.

Kendall, Brent, Jess Bravin, and Michelle Hackman. "Trump's Bid to End DACA Blocked by Supreme Court." *Wall Street Journal*, 18 June 2020. https://tinyurl.com/SBL03108t.

Kendi, Ibram X. "Is This the Beginning of the End of American Racism?" *The Atlantic*, September 2020. https://tinyurl.com/SBL03108ae.

Knuckey, Jonathan, and Komysha Hassan. "Authoritarianism and Support for Trump in the 2016 Presidential Election." *SSJ* 57 (2020): 1–14.

Kristiansen, Lars J., and Bernd Kaussler. "The B——t Doctrine: Fabrications, Lies, and Nonsense in the Age of Trump." *IL* 38 (2018): 13–52.

Leonhardt, David, and Ian Prasad Philbrick. "Donald Trump's Racism: The Definitive List, Updated." *New York Times*, 15 January 2018. https://tinyurl.com/SBL03108w.

MacKenzie, Alison, and Ibrar Bhatt. "Lies, B——t, and Fake News: Some Epistemological Concerns." *PSE* 2 (2020): 9–13.

MacWilliams, Matthew. "Who Decides When the Party Doesn't? Authoritarian Voters and the Rise of Donald Trump." *PSP* 49 (2016): 716–21.

Man, Paul de. "The Return to Philology." Pages 21–26 in *The Resistance to Theory*. THL 33. Minneapolis: University of Minnesota Press, 1986.

McGrew, Sarah, Teresa Ortega, Joel Breakstone, and Sam Wineburg. "The Challenge That's Bigger than Fake News: Civic Reasoning in a Social Media Environment." *AE* (Fall 2017). https://tinyurl.com/SBL03108aj.

Mroczek, Eva. *The Literary Imagination in Jewish Antiquity*. Oxford: Oxford University Press, 2016.

Newman, Benjamin, Jennifer L. Merolla, Sono Shah, and Danielle Casarez Lemi. "The Trump Effect: An Experimental Investigation of the Emboldening Effect of Racially Inflammatory Elite Communication." *BJPS* 50 (2020): 1–22.

Niditch, Susan. *Oral World and Written Word: Ancient Israelite Literature*. LAI. Louisville: Westminster John Knox, 1996.

Ray, Rashawn, and Keon L. Gilbert. "Has Trump Failed Black Americans?" Brookings Institution, 15 October 2020. https://tinyurl.com/SBL03108r.

Rini, Regina. "Fake News and Partisan Epistemology." *KIEJ* 27.2 supplement (2017): E-43–E-64.

Rogers, Katie, and Nicholas Fandos. "Trump Tells Congresswomen to 'Go Back' to the Countries They Came From." *New York Times*, 14 July 2019. https://tinyurl.com/SBL03108z.

Rowland, Robert. "The Populist and Nationalist Roots of Trump's Rhetoric." *RPA* 22 (2019): 343–88.

Sacchetti, Maria. "Trump Administration to Expand Its Power to Deport Undocumented Immigrants." *Washington Post*, 22 July 2019. https://tinyurl.com/SBL03108s.

Swalwell, Katy. *Educating Activist Allies: Social Justice Pedagogy with the Suburban and Urban Elite.* CSTS. New York: Routledge, 2013.

Thrush, Glenn, and Rebecca R. Ruiz. "White House Acts to Stem Fallout from Trump's First Charlottesville Remarks." *New York Times*, 13 August 2017. https://tinyurl.com/SBL03108ac.

Watson, Dyan. "Staying in the Conversation: Having Difficult Conversations about Race in Teacher Education." Pages 40–49 in *Exploring Race in Predominantly White Classrooms.* Edited by George Yancy and Maria del Guadalupe Davidson. New York: Routledge, 2014.

White, Daniel. "Donald Trump Ramps Up Attacks against Judge in Trump University Case." *Time*, 2 June 2016. https://tinyurl.com/SBL03108ab.

Wiggins, Grant, and Jay McTighe. *Understanding by Design.* 2nd ed. MEACTS. Upper Saddle River, NJ: Pearson.

Yglesias, Matthew. "The B——ter in Chief." *Vox*, 30 May 2017. https://tinyurl.com/SBL03108ah.

Quick Tip
Answering Critical Questions

GEORGE BRANCH-TREVATHAN

Every spring I teach an honors course titled Interpreting Scriptures. The students are in their first year at a small liberal arts college. Many aim to be the first in their family to earn a bachelor's degree. I aim to introduce them to the Hebrew Bible, New Testament, and Qur'an as well as to higher education. Because Interpreting Scriptures serves both the religion department and the honors program, it has two sets of learning goals. The religion department sets disciplinary goals. It asks students to learn something about the contents of the Jewish, Christian, and Islamic canons, the exegetical methods applied to them, and the questions those methods seek to answer. The honors program sets general educational goals. It asks students to improve their ability to locate and evaluate secondary sources as well as to communicate orally and in writing. Like many instructors, I serve two masters. To do so coherently and efficiently, I have developed a critical-introduction omnibus assignment for my unit on the Hebrew Bible.

To complete this assignment, students must answer six fundamental questions: Who wrote this composition? When was it written? Was the work originally written as it appears now or were parts added at different times? What is the work's structure? What main claims does the work make? What does the author intend to accomplish with this writing?[1] As students answer these questions about authorship, date, literary integrity, outline, themes, and purpose, they begin to see how historical and literary criticism function.

---

1. I have adapted these parameters for a critical introduction from Jerry L. Sumney, *The Bible: An Introduction* (Minneapolis: Fortress, 2010), 50.

To answer these questions, students work in groups of two or three. They choose a book from the Hebrew Bible and read it in its entirety. They also utilize at least three standard secondary sources. To ensure familiarity with scholarly reference works, I require them to use the entry for their biblical book in either the *Anchor Bible Dictionary* or the *New Interpreter's Dictionary of the Bible*. For their other two sources, I recommend various commentaries and introductions. In an online course without easy student access to electronic copies of appropriate resources, I would instead instruct students to use websites written by biblical scholars. Examples include Enter the Bible and Bibledex.[2] For each source, students must note its answer to each critical question as well as how the author(s) reached that answer. They must then compare and assess the answers and rationales found in those sources. "The secondary sources you read may differ in their answers to these questions," I explain in the written assignment. "If so, compare and assess the quality and quantity of evidence each source provides in support of its claims. You may conclude that one source has a more persuasive argument than another or that the arguments are equally meritorious (and hence the question admits of multiple answers), or you may propose a different answer altogether."

Students then introduce their writing to the class by offering a twelve-to fifteen-minute presentation in which they answer the critical questions and highlight the evidence and the reasoning behind their answers. If the biblical text they have selected is on the syllabus, they present on that day. If not, they present on a day we discuss a nearby writing in the canonical order of any major religion. A question-and-answer period follows the presentation. The class typically uses that period to discuss the degree to which the evidence adduced indeed supports the answers offered.

The assignment furthers disciplinary goals by requiring students to familiarize themselves with the contents of one Hebrew Bible book and to answer some basic critical questions about it. Students learn to reason like modern biblical scholars. The assignment also furthers general educational goals by requiring students to locate resources regularly consulted by biblical scholars and to scrutinize, compare, and assess the scholarly opinions therein. They engage in library research, critical thinking, and argumentation. They also improve their oral communication skills by

---

2. Enter the Bible, Luther Seminary, https://www.enterthebible.org; Bibledex, University of Nottingham, http://www.bibledex.com.

presenting their findings to the class. As an ancillary benefit, small group work prompts students to discuss biblical texts and biblical interpretation outside class, without the professor's mediation. In all these ways, this omnibus assignment acquaints students with biblical literature, biblical studies, and college-level learning.

Bibliography

Bibledex. University of Nottingham. http://www.bibledex.com.
Enter the Bible. Luther Seminary. https://www.enterthebible.org.
Sumney, Jerry L. *The Bible: An Introduction*. Minneapolis: Fortress, 2010.

QUICK TIP
ACTS IN ACTION

SYLVIE T. RAQUEL

I teach in a small Christian liberal arts college where all students take several Bible classes, including my Introduction to the New Testament course. To respond to my current students' needs, I wanted to revitalize my class and incorporate more student-centered activities that promoted quality, advanced equity, valued democracy, and emphasized discovery. As my students' attention span would dramatically drop in the middle of the semester, I also needed to reenergize the class at that time. I decided to experiment with the book of Acts.

My first task was to reflect on my overarching purpose and my objectives. I had covered the historical, social, religious, and geographical background of the book, so I decided to focus on the dynamics of the text. Overall, I wanted my students to experience the vibrancy of the book that centers on the momentum of Christianity in the first century. Acts is indeed an action-packed, thrilling race against time, status quo, and preconceptions where the contestants keep breaking down the racial, social, and religious conventions of the first-century world.

I decided to design an activity that would reflect my strategic goals. At the conclusion of the activity, I wanted my students to be able to

1. Describe Luke's central theological teachings.
2. Identify reliable New Testament materials from the library and online resources.
3. Analyze scholarly works on Acts, thinking critically and creatively.
4. Assume personal and collective responsibility.
5. Organize and summarize the essence of their learning.
6. Apply it to contemporary situations both locally and globally.

Next, I chose topics that would help my students embark on a journey of discovery about the amazing race that started in Jerusalem and spread through the heart of the Roman Empire. I settled on nine. The first three—the Holy Spirit, prayer, and persecution—combine to motivate the spread of the gospel in Acts.[1] The Holy Spirit is the driving force behind the entire story, as he guides, rebukes, and inspires the new Christians. Prayer unleashes God's power to perform miracles and wonders. Persecution forces Christians to move away from their homes, which gives them the opportunity to share their faith all over the Roman Empire.

With these three topics in place, I then concentrated on Acts' characters. The story focuses on two main characters, Peter leading the Jewish mission and Paul advancing the gentile mission. Yet, these leading figures cannot fulfill their mission without the help (or hindrance) of minor characters who, when they repent, become vital instruments for carrying on the Christian mission. A by-product of their salvation is their transformed relationship with the wealth, magic, and social and religious powers that once defined them. I had my next three topics: the role of the minor characters in Acts, riches and poverty, and "just like magic."

After what and who propelled the growth of Christianity, I needed to address how this peasant movement became an indestructible force that spread in the Roman world like a tsunami wave. I reflected on turning points in the narrative that propelled the gospel into new territories. They stood at the intersection of God's initiative through the Holy Spirit and human responses in the Holy Spirit: the Jerusalem Council, which recognized the Holy Spirit's work among gentiles; the vision and missionary support of the believers in Antioch; and Paul's missionary journeys. One of the book's geniuses is its open-ended conclusion, in which Luke invites his readers to continue God's story. I nailed my last three topics: the Jerusalem Council, the Antioch church, and Paul's amazing race.[2]

Each of my forty-five to fifty-five students chose one of the nine topics, with a maximum of five students per group. I asked each group to read and interpret relevant passages from Acts. I also assigned readings from secondary sources. Every group member read a specific book chapter or

---

1. One of my former professors, Dr. Gerald Stevens, inspired some of these topics.

2. I was inspired to create this exercise by Sandie Gravett's article "Paul and the Amazing Race," in *Teaching the Bible: Practical Strategies for Classroom Instruction*, ed. Mark Roncace and Patrick Gray (Atlanta: Society of Biblical Literature, 2005), 333.

article, and each individual student chose and read another relevant article from a Bible dictionary, encyclopedia, or another scholarly resource. I made students responsible for outlining these articles and sharing what they had learned with the rest of their group. I had to recruit our librarians to help guide the students.

I then asked each group to write a paper that used all of their sources. Finally, each group presented their findings to the entire class (see fig. 2 on p. 64). They used drama, video, PowerPoint, board, creative writing, and simple exposition. They even wrote musicals and adopted eclectic approaches. Students were creative and well invested in their assignments.

Before each presentation, the presenters distributed five questions for their classmates to answer. The questions helped students stay engaged and alert during their peers' presentations. Creating five thought-provoking questions has been the most challenging part of the whole activity. Students either prepared questions that prompted only yes-or-no answers, or did not articulate their thoughts properly. I now ask students to send me their questions in advance, which gives me the chance to send suggestions for improvement. In general, it takes three to five email exchanges to obtain a decent set of questions. It is time consuming but truly formative for self-assessment.

Most students indicate that they enjoyed this activity and learned much. I was delighted that I succeeded in achieving my six learning outcomes. Students learned the central points of Luke's theology, the benefits of using secondary sources, and the art of interpreting a biblical book. They also learned to assume responsibility for their group and the class, synthesize what they learned, and apply their findings to the twenty-first century.

Bibliography

Gravett, Sandie. "Paul and the Amazing Race." Page 333 in *Teaching the Bible: Practical Strategies for Classroom Instruction*. Edited by Mark Roncace and Patrick Gray. RBS 49. Atlanta: Society of Biblical Literature, 2005.

Riches and Poverty

A. Read the following three passages:
    1. Acts 2:42–47, Acts 5:1–11, Acts 6:1–4, Acts 8:18–23.
    2. An article on riches and/or poverty in a Bible encyclo-
        pedia or Bible dictionary or from the ATLA Religion
        Database.
    3. Chapter 5 in Craig Blomberg, *Neither Poverty nor
        Riches: A Biblical Theology of Possessions* (IVP Aca-
        demic, 2000), 147, 160–75.

B. In each of the passages mentioned above, describe what the
    text teaches on the issue of wealth and poverty and how the
    early church responded to it.

C. Compare and contrast what Christians lived in Acts with the
    way the American churches respond to the United States'
    economic reality.

D. Jesus did not seem to concern himself with government or
    economic systems, so why should his followers do so?*

Give a 15-minute oral presentation of your research. You can
use drama, video, PowerPoint, board, creative writing, plain
exposition, or any means you deem appropriate.

* Question adapted from Craig Blomberg, *Christians in an Age of Wealth: A
Biblical Theology of Stewardship* (Grand Rapids: Zondervan, 2013), 213.

Fig. 2. Sample of group's assignment

PART 2
READING

To Read or Not to Read? That Is the Question!

SYLVIE T. RAQUEL

Students now entering college belong to what we call Generation Z, also known as Gen Z. In general, Gen Z includes people born between 1996 and 2016.[1] They will be tomorrow's students for the next fifteen years. They differ from the Millennials who have filled the college seats for the past twenty years because they grew up in a different world. They have distinct aspirations and unique habits. Significantly for me, they spend more time on social media, gaming, and video watching than on reading activities. I now face the challenge of teaching college students who are unprepared for disciplinary literacy and uninterested in the literary endeavor.

Added to this challenge, my subject matter is becoming more unfamiliar, perhaps unattractive, to many of my first-year students who populate my New Testament survey course, as required by the general education curriculum at my Christian liberal arts institution. Without sufficient reading skills, my students are less likely to succeed. Skilled reading supports learning competence. It promotes knowledge, critical thinking, and personal responsibility. I wondered what I could do to motivate my students to engage in disciplinary reading activities and grow in their reading skills.

As I tried to answer this question, I realized I needed first to understand more about my students' distinctiveness and their reading identity—that is, their sense of themselves as readers and the value they place on reading. As the digital-native generation, Gen Z's perception and understanding of the world—and education—is quite different from that of previous generations.

---

1. The Pew Research Center considers 1996 as "a meaningful cutoff between Millennials and Gen Z." See Michael Dimock, "Defining Generations: Where Millennials End and Generation Z Begins," Pew Research Center, 17 January 2019, https://tinyurl.com/SBL03108ak.

In general, Gen Z students do not have a strong reading identity. They place little value on reading, doubt their reading competence, and lack background knowledge. My task was to persuade them that reading matters, to build their self-confidence, and to motivate them to read. I changed some of my strategies for others that enhanced my students' reading engagement. In this essay, I will share my reflections on these questions and offer some practical ideas for building student confidence with reading, interest in reading, and growth in reading comprehension.

Why Does Advanced Reading Matter?

The compromised reading identity of Gen Z students is a reality that all college professors face today. We can close our eyes and ignore the problem, or we can take action and help our students understand the importance of graduating with advanced reading skills. I opted for taking action. I believe that advanced reading skills help students become accomplished citizens in three ways. They give access to information, support reasoning, and prompt responsibility.

First, advanced reading skills give access to relevant information. Our students certainly know how to read a recipe, an application form, or instructions for completing an assignment. They engage in literate practices such as "reading graphic novels, e-mailing, instant messaging, participating in chat rooms and blogs, and consulting computer and video game magazines for strategies."[2] But the relevance of reading goes beyond daily tasks or a quick look at information that aligns with personal views. Reading has lifelong implications. It helps students navigate complex situations in their social and professional environments.[3] The relevance of disciplinary literacy also goes beyond being able to adapt to a career or job change.[4] In this fast-changing world, knowledge production matters for

---

2. William G. Brozo and E. Sutton Flynt, "Motivating Students to Read in the Content Classroom: Six Evidence-Based Principles," *RT* 62 (2008): 173.

3. The Association of American Colleges and Universities defines lifelong learning as the "all purposeful learning activity, undertaken on an ongoing basis with the aim of improving knowledge, skills, and competence." See "Foundations and Skills for Lifelong Learning VALUE Rubric," Association of American Colleges and Universities, https://tinyurl.com/SBL03108al.

4. Some claim that the average person will change career five to seven times in a lifetime. However, the Bureau of Labor Statistics states that "no consensus has

our students who will have to adapt to swift transformations in their areas of expertise.[5] Additionally, the concept of specialization has evolved. Students more than ever require skills and expertise across a variety of subject matters. Business majors will need to understand and analyze complex reports; political science majors will have to explore intricate discourses beyond podcasts and brief snippets of texts; biology majors will want to understand, evaluate, and use information from emerging research. Advanced reading skills and disciplinary literacy will enable students to become fluent in their areas of expertise as well as to keep up with new knowledge and new ways of thinking.

Second, advanced reading skills support reasoning. A reading person is a thinking person. Reading, especially critical reading, supports critical thinking because it involves "predicting, acknowledging, comparing, evaluating and decision-making.... [It] is a sophisticated activity, which includes psychological, linguistic, and sociological aspects.... The reader needs to think while reading and bridge his own prior knowledge and new knowledge coming from outside."[6] Readers encounter new ideas. Reading develops the cognitive aptitudes, analytical perception, and rational thinking that enhance interaction among the reader, the text, and the writer. In these ways, reading expands the life of the mind.[7]

Reading also strengthens ethical reasoning. It appeals not only to the logos (logic and reason) but also to the ethos and pathos. An educated citizenry is more apt to develop "ethical reasoning and action."[8] Reading

---

emerged on what constitutes a career change," and therefore does not make any estimate. See "National Longitudinal Surveys Frequently Asked Questions," US Bureau of Labor Statistics, https://tinyurl.com/SBL03108am. Others advocate for speaking of a change of job versus a change of career. See, e.g., Carl Bialik, "Seven Careers in a Lifetime? Think Twice, Researchers Say," *Wall Street Journal*, 4 September 2010, https://tinyurl.com/SBL03108an.

5. The National Endowment for the Arts argues for the competitive value of advanced literacy in the American workplace. See "To Read or Not to Read: A Question of National Consequence," RR 47, National Endowment for the Arts, November 2007.

6. Ibrahim Abu Shihab, "Reading as Critical Thinking," *AsianSocSci* 7.8 (2011): 209, 212.

7. On that topic, consult the work of Cliff Williams, *The Life of the Mind* (Grand Rapids: Baker Academic, 2002).

8. See "Essential Learning Outcomes," Association of American Colleges and Universities, https://tinyurl.com/SBL03108k.

develops the imagination and can inspire people to dream and act on others' behalf.[9] It confronts people with new perspectives and helps form opinions and strategies. Reading also helps improve one's vocabulary for expressing personal views to a wide audience. By penning their thoughts, readers can propagate their views and persuade others.[10]

Third, advanced reading skills open a world of responsibility. According to the Association of American Colleges and Universities, civic engagement leading to intercultural competence prepares undergraduates for responsible citizenship and professional life.[11] Advanced reading skills play an important role in building a more literate, responsible citizenry.[12] The National Endowment for the Arts reports that "reading is an irreplaceable activity in developing productive and active adults as well as healthy communities."[13] In contrast, "deficient readers are less likely to become active in civic and cultural life, most notably in volunteerism and voting."[14] Moreover, nonreading citizens are vulnerable. They can be swayed by arguments not because of their validity but because of their appeal. A generation without advanced reading skills will not develop the necessary expertise to sort out which arguments are evidence-based, logical, causal, or correlational. And fewer citizens with

---

9. Professor Gregory S. Berns and his assistants found that reading increases the somatosensory cortex connectivity. He claims that "it is plausible that the act of reading a novel places the reader in the body of the protagonist, which may alter somatosensory and motor cortex connectivity." See Berns et al., "Short- and Long-Term Effects of a Novel on Connectivity in the Brain," *BC* 3 (2013): 598.

10. Reformers such as Martin Luther King were erudite. King read books of different genres. Some of the books that most influenced him include the Bible, Thomas Aquinas's *Summa Theologica*, Aristotle's *Politics*, Aristotle's *Nicomachean Ethics*, Plato's *Republic*, Augustine's *City of God*, William Bryant's *Poems*, Niccolo Machavielli's *The Prince*, Thomas Carlyle's *The French Revolution*, Mahatma Gandhi's *Collected Works*, Henry George's *Progress and Poverty*, Henry Longfellow's *Poems and Other Writings*, Jean-Jacques Rousseau's *Social Contract*, and Henry David Thoreau's "Civil Disobedience."

11. "Civic Engagement VALUE Rubric," Association of American Colleges and Universities, https://tinyurl.com/SBL03108ao.

12. Elizabeth Birr Moje, "Disciplinary Literacy: Why It Matters and What We Should Do about It" (paper presented at the National Reading Initiative Conference, New Orleans, 6 March 2010).

13. "To Read or Not to Read," 6.

14. "To Read or Not to Read," 5.

reasoning skills means fewer perspectives in think tanks.[15] Educators must therefore teach the reading proficiencies necessary for students to access a variety of arguments, weigh them, nurture their minds, and help build a better society.[16]

Our Students' Reading Challenges

Knowing that reading matters is one thing. Convincing our students is another. Although Gen Z is considered more educated than previous generations, we are now working with many students who have no desire to read or lack the sufficient comprehension skills to succeed in higher education. This does not mean that our students cannot read. It simply characterizes their reading identity. According to Leigh A. Hall, "The term reading identity refers to how capable individuals believe they are in comprehending texts, the value they place on reading and their understanding of what it means to be a particular type of reader within a given context."[17] Many current students do not exhibit strong reading identities. They feel inadequate in a college-level learning environment, place little or no value on reading, and do not navigate easily among reading contexts.

Instead, Gen Z students are busy honing other skills and navigating other contexts. Most of them have enjoyed an uninterrupted technological environment with constant access to the internet, social media, on-demand entertainment, and instant communication. They easily flip between platforms and technologies and quickly learn to use new software. Yet, growing up in times of accelerated technological, social, and

---

15. Juan Botero, Alejandro Ponce, and Andrei Shleifer suggest that more-educated societies make more-accountable governments, possibly because educated people are more likely to complain about government misconduct and that more frequent complaints encourage better behavior from officials. See Botero, Ponce, and Shleifer, "Education, Complaints, and Accountability," *JLE* 56 (2013): 965.

16. Under "Personal and Social Responsibility," the Association of American Colleges and Universities lists the following essential learning outcomes: civic knowledge and engagement—local and global, intercultural knowledge and competence, ethical reasoning and action, and foundations and skills for lifelong learning ("Essential Learning Outcomes").

17. Leigh A. Hall, "Rewriting Identities: Creating Spaces for Students and Teachers to Challenge the Norms of What It Means to Be a Reader in School," *JAAL* 55 (2012): 369.

political changes created, for many, a sense of instability and insecurity. The American Psychological Association reports that news of mass shootings and threats to immigrants, along with general concerns about their own finances (perhaps due to fallout from the Great Recession of 2008–2009), has left Gen Zers feeling anxious and stressed out. At least 91 percent have experienced feeling depressed, unmotivated, or lethargic.[18] This disposition also affects their sense of academic performance.

Our students' dependence on technology affects their reading identity in two ways. First, since they can access information in audio-visual as well as written formats, they usually favor listening or watching over reading. The more they feed on audio-visual tidbits, the less they concentrate on sustained reading about complex matters. And the less they read, the less familiar they become with various reading contexts. They may be champions in navigating digital platforms, but they do not always know how to adapt their reading skills to college textbooks or, in my context, to the Bible. As Doug Buehl points out, "[The current] unprecedented access to information and an ever-expanding core of disciplinary knowledge … is unrealized if our students are not able to successfully interact with the wide array of written texts that are available literally at their fingertips."[19] According to cognitive scientists, "Reading is a complex, active process of constructing meaning—not skill application."[20] This process is "interactive," "strategic," and "adaptable."[21] Proficient readers are strategic readers. Their metacognitive awareness allows them to select the appropriate strategy for comprehending a given

---

18. Sophie Bethune, "Gen Z More Likely to Report Mental Health Problems," *MP* 50 (2019): 20. See "Stress in America 2020: A National Mental Health Crisis," American Psychological Association, 2020, https://tinyurl.com/SBL03108ap.

19. Doug Buehl, *Developing Readers in the Academic Disciplines*, 2nd ed. (Portsmouth, NH: Stenhouse, 2017), 26.

20. Texas Education Agency, "What Research Tells Us about Reading Comprehension and Comprehension Instruction," Texas Reading Initiative, 2002, https://tinyurl.com/SBL03108aq, 4–8. The statement is based on conclusions from Janice A. Dole et al., "Moving from the Old to the New: Research on Reading Comprehension Instruction," *RER* 61 (1991): 239–64.

21. Dole et al., "Moving from the Old," 241, 246, especially on strategic reading. On interactive reading, see Arthur W. Heilman, Timothy R. Blair, and William R. Rupley, *Principles and Practices of Teaching Reading*, 10th ed. (New York: Pearson, 2002). On adaptable reading, see Michael Pressley and Peter Afflerbach, *Verbal Protocols of Reading: The Nature of Constructively Responsive Reading* (Hillsdale, NJ: Erlbaum, 1995).

text.[22] They also have a proper assessment of the level of their own thinking. Ineffective readers are unaware of the organizational structure of the text and have difficulty understanding it. Their underdeveloped metacognitive skills lead them to over- or underestimate their level of comprehension. They tend not to reflect on what they have read.[23]

It is no wonder, then, that many Gen Z students feel incapable of comprehending college-level texts, devalue reading, and lack the ability to navigate various reading contexts. According to Donalyn Miller, they have probably been this way since middle school.[24] College professors therefore face the challenge of deconstructing students' long-held beliefs about the value of reading and their ability to do it. Biblical studies professors experience the extra challenge of teaching students who, for the most part, have never studied religious literature. Many are disinclined to open a Bible because they do not identify with any particular religion.[25] It does not necessarily mean that they are uninterested in religion. Indeed, Kevin Eagan and colleagues report that, in 2015, 80.2 percent of incoming students had frequently or occasionally discussed religion.[26] Still, they have a tendency not to tie their religiosity to specific institutions, which means that they are less likely to be familiar with a particular sacred text. Others, even if raised in a religious environment, are biblically illiterate. They enter the biblical studies classroom assuming that they will never understand the topic. They will therefore hesitate to engage in a course that will expose their illiteracy.[27] They can then get caught up in a self-defeating cycle of less comprehension, less proficiency, and less engagement.[28] To alleviate

---

22. James M. Lang, "Metacognition and Student Learning," *Chronicle of Higher Education*, 17 January 2012, https://tinyurl.com/SBL03108ar. Metacognition is the ability to assess one's own skills, knowledge, and learning. Lang adds, "That ability affects how well and how long students study—which, of course, affects how much and how deeply they learn."

23. Texas Education Agency, "What Research Tells Us," 8.

24. Donalyn Miller, *The Book Whisperer* (New York: Scholastic, 2009), 23.

25. Kevin Eagan et al., *The American Freshman: Fifty-Year Trends; 1966–2015* (Los Angeles: Higher Education Research Institute, 2016), 7.

26. Eagan et al., *American Freshman*, 7.

27. Deep Patel, "8 Ways Generation Z Will Differ from Millennials in the Workplace," *Forbes*, 21 September 2017, https://tinyurl.com/SBL03108as.

28. See Paul R. Pintrich, Judith R. Meece, and Dale H. Schunk, *Motivation in Education Theory, Research and Applications*, 4th ed. (Englewood Cliffs, NJ: Prentice Hall, 2014). They show that confident students outperform less-engaged peers.

any kind of apprehension our courses may create, therefore, we have to offer learning experiences that will help students grow in fluency with the content of biblical studies.

Our Challenge

We cannot expect our students to transform their reading identity in a heartbeat. Our main goal is to lead them to become autonomous, creative, and interactive readers. In biblical studies courses, we need to equip them with disciplinary literacy. William G. Brozo and E. Sutton Flynt say, "Students who don't read content texts run the risk of never acquiring critical background knowledge, which is the foundation for academic success."[29] As Elizabeth Birr Moje points out, making knowledge accessible to all is an issue of social justice. When we help students move with proficiency from one domain to the next, we give them access to "knowledge production and critique."[30] The goal is not to turn them into savants (disciplinary literacy is not only for advanced students) but to give them tools that will allow them to ask better questions and enter into conversation with the discipline. If Gen Z college students come to us unmotivated and skeptical of their abilities and preparedness for higher education, then motivating them to read at the college level is a priority.

Their motivation will determine their involvement in the course. It is the key ingredient for addressing Gen Z students' lack of confidence, interest, or comprehension. Proper motivation will take into consideration the diversity of readers in the classroom and offer a variety of experiences. Miller classifies readers into three categories: developing readers who struggle in spite of their effort; dormant (or reluctant) readers who fulfill their assigned reading out of duty, not of pleasure; and underground readers who, while gifted and avid readers, do not connect with the required readings.[31] Developing readers need to feel successful, dormant readers need to discover that reading is engaging, and underground readers need to access challenging and stimulating texts. Reading is not just an intellectual activity. It is "both a cog-

---

29. Brozo and Flynt, "Motivating Students," 172. They refer to E. D. Hirsch, "The Knowledge Connection," *Washington Post*, 16 February 2008, https://tinyurl.com/SBL03108at.

30. Moje, "Disciplinary Literacy."

31. Miller, *Book Whisperer*, 24–31.

nitive and an emotional journey."[32] If a reading assignment creates emotional or psychological disturbance, it will affect the whole learning experience.[33] Therefore, professors who motivate their students can improve their learning and generate changes. "People can change," writes Ken Bain, "and those changes, not just the accumulation of information, represent true learning. More than anything else, this central set of beliefs distinguishes the most effective teachers from many of their colleagues."[34]

How, then, might we best motivate our current students? We need to begin by considering their dispositions. Each generation has its preferences. The art of education is to be able to adapt to those preferences. Deep Patel identifies eight of them for Gen Zers:

1. Gen Z young people are pragmatic.
2. They are competitive and want to be judged on their own merits.
3. They want independence and like to work alone.
4. They multitask more than Millennials.
5. They are entrepreneurial.
6. They want to communicate face-to-face.
7. They are true digital natives.
8. They expect the workplace to conform to their needs.[35]

This information should guide us to find strategies suitable for our students—strategies that allow them to apply their learning, be in charge of their education, make choices, use diverse platforms, express their creativity, and promote interaction and collaboration.

We should also be aware that Gen Z young people are labeled as social-justice warriors. The Pew Research Center defines Gen Z as not only the most progressive generation in American history but also the most racially and ethnically diverse.[36] Gen Z students grew up in a mul-

---

32. Miller, *Book Whisperer*, 16.

33. As psychologists and physicians have revealed, emotional and psychological health affect every aspect of life. See Harvard Medical School, "Mind and Mood," Harvard Health Publishing, https://tinyurl.com/SBL03108au.

34. Ken Bain, *What the Best College Teachers Do* (Cambridge: Harvard University Press, 2004), 83.

35. Patel, "8 Ways."

36. See Kim Parker and Ruth Igielnik, "On the Cusp of Adulthood and Facing an Uncertain Future: What We Know About Gen Z So Far," Pew Research Center, 14 May 2020, https://tinyurl.com/SBL03108a.

tiracial society, and many are not afraid to take a stand for racial equality and racial reconciliation.[37] They like to hear diverse voices. Educators can benefit from these dispositions to train students in reading the works of diverse scholars in various disciplines. They must also create spaces that will promote meaningful and equitable conversations. Corey Seemiller and Meghan Grace confirm that Gen Z strives for openness.[38] Educators can capitalize on this forthrightness, build rapport, and collaborate with their students to create a safe and motivational space that fosters student confidence.

Some Strategies

Brozo and Flynt remind us that "being aware of the importance of motivating students to be active readers is one thing; finding the right way to do so is often quite another."[39] Michael Pressley and Richard Allington state, "For academic motivation to remain high, students must be successful and perceive they are successful."[40] Therefore, the best motivator is a conducive climate that promotes success.[41] In order to create such a climate, I propose three strategies that address students' lack of confidence, lack of interest, and lack of comprehension in advanced reading. These strategies focus on the motivation, relevance, responsibility, and reasoning that build students reading identities. Since I developed them for my required New Testament course, they work well with students at various levels of reading proficiency.

---

37. Gen Z's twenty-four-hour access to culture and ideas has made them more socially aware. They also came of age amid accelerating changes in the treatment of minorities. See Jeremy Cliffe, "Can Gen Z Succeed Where Others Failed?," *Financial Review*, 19 June 2020, https://tinyurl.com/SBL03108av. Some of the 2020 American antiracism protests in all fifty American states, as well as the youth-led protests in Algeria, Iraq, Lebanon, and Chile, testify to their social involvement.

38. Corey Seemiller and Meghan Grace, *Generation Z Goes to College* (San Francisco: Jossey-Bass, 2016), 10.

39. Brozo and Flynt, "Motivating Students," 172.

40. Michael Pressley and Richard Allington, *Reading Instruction That Works: The Case for Balanced Teaching*, 4th ed. (New York: Guilford, 2004), 378.

41. For an introduction on the psychological effect of motivation, consult Kou Murayama's article and his attached bibliography. See Murayama, "The Science of Motivation: Multidisciplinary Approaches Advance Research on the Nature and Effects of Motivation," *PSA* (June 2018), https://tinyurl.com/SBL03108aw.

The strategies also involve relevance and collaboration. I find that collaborative work brings the most positive results, as expected with Gen Z students, so I implement group work as much as possible. Buehl supports this choice. "We frequently conceptualize reading as a solitary act," he says, "[but] researchers are increasingly examining the critical role that dialogue … plays in reading comprehension."[42] I also rely on Bain's principles that people learn most effectively when they are trying to solve problems that they care about; enjoy a challenging, supportive environment; collaborate with others; receive fair, honest consideration for their contributions; and can try, fail, and receive feedback from others.[43] These principles apply well to Gen Z students.

Building Confidence

In order to address the students' lack of confidence in reading, I recommend the tactic of guided reading. Guided reading resembles apprenticeship. What better way to build credibility than to model—not just teach—an important skill? Buehl agrees with this view. He encourages educators to act as mentors instead of supervisors or managers. "[Students] learn by witnessing the expert (the professor) engaged in an activity."[44] If we want our students to read successfully, we should engage in discovering, comprehending, analyzing, and interpreting biblical texts with them. Miller recommends transforming the classroom into a workshop, "a place where apprentices hone a craft under the tutelage of a master."[45]

Guided reading tactics encourage confidence in reading proficiency. A simple way to help students read more analytically is by asking specific

---

42. Buehl, *Developing Readers*, 29.

43. Adapted from Bain, *What the Best College Teachers*, 108–9. Brian Cambourne identifies the following factors that create the proper conditions for successful learning: (1) immersion (surround students with books); (2) demonstrations (demonstrate the structure and features of texts); (3) expectations (students will rise to the level of the expectation); (4) responsibility (students need to make some of their own choices); (5) use (let students practice the learning); (6) approximations (allow for some mistakes); (7) response (provide nonthreatening immediate feedback); (8) engagement (create a condition where learning has value to the students, that is perceived as doable, free from anxiety, and modeled by someone they respect and trust). See Cambourne, "Toward an Educationally Relevant Theory of Literacy Learning: Twenty Years of Inquiry," *RT* 49 (1995): 182–90, quoted in Miller, *Book Whisperer*, 35–36.

44. Buehl, *Developing Readers*, 23.

45. Miller, *Book Whisperer*, 15.

questions about the reading, such as "How does this author develop authentic reasons to write?" "Do you agree with their method? Why?" Questions such as these help students focus on essential matters and teach them to respond to the author. Education professor Susan Corapi proposes starting the semester with a close-reading technique in which the educator models in class how to read a text.[46] While the class reads together, the professor guides the students in annotating it, paragraph by paragraph. The professor can either create a specific system of annotation or let students develop their own, individually or collectively.[47] Corapi's preferred system includes surveying titles, skimming subheadings, and analyzing paragraphs with attention to structure and content. Her approach has three benefits. First, it creates a safe environment. Second, it teaches students how to dialogue with the text.[48] Third, it gives a chance for the educator to exemplify the values of higher education by collaborating with students.

In my New Testament class, I apply a similar approach when I ask my students to draw a text. Drawing a text is a different kind of guided reading. It harnesses visual representation and student imagination to outline a plot, compelling them to differentiate between the primary and auxiliary details of the narrative. For this type of exercise, it is best to use narratives or other vivid texts. Students can create a drawing, a pamphlet, an advertising sign, a road sign, or some other appropriate artifact. I use this technique to help my students visualize the narrative elements of the book of Revelation. Because the activity takes place toward the end of the semester, I have already worked with my students on guided reading. We have also discussed what I consider the fourfold genre of Revelation (epistle, apocalypse, prophecy, and drama) and its implication for the interpretation of the text.[49]

---

46. Susan Corapi, email to author, 18 November 2020. Corapi commends Kylene Beer and Robert E. Probst, *Notice and Note: Strategies for Close Reading* (Portsmouth, NH: Heinemann, 2012).

47. Corapi insists that summarizing a text kills motivation (Corapi, email to author). She prefers annotating texts, either by writing on the book or article or by using sticky notes. She recommends consulting Kylene Beer and Robert E. Probst, *Reading Nonfiction: Notice and Note; Stances, Signposts, and Strategies* (Portsmouth, NH: Heinemann, 2016).

48. See Kimberly Bauser McBrien's essay in this volume.

49. On Revelation as a drama, see Sylvie T. Raquel, "Revelation as a Drama: A Staging of the Apocalypse," in *Essays on Revelation: Appropriating Yesterday's Apocalypse in Today's World*, ed. Gerald Stevens (Eugene, OR: Pickwick, 2011), 156–74.

I divide students into ten groups of four and assign a chapter to each group.[50] I provide various drawing material (crayons, markers, pencils, paint, paper) and give each group thirty minutes to draw a representation of its assigned chapter. I then line up representatives from each group in the order of their chapters. As each representative explains the group's drawing to the class, I summarize the content of intervening chapters. With this method, we go through the entire narrative of Revelation in twenty minutes. By the end of the session, students have received a visual overview of the entire plot of the book while participating in telling the story.

This is an excellent activity for building students' confidence. Most of them never dared to study Revelation because of its complexity. By the end of the exercise, however, they grasp the story line. Drawing the text gives them enough assurance to study the narrative's details and to uncover its theological intricacy.

This type of exercise can be used at any point of the semester, whether to illustrate the life of Jesus, the formation of the church, or the first missiological movement. Students need no prior knowledge of the Bible to complete this activity. They just need to be observant readers.

Building Interest

To address students' lack of interest in reading, we need to bolster their reading engagement. Linda Gambrell points out that intrinsic motivation facilitates reading engagement, which leads in turn to reading comprehension.[51] Since engaged readers are intrinsically motivated by a variety of personal reasons, we need to diversify our approaches. Gambrell, together with Brozo and Flynt, advocates for seven research-based rules of engagement.[52] The first three are as follows:

1. Make the reading activities relevant to the students' lives. For example, have them keep a reading diary where they relate what

---

50. Chapters include Rev 1; 4; 5; 6; 8; 12; 13; 16; 19; 22.

51. Linda B. Gambrell, "Seven Rules of Engagement: What's Most Important to Know about Motivation to Read," *RT* 65 (2011): 172. She defines motivation to read as the likelihood of engaging in reading or choosing to read.

52. Gambrell and Brozo and Flynt advocate for the same evidence-based principles for motivating and engaging students (Gambrell, "Seven Rules of Engagement," 172; Brozo and Flynt, "Motivating Students," 172–74).

they have learned to their experience. Students can also connect assigned reading to text that they encounter outside class.[53]

2. Involve students in conversation about the text.[54] In remote learning, break rooms can create intimate spaces where students feel comfortable sharing ideas. Collaboration can take place among peers or between the professor and students.[55] When guided by clear principles of engagement, interaction and cooperation affirm that education takes place in community.

3. Introduce students to challenging texts. We may feel compelled to lower expectation levels because of student unfamiliarity with our subject. Doing so, however, insults their intelligence. We need to choose texts that take students to the next level, giving them a sense of accomplishment and perceptions of improved competence.[56]

Gambrell's last four rules of engagement suggest involving students' choices, providing access to a wide range of reading materials and genres, giving opportunities for students to engage in sustained reading, and offering incentives that reflect the value of reading.[57]

---

53. See Lesley DiFransico's essay in this volume. See also Kathleen A. Hinchman et al., "Supporting Older Students' In- and Out-of-School Literacies," *JAAL* 47 (2003/2004): 304–10.

54. Gambrell, "Seven Rules of Engagement," 175. She notes that several studies have shown that incorporating "social interaction about text increases students' motivation to read and reading comprehension achievement." See also Doug Buehl, *Classroom Strategies for Interactive Learning*, 4th ed. (Newark, DE: International Reading Association, 2014).

55. See also John T. Guthrie, *Engaging Adolescents in Reading* (Thousand Oaks, CA: Corwin, 2008).

56. See also Pintrich et al., *Motivation in Education*.

57. By essence, biblical studies encompasses a broad spectrum of genres that requires a variety of reading strategies. On the last four rules of engagement, see also John T. Guthrie and Nicole M. Humenick, "Motivating Students to Read: Evidence for Classroom Practices That Increase Motivation and Achievement," in *The Voice of Evidence in Reading Research*, ed. Peggy McCardle and Vinita Chhabra (Baltimore: Brookes, 2004), 329–54; John T. Guthrie, Allan Wigfield, and Kathleen C. Perencevich, eds., *Motivating Reading Comprehension: Concept-Oriented Reading Instruction* (Mahwah, NJ: Erlbaum, 2004); James Rycik and Judith Irvin, eds., *What Adolescents Deserve: A Commitment to Students' Literacy Learning* (Newark, DE: International Reading Association, 2001); Kou Murayama et al., "People's Naiveté about How Extrinsic Rewards Influence Intrinsic Motivation," *MS* 2 (2016), 138–42; Allan Wig-

In my New Testament class, I offer an exercise in collaborative reading and contemporary application of challenging texts. I start by letting each student choose one of Jesus's parables, making sure that four or five students study the same one. I try to diversify the religious, ethnic, and gender makeup of each group so that it will lead to stimulating conversations.

Before the groups meet, students read their assigned parables, short instructions on how to interpret them, and short commentaries that supply the necessary background information. I also provide a series of questions that help them navigate these sources and lead them to answer the ultimate question: what is/are the timeless principle(s) of the parable? Students share the result of their analysis with me.

In class, then, I give each group the following instruction: "Based on the timeless principle(s) you have discovered in the message of the parable, rewrite the story as a skit that suits a twenty-first-century North American setting." Students have about thirty minutes to discuss the principle(s), create a short sketch, and perform it in front of the class. I find that the exercise builds student interest in reading. It guides them in interpreting a parable and then harnesses visual, auditory, and dramatic representation to communicate its basic point in a parallel situation with contemporary relevance.

Building Comprehension

To address student inability to navigate among various reading contexts, we need to build comprehension. Frequent failures lead students to discouragement and potential withdrawal. The first step toward reading success is to build the background knowledge undergraduate students need.[58] Buehl advocates for "adequate instructional scaffolds" to help our students move the ladder up to disciplinary texts.[59] He offers a three-step process: start with primary literacy, move to intermediate literacy, and end with disciplinary literacy. The last stage is the one that "requires skills

---

field et al., "The Nature of Children's Motivation for Reading, and Their Relations to Reading Frequency and Reading Performance," ReadRep 63, National Reading Research Center, 1996, https://tinyurl.com/SBL03108ax, 5.

58. Brozo and Flynt, "Motivating Students," 172; Moje, "Disciplinary Literacy"; Corapi, email to author.

59. Buehl, *Developing Readers*, 25.

and knowledge and reasoning that are specific to particular disciplines."[60] Buehl also emphasizes that collaboration is important for scaffolding.[61] If we only assign worksheets to complete or questions to answer, we only address students' basic reading comprehension. We must lead them together into critical thinking, analysis, and critical self-reflection.[62]

In my New Testament class, I offer position-paper exercises that build comprehension and critical thinking through collaborative reading. For each exercise, students read a short article on a contemporary issue with New Testament antecedents. I try to assign engaging and relevant questions. Is the Bible reliable? Do all spiritual gifts still operate today? Can women be pastors? Is Jesus the only way to salvation?[63] We treat each topic separately. Students read different articles whose authors embrace a variety of theological views. The articles are no longer than three pages. They are easy to read and provide enough biblical and theological references to help students without prior knowledge of these issues.

Once students have read their article, they meet with peers assigned to papers with opposing or eclectic opinions. Using biblical evidence and theological arguments, they try to persuade their group members of the validity or shortcomings of the position laid out in their assigned article.[64] This exercise generates lively conversations and leads to in-depth discussions of the writers' opinions. I follow Buehl's principle of scaffolding by introducing progressively more complex resources each time we engage in a debate. The collaborative reading exercise builds comprehension and critical thinking because it guides students in interpreting arguments from the Bible as well as interpreting and evaluating the arguments of other interpreters.

Conclusion

The current Gen Z college population presents new challenges because many—if not most—students lack disciplinary literacy and are not competent readers. They are not confident in their reading skills, do not value

---

60. Buehl, *Developing Readers*, 11.

61. Buehl, *Developing Readers*, 29.

62. Two other essential learning outcomes in a liberal arts education are "critical and creative thinking" and "inquiry and analysis" (see "Essential Learning Outcomes").

63. I am indebted to Jillian Ross for some of these topics.

64. With this exercise, I follow Gambrell's seven rules of engagement.

reading, and do not navigate well among reading contexts. In response, we have to modify our objectives, methodologies, and strategies to foster classroom encounters that are meaningful to both students and instructors. We first need to become familiar with Gen Z's competitive, entrepreneurial, creative, and multitasking dispositions. The more we learn about our students, the more we become relevant in our instruction. To motivate them to read, build their confidence in reading, and expand their reading skills, we need to offer classroom experiences that will help our students move to reading independence and complexity, which will lead them to academic freedom. We can choose readings relevant to their lives, invite collaboration, scaffold reading levels, provide guided reading, offer a variety of genres and reading contexts, stimulate creativity, honor autonomy, inspire responsibility, and offer appropriate challenges. To echo Brian Cambourne, when educators add the correct processes that enable learning—namely, transformation, discussion/reflection, application, and evaluation— they can bring students to change their understanding, values, and skills about literacy learning.[65] We do not have to revise our entire courses all at once to achieve our goal. As Ruth Bader Ginsburg would say, "Real change, enduring change, happens one step at a time."[66]

Bibliography

Bain, Ken. *What the Best College Teachers Do.* Cambridge: Harvard University Press, 2004.

Beer, Kylene, and Robert E. Probst. *Notice and Note: Strategies for Close Reading.* Portsmouth, NH: Heinemann, 2012.

———. *Reading Nonfiction: Notice and Note; Stances, Signposts, and Strategies.* Portsmouth, NH: Heinemann, 2016.

Berns, Gregory S., Kristina Blaine, Michael J. Prietula, and Brandon E. Pye. "Short- and Long-Term Effects of a Novel on Connectivity in the Brain." *BC* 3 (2013): 590–600.

Bethune, Sophie. "Gen Z More Likely to Report Mental Health Problems." *MP* 50 (2019): 20.

---

65. See his blog at Cambourne's Conditions of Learning, https://tinyurl.com/SBLPress03108c1.

66. Irin Carmon, *Notorious RBG: The Life and Times of Ruth Bader Ginsburg* (New York: Morrow, 2015), 60.

Bialik, Carl. "Seven Careers in a Lifetime? Think Twice, Researchers Say." *Wall Street Journal*, 4 September 2010. https://tinyurl.com/SBL03108an.

Botero, Juan, Alejandro Ponce, and Andrei Shleifer. "Education, Complaints, and Accountability." *JLE* 56 (2013): 959–96.

Brozo, William G., and E. Sutton Flynt. "Motivating Students to Read in the Content Classroom: Six-Evidence-Based Principles." *RT* 62 (2008): 172–74.

Buehl, Doug. *Classroom Strategies for Interactive Learning*. 4th ed. Newark, DE: International Reading Association, 2014.

———. *Developing Readers in the Academic Disciplines*. 2nd ed. Portsmouth, NH: Stenhouse, 2017.

Cambourne, Brian. Cambourne's Conditions of Learning (blog). https://tinyurl.com/SBLPress03108c1.

———. "Toward an Educationally Relevant Theory of Literacy Learning: Twenty Years of Inquiry." *RT* 49 (1995): 182–90.

Carmon, Irin. *Notorious RBG: The Life and Times of Ruth Bader Ginsburg*. New York: Morrow, 2015.

"Civic Engagement VALUE Rubric." American Association of Colleges and Universities. https://tinyurl.com/SBL03108ao.

Cliffe, Jeremy. "Can Gen Z Succeed Where Others Failed?" *Financial Review*, 19 June 2020. https://tinyurl.com/SBL03108av.

Dimock, Michael. "Defining Generations: Where Millennials End and Generation Z Begins." Pew Research Center, 17 January 2019. https://tinyurl.com/SBL03108ak.

Dole, Janice A., Gerald G. Duffy, Laura R. Roehler, and P. David Pearson. "Moving from the Old to the New: Research on Reading Comprehension Instruction." *RRE* 61 (1991): 239–64.

Eagan, Kevin, Ellen Bara Stolzenberg, Joseph J. Ramirez, Melissa C. Aragon, Maria Ramirez Suchard, and Cecilia Rios-Aguilar. *The American Freshman: Fifty-Year Trends; 1966–2015*. Los Angeles: Higher Education Research Institute, 2016.

"Essential Learning Outcomes." American Association of Colleges and Universities. https://tinyurl.com/SBL03108k.

"Foundations and Skills for Lifelong Learning VALUE Rubric." American Association of Colleges and Universities. https://tinyurl.com/SBL03108al.

Gambrell, Linda B. "Seven Rules of Engagement: What's Most Important to Know about Motivation to Read." *RT* 65 (2011): 172–78.

Guthrie, John T. *Engaging Adolescents in Reading.* Thousand Oaks, CA: Corwin, 2008.

Guthrie, John T., and Nicole M. Humenick. "Motivating Students to Read: Evidence for Classroom Practices That Increase Motivation and Achievement." Pages 329–54 in *The Voice of Evidence in Reading Research.* Edited by Peggy McCardle and Vinita Chhabra. Baltimore: Brookes, 2004.

Guthrie, John T., Allan Wigfield, and Kathleen C. Perencevich, eds. *Motivating Reading Comprehension: Concept-Oriented Reading Instruction.* Mahwah, NJ: Erlbaum, 2004.

Hall, Leigh A. "Rewriting Identities: Creating Spaces for Students and Teachers to Challenge the Norms of What It Means to Be a Reader in School." *JAAL* 55 (2012): 368–73.

Harvard Medical School. "Mind and Mood." Harvard Health Publishing. https://tinyurl.com/SBL03108au.

Heilman, Arthur W., Timothy R. Blair, and William R. Rupley. *Principles and Practices of Teaching Reading.* 10th ed. New York: Pearson, 2002.

Hinchman, Kathleen A., Donna E. Alvermann, Fenice B. Boyd, William G. Brozo, and Richard T. Vacca. "Supporting Older Students' In- and Out-of-School Literacies." *JAAL* 47 (2003/2004): 304–10.

Hirsch, E. D. "The Knowledge Connection." *Washington Post,* 16 February 2008. https://tinyurl.com/SBL03108at.

Lang, James M. "Metacognition and Student Learning." *Chronicle of Higher Education,* 17 January 2012. https://tinyurl.com/SBL03108ar.

Miller, Donalyn. *The Book Whisperer.* New York: Scholastic, 2009.

Moje, Elizabeth Birr. "Disciplinary Literacy: Why It Matters and What We Should Do about It." Paper presented at the National Reading Initiative Conference. New Orleans, 6 March 2010.

Murayama, Kou. "The Science of Motivation: Multidisciplinary Approaches Advance Research on the Nature and Effects of Motivation." *PSA* (June 2018). https://tinyurl.com/SBL03108aw.

Murayama, Kou, Shinji Kitagami, Ayumi Tanaka, and Jasmine A. L. Raw. "People's Naiveté about How Extrinsic Rewards Influence Intrinsic Motivation." *MS* 2 (2016): 138–42.

"National Longitudinal Surveys Frequently Asked Questions." US Bureau of Labor Statistics. https://tinyurl.com/SBL03108am.

Parker, Kim, and Ruth Igielnik. "On the Cusp of Adulthood and Facing an Uncertain Future: What We Know about Gen Z So Far." Pew Research Center, 14 May 2020. https://tinyurl.com/SBL03108a.

Patel, Deep. "8 Ways Generation Z Will Differ from Millennials in the Workplace." *Forbes*, 21 September 2017. https://tinyurl.com/SBL03108as.

Pintrich, Paul R., Judith R. Meece, and Dale H. Schunk. *Motivation in Education Theory, Research and Applications*. 4th ed. Englewood Cliffs, NJ: Prentice Hall, 2014.

Pressley, Michael, and Peter Afflerbach. *Verbal Protocols of Reading: The Nature of Constructively Responsive Reading*. Hillsdale, NJ: Erlbaum, 1995.

Pressley, Michael, and Richard Allington. *Reading Instruction That Works: The Case for Balanced Teaching*. 4th ed. New York: Guilford, 2004.

Raquel, Sylvie T. "Revelation as a Drama: A Staging of the Apocalypse." Pages 156–74 in *Essays on Revelation: Appropriating Yesterday's Apocalypse in Today's World*. Edited by Gerald Stevens. Eugene, OR: Pickwick, 2011.

Rycik, James, and Judith Irvin, eds. *What Adolescents Deserve: A Commitment to Students' Literacy Learning*. Newark, DE: International Reading Association, 2001.

Seemiller, Corey, and Meghan Grace. *Generation Z Goes to College*. San Francisco: Jossey-Bass, 2016.

Shihab, Ibrahim Abu. "Reading as Critical Thinking." *AsianSocSci* 7.8 (2011): 209–18.

"Stress in America 2020: A National Mental Health Crisis." American Psychological Association, 2020. https://tinyurl.com/SBL03108ap.

Texas Education Agency. "What Research Tells Us about Reading Comprehension and Comprehension Instruction." Texas Reading Initiative, 2002. https://tinyurl.com/SBL03108aq.

"To Read or Not to Read: A Question of National Consequence." RR 47. National Endowment for the Arts, November 2007.

Wigfield, Allan, Kathleen Wilde, Linda Baker, Deborah Scher, and Sylvia Fernandez-Fein. "The Nature of Children's Motivation for Reading, and Their Relations to Reading Frequency and Reading Performance." ReadRep 63. National Reading Research Center, 1996. https://tinyurl.com/SBL03108ax.

Williams, Cliff. *The Life of the Mind*. Grand Rapids: Baker Academic, 2002.

READING TOGETHER APART: SOCIAL ANNOTATION

KIMBERLY BAUSER MCBRIEN

Undergraduate instructors may be familiar with the looks of confusion, consternation, or confidence that I see on my students' faces on the first day of class. In a course they thought was going to teach them about the New Testament, I tell them that one thing—perhaps even the primary thing—they are going to learn in the course is how to read. They assume that they already know how to read. Many even assume that they know how to read the Bible. The kind of reading I expect them to do in a college-level Bible course, however, is different from their previous reading. I explain that they will need to learn this essential skill anew. In class, we accomplish that goal by reading the Bible together, considering whole books, focusing on short passages, and sometimes dwelling on a single word, phrase, or idea. We read slowly and supplement our reading with relevant outside resources. Our work is enriched by our learning community, each of us bringing our own knowledge and perspectives to the collective task. We learn to read together. But what am I to do with the fact that most of my students' reading happens apart? How might a biblical studies course foster the skills of close reading and the methods of academic biblical study while harnessing the benefits of reciprocity and cooperation even outside class?

In my experience, online social annotation effectively meets these challenges. While different online platforms come with their own particular strengths and weaknesses, online social annotation mimics in-class practice with something similar to an augmented-reality version of reading. It allows faculty to guide student reading activity to deepen engagement with the text. It allows students to benefit from that guidance and to interact with the text itself, their peers, and the professor in a dialogic format anchored directly in the text. Using social annotation, my students have created collaboratively authored, dynamic records of their collective engagement with the text. These records serve not just as metatext documents but as powerful resources for teaching and learning. Social annotation is no panacea for all the reading woes of the undergraduate biblical studies classroom. When carefully integrated both in and out of the classroom, however, it transforms out-of-class reading to feel more like the active, dynamic, dialogic, and learner-centered practice of our in-class participation in biblical scholarship.[1]

The Benefits of Reading Together

From an informal survey of syllabi available online, it would seem that I am not alone in wanting Bible students to learn a particular way, or set of ways, of reading the Bible. Many Bible instructors include learning to read—whether "closely," "critically," "with the methods of academic biblical scholarship," or "by applying various hermeneutical lenses"—among their primary learning outcomes. We also regularly include critical reading among the essential transferable skills of the humanities, including biblical studies. Carolyn Jones Medine describes critical reading as a "superpower," one that can be finely honed in the religious studies classroom.[2] With this goal in mind, we model and practice careful reading in our classrooms. We then send our students out of the classroom, telling them to go and do likewise on their own, with the assigned readings for the next class. My students, rather like the disciples when left to their own devices, may try but do not quite succeed. This is not, or not entirely, their fault. Learning to read closely and critically is not only a matter of time and attention. It requires guidance. In the classroom I might stop my students midsentence to invite them to think about a particular word or phrase or idea. I incorporate outside resources to clarify foreign concepts and prompt my students to make connections among multiple texts or ideas. I ask hermeneutical questions that disrupt the expectations of a straightforward reading. Reading together, my students and I engage in conversations that

---

1. Though my experience at the time of writing was using social annotation primarily as an out-of-class supplement to in-person and emergency remote teaching, the tools and several of the strategies discussed here are readily transferable also to hybrid and online teaching models.

2. Carolyn M. Jones Medine, "Through Literacy to Fluency: Reading in the Religious Studies Classroom," *TTR* 19 (2016): 359–77.

expose assumptions, explore curiosities, highlight diversity, and destabi-lize the notion of a single interpretation.

As we read in class, students occasionally annotate with highlight-ers, pens, and sticky notes. To encourage this process, I show my students pages of my own heavily annotated Bible. I encourage them to follow suit: to make note of unfamiliar expressions or ideas, to mark key phrases or outline the logic of an argument, and to include their own thoughts, all in the margins of their text. Though some may hesitate at defacing a sacred text, with a little in-class guidance most come around and develop some system for marking particular passages, often those that have been identified as likely to show up on an exam. They place neon notes, insert simple symbols, and write their own questions and commentary around the edges of the page. Medine has described how teaching critical annota-tion in religious studies classrooms can help students move from simple literacy to fluency with relevant vocabulary and ideas.[3] Whatever methods we choose, this is all part of the work we do with our students in the class-room to help them learn to read together.

The Costs of Reading Apart

Most of the time, however, my students and I read apart. I assign read-ings for each class and expect them to complete those readings on their own before we meet. When they seem unable to engage thoughtfully with the text during class discussion, it is easy for me to assume that this is because they simply have not read.[4] I have often thought that if students would simply do the reading, the problem would be solved. Following that logic, I have incentivized reading or penalized not-reading through comprehension quizzes or similar forms of assessment. I have found this type of assessment, however, to be more effective for measuring objective knowledge than actual engagement with the biblical text or critical read-ing methods. Furthermore, my assumption about the root problem has not always aligned with students' self-reporting. When asked, most of my students claim to have read. Many admit, however, that although they try to read, their reading does not always feel productive.

---

3. Medine, "Through Literacy to Fluency," passim.

4. Steven Johnson, "The Fall, and Rise, of Reading," *Chronicle of Higher Education*, 26 April 2019, https://tinyurl.com/SBL03108ay.

Many students are not used to reading the Bible at all. Even in contemporary translations, the language and style of the Bible can be unfamiliar and discomfiting. Students feel lost. They do not know what aspects of the texts deserve close attention. Because they are more familiar with textbooks, many students try to scan Bible readings for important information. They come away with the editors' headings but no sense of the language or logic of the biblical text. Others have read the Bible previously but find it difficult to break out of the modes of reading they have practiced in religious settings. Students are reading, but they are not reading well. They are not transferring our in-class practice of close, critical reading to their practice of reading on their own.

Online guided reading questions and discussion boards approach the problem from this angle. Both seem to have some positive impact on student engagement and thinking. In a survey of research comparing online and face-to-face discussion, Margaret Perrow has found that online discussion of the sort found in an asynchronous forum evokes higher-order thinking more effectively than does in-person conversation.[5] In guided reading questions and open discussion forums, students can participate at their own pace and draw on outside resources for their responses. Students can also benefit from reading peer responses and integrating them into their own contributions. Perrow has shown that online discussion boards increase the frequency and length of contributions from women, students of color, and other underrepresented groups.[6] Still, students all too often fail to ground their interpretations in specific textual evidence. Even online, it is still too easy for students to dissociate their comments from the biblical text as well as from the skills and techniques we practice together in class. An additional tool is needed, one that will focus students on the text.

---

5. Margaret Perrow, "Strengthening the Conversation in Blended and Face-to-Face Courses: Connecting Online and In-Person Learning with Crossover Protocols," *CT* 65.3 (2017): 97–105. Sara Brierton et al. support this conclusion concerning the higher-order thinking demonstrated on asynchronous online discussion boards, though their study compared this type of forum primarily to online synchronous chat or messaging platforms. See Brierton et al., "A Comparison of Higher Order Thinking Skills Demonstrated in Synchronous and Asynchronous Online College Discussion Posts," *NACTAJ* 60 (2016): 14–21.

6. Perrow, "Strengthening the Conversation," 98.

Reading Together Apart

Social annotation encourages text-focused reading. The practice of annotation in general has deep roots in traditional Bible reading. Ancient scribes scribbled in margins, medieval monks added commentary and cartoons, and modern scholars append study aids. These notations, shared for the benefit of readers and copyists, feature a social component. Online social-annotation tools bring those ancient practices and social dynamics into the digital age, proving their pedagogical value as well as their historical precedent.

At its most basic level, say Antero Garcia and Remi H. Kalir, annotation might consist of "a note added to a text." It is also a mark of intellectual conversation—a talking back to an author and their text—and as such an exercise of power.[7] Annotation is all around us as handwritten suggestions in a cookbook, comment threads on a YouTube video, or graffiti on a park fence declaring "Black Lives Matter."[8] Such notes added to various texts participate in a social and dynamic dialogue, speaking one person's truth to another's power. Students regularly participate in this dialogue, offering their own commentary (via text, GIFs, emojis, or other imagery) in a retweet or on a shared Instagram post. With guidance, they are able to translate these natural annotation skills to improve their Bible-reading skills through social annotation.

Annotation does what guided questions and discussion forums fail to do. It links commentary to the text. It recasts reading not as passive information absorption but as part of an active learning practice. It also improves student writing. Carol Porter-O'Donnell has demonstrated that annotation, as a writing-to-learn strategy, can improve reading comprehension and deepen engagement with a text by inviting students to process and express their own ideas directly alongside

---

7. Antero Garcia and Remi H. Kalir, *Annotation* (Cambridge: MIT Press Open, 2019), 12–18.

8. Mark Leibovich describes signs affixed to the fence around Lafayette Square memorializing George Floyd and supporting the Black Lives Matter movement in summer 2020 as modern examples of a long tradition of annotation of physical spaces, which includes Martin Luther's theses and Wei Jingsheng's "The Fifth Modernization." See Leibovich, "An Eyesore in Washington Becomes an Icon," *New York Times*, 10 June 2020, https://tinyurl.com/SBL03108az.

those of the text itself.[9] Medine makes similar observations in her case for teaching annotation in the religious studies classroom, mentioning that annotation "slows down the reading process and invites thinking."[10] Additionally, she says, annotation marries the reading and writing processes. Students are writing as they read, identifying the key elements of the text and beginning to articulate their own thoughts, thus laying the groundwork for future writing assignments. In this way, according to Anke Geertsma, annotation can help to shift student focus "from product to process."[11] Students who are used to skimming must read more slowly in order to annotate as they go. At this slowed pace they uncover more information, discover more meaning, and create a record of their thinking process.

Social annotation combines the pedagogical benefits of annotation with those of in-person reading and discussion and carries them beyond the classroom. As the name would suggest, social annotation refers to "a genre of learning technology that enables the annotation of digital resources for information sharing, social interaction and knowledge production."[12] These digital platforms allow for multiple participants to interact with a shared text and with one another via multimodal comments. Because this still-emerging technology has flourished especially in the last decade, educators and lay annotators alike can now choose from a plethora of annotation options for commenting on websites, PDFs, ebooks, images, and videos. Some are open in that anyone with internet access can contribute to their annotations. Others are social in that texts and annotations circulate only within an established community. The proliferation of these platforms has been fed in part by the social dynamics inherent in annotation. Proponents of social-annotation tools, especially open options, champion them as means of radical democratic practice, capable of superimposing the voices of the people on various canons of

---

9. Carol Porter-O'Donnell, "Beyond the Yellow Highlighter: Teaching Annotation Skills to Improve Reading Comprehension," *EJ* 93.5 (2004): 82–89.

10. Medine, "Through Literacy to Fluency," 367.

11. Anke Geertsma and Mary Catherine Kinniburgh, "Annotation Tools: A Resource for College Instructors," CUNY Academic Commons, https://annotation.commons.gc.cuny.edu/tools/.

12. Jeremiah Holden Kalir et al., "'When I Saw My Peers Annotating': Student Perceptions of Social Annotation for Learning in Multiple Courses," *JILS* 121 (2020), doi:10.1108/ILS-12-2019-0128/full/html.

literature and lyrics alike.[13] Increasingly, researchers also champion them as tools to improve student engagement with course content.[14]

Because of the abundance of platforms now available and the pace at which technologies change and develop, I am not going to provide a survey or review of social-annotation tools.[15] Any educator interested in incorporating social annotation into their course should consult with the academic technology professionals at their institution or search the web to see what tools are available, accessible to their target population, and suited to student learning outcomes.[16] For my classes, I have chosen a platform called Perusall.

According to its mission, Perusall aims "to change the nature of reading—from the traditional solitary experience to an engaging and collective one."[17] In line with this mission, it provides a free, online social-annotation platform. Users can access the platform via a Perusall account or their Google, Facebook, or Twitter credentials. For each of my classes I am able to set up a unique course, which provides a social but closed system for that learning community. This closed system offers safety and privacy for my students and myself. Setting up the course involves creating a course

---

13. Monica Brown and Benjamin Croft, "Social Annotation and an Inclusive Praxis for Open Pedagogy in the College Classroom," *JIME* 1 (2020), doi:10.5334/jime.561; Jeremiah H. Kalir, "Open Web Annotations as Collaborative Learning," *FM* 24 (2019), https://tinyurl.com/SBL03108ba; Garcia and Kalir, *Annotation*.

14. See, e.g., the research and literature reviews in support of social annotation in higher education provided by Brown and Croft, "Social Annotation"; Fei Gao, "A Case Study of Using a Social Annotation Tool to Support Collaboratively Learning," *VCTEFP* 21 (2013), https://tinyurl.com/SBL03108bb; Geertsma, "Annotation Tools"; Kalir et al., "When I Saw My Peers"; Elena Novak, Rim Razzouk, and Tristan E. Johnson, "The Educational Use of Social Annotation Tools in Higher Education: A Literature Review," *IHE* 15 (2012): 39–49, doi:10.1016/j.iheduc.2011.09.00; Paul Schacht, "Annotation," Modern Language Association, https://tinyurl.com/SBL03108bc.

15. At the time of writing, several of the more helpful surveys available were those of Geertsma and Kinniburgh, "Annotation Tools"; Lindsey Seatter, "Towards Open Annotation: Examples and Experiments," *KULA* 3 (2019), doi:10.5334/kula.49; Ray Siemens et al., "The Value of Plurality in 'The Network with a Thousand Entrances,'" *IJHAC* 11.2 (2107): 153–73.

16. Lindsey Seatter offers a helpful model for evaluating social-annotation tools, particularly in terms of their "flexibility," "usability," and "sociality," but these criteria could be amended or adapted as needed for any particular context and course ("Towards Open Annotation").

17. "About Perusall," Perusall, https://tinyurl.com/SBL03108bd.

library, whether from Perusall's collection of more than two hundred thousand ebooks and e-textbooks or from uploaded PDFs. I appreciate that these options allow me to make materials available to my students at low or no cost and in formats optimized for accessibility.[18] Whatever the text, Perusall's developers have identified sociality as a crucial factor in motivating and improving student reading. Therefore, enabling social reading lies at the core of the Perusall experience.[19]

Teaching with Social Annotation

I have found that social annotation does indeed motivate and improve student reading by bringing it in line with at least five of the seven classic principles of good practice in undergraduate education articulated by Arthur Chickering and Zelda Gamson.[20] It "encourages student-faculty

---

18. Perusall's "Accessibility Statement" adds that "students can have course materials read aloud to them from within Perusall without having to use specialized screen reader software." See "Accessibility Statement," Perusall, https://tinyurl.com/ SBL03108be. None of my students has reported using this feature so I cannot comment on it. But I appreciate Perusall's attention to issues of accessibility.

19. Gary King, "An Introduction to Perusall," Harvard University, 5 April 2016, https://tinyurl.com/SBL03108bf. The Perusall team provides links to "Scientific Research about the Perusall Platform" (both internal conducted by members of their team and external) in support of their platform and claims concerning its efficacy. See "Scientific Research about the Perusall Platform," Perusall, https:// perusall.com/ research. These include Andrew J. Clarke, "Perusall: Social Learning Platform for Reading and Annotating (perusall LLC, perusall.com)," *JPSE* 17 (2019), doi:10.1080/ 15512169.2019.1649151; Seow Chong Lee and Foong May Yeong, "Fostering Student Engagement Using Online, Collaborative Reading Assignments Mediated by Perusall," *APS* 3.3 (2018): 46–48; Timothy McFarlin, "Using Open-Source, Collaborative Online Reading to Teach Property," *SLULJ* 355 (2020), doi:10.2139/ssrn.3558169; Kelly Miller et al., "Use of a Social Annotation Platform for Pre-class Reading Assignments in a Flipped Introductory Physics Class," *FE* 3 (2018): 1–12.

20. Arthur W. Chickering and Zelda F. Gamson, "Seven Principles for Good Practice in Undergraduate Education," *AAHEB* 3 (1987): 2–6; Arthur W. Chickering and Stephen C. Ehrmann, "Implementing the Seven Principles: Technology as a Lever," *AAHEB* 49.2 (1996): 3–6; Tena B. Crews, Kelly Wilkinson, and Jason K. Neill, "Principles for Good Practice in Undergraduate Education: Effective Online Course Design to Assist Students' Success," *MERLOT* 11 (2015): 87–103; Sherryl Johnson, "Applying the Seven Principles of Good Practice: Technology as a Lever—In an Online Research Course," *JIOL* 13.2 (2014): 41–50.

contact," "develops reciprocation and cooperation among students," "uses active learning," "gives prompt feedback," and "respects diverse talents and ways of learning."[21]

Perusall allows me to provide clickable commentary on a text, which can encourage student-faculty contact and respect diverse ways of learning. I am able to orient students to their assigned readings by providing notes right beside the text. Housing this type of information alongside the text itself helps keep it at the forefront of students' minds while reading. Their attention is not lost in the process of toggling between assignment and text. These annotations at the beginning of the text might set the historical context, sketch an outline of the text, or point out its dominant themes. In an introduction to 1 Thessalonians, for example, I might remind students that this text, Paul's earliest extant letter, contains certain formulaic elements of an ancient letter. Sometimes I use a prefatory annotation to set a guiding question for students to consider concerning the text as a whole. I might encourage students to look for the epistolary elements, to compare this letter to a modern letter they might have received, or to look for clues about the occasion for the letter and thus the situation faced by its recipients.

I also make strategic annotations throughout the text. I provide definitions or cross-references for new or unfamiliar vocabulary, explanations of Greek language or syntax, links to online resources, or my own exegetical notes. As with in-class close reading and annotation practices, these notes can serve to slow or pause the reading process so as to make space for critical thinking and active learning. Since 1 Thessalonians is usually the first epistle my students read in the New Testament course, I might identify the standard elements of a letter for them as they appear in the text, making note of their distinctive features. Highlighting and commenting on the first line, for instance, I might label the opening greeting, identify the multiple named senders, and consider some possibilities for the relationship of each to the others and to the text. Alternatively, I might link to an image of *Saint Paul Writing His Epistles* on bibleodyssey.org and encourage students to compare this depiction to what we have learned about Paul and his letter-writing process and to come to class ready to

---

21. Chickering and Gamson, "Seven Principles." The case could certainly be made that social annotation can also meet the remaining two principles ("emphasizes time on task" and "communicates high expectations"), but I have chosen to focus on the five principles where I see it make the most significant change.

discuss the painting. My annotation makes the text a context for multi-modal commentary that involves students in multiple ways of learning and provides them with resources to explore their own curiosity.[22] It aids communication between faculty and students in a way that reading alone generally does not.[23]

Further benefits of social annotation come into play when students join the conversation. The tools allow all participants to produce their own notes, interacting with the text and with one another. Class participation in the annotation process fosters student-faculty contact, reciprocation and cooperation among students, active learning, and prompt feedback. In order to facilitate productive interactions, I find it necessary to strike a balance between freedom and structure. When I invite students to report on points of confusion or curiosity (anonymously, if they prefer), some share interesting observations and questions about the text. In Perusall, they can use the familiar hashtags (#) and "at" symbols (@) to tag their comments to course themes or class members. They can also add emojis, other images, GIFs, videos, and hyperlinks.[24] The digital format thus invites students into a new and more open learning space in which some seem to flourish. They often make comments online that they would not have shared in class, whether due to time constraints or their own reticence. Sometimes the conversation continues with further annotation, via threaded discussion, from other students or me. Other times, their comments become fodder for in-class conversation.[25]

While I always leave an open invitation to annotate any assigned text, I also occasionally require students to respond to prompts from

---

22. Chickering and Gamson, "Seven Principles," 3–5.

23. Chickering and Gamson, "Seven Principles," 3.

24. These tools facilitate synthetic thought and collaboration. Additionally, relaxing the expectations of academic writing and allowing students to employ their own social media vernaculars seems to grant students the freedom to focus on expressing their ideas authentically, and sometimes more creatively than I could have anticipated (Chickering and Gamson, "Seven Principles," 5).

25. Chickering and Gamson, "Seven Principles," 3–4. Perrow has made the case that this type of "crossover protocol," as she describes it, explicitly linking what happens online with what happens in person (or asynchronously with synchronously), is the "key to strengthening the overall academic conversation." She also includes a number of helpful examples of these crossover protocols, many of which could be easily integrated with social-annotation tools (Perrow, "Strengthening the Conversation," 98–104).

me.[26] Embedding these prompts as annotations keeps students' attention focused on the text. For example, I use a comment at the top of the first page to instruct students reading Mark's Gospel to identify the climax of the narrative and to explain their choice. Students reading Galatians must identify and explain one or two examples of Paul's use of *law* in the letter. We use their annotations as a starting point for class conversation. My students particularly enjoy this kind of scavenger hunt, and Perusall allows me to divide them into competing teams to further enhance the gaming experience. They report that competitively collaborative work like this enhances their reading, making them more attentive than they would be for an assignment submitted only to me.[27] Sometimes I embed the prompt in the body of the text. To get students to compare two perspectives on faith and works, for example, I make a note on Jas 2:24 and include a link to Gal 2:16. The same note prompts them to annotate one of these two texts or any other relevant passages in order to explain the seeming contradiction.

With the biblical text as the context for class conversation, responses refer more frequently to the text and demonstrate closer reading of it.[28] Students learn by linking various verses with similar themes, reading each other's comments, and interacting with me. Students whose interpretations draw from multiple passages can use hashtags to connect the relevant verses, thus creating even more points of contact with the text. They can click on others' comments as they read and draw on them as inspiration for their own reading and response.[29] By keeping the text in

---

26. At least one team of researchers has found there is a danger of overengineering social-annotation assignments to the point that they inhibit students' critical thinking, but the following examples seem to have struck a reasonable balance. See Tristan E. Johnson, Thomas N. Archibald, and Gershon Tenenbaum, "Individual and Team Annotation Effects on Students' Reading Comprehension, Critical Thinking, and Meta-cognitive Skills," *CHB* 26.6 (2010), doi:10.1016/j.chb.2010.05.014.

27. Chickering and Gamson, "Seven Principles," 4.

28. Several studies support this anecdotal observation. See Gao, "Case Study of Using"; Yanyan Sun and Fei Gao, "Comparing the Use of a Social Annotation Tool and a Threaded Discussion Forum to Support Online Discussions," *IHE* 32 (2017): 72–79.

29. Gao reports on at least one study that found that, for some students, mini-discussions appearing alongside the text can be distracting to their reading of the text itself ("Case Study of Using"). Having likely been designed with this type of concern in mind, Perusall allows users to close the discussion window while reading, so that the highlighting remains visible but the comments do not unless users click on them.

front of them, social annotation allows students to practice close reading. Additionally, I can track whether and how students are reading. I can link my comments directly to the text. Together, the class annotations serve as a record of our collective reading process and a resource for students' future thinking and writing.

I have found this to be especially true in upper-level courses. Taking advantage of Perusall's searchable hashtag function, I once worked with the six students in a course on the letters of Paul to tag them all. A few weeks into the semester, I explained to them the plan. First, we would develop hashtags related to Paul's words and topics that seemed important or that interested us, particularly with an eye toward the semester's final research project. In a shared Google Doc, the students and I brainstormed a list, including #adelphoi, #bodies, #doulos, #ethne, #GenderRoles, #ParentalPaul, #PowerStruggle, and #SassyPaul. In class, we whittled the list down by eliminating redundancies, combining some, and omitting others. We then distributed the hashtags so that each of us was responsible for approximately six. As we annotated the text over the course of the semester, we each tagged the relevant texts with our assigned hashtags along with any necessary explanations.[30] In this way, we produced a useful resource that enabled us to notice and review common words and themes. By the end of the semester, we had created a unique tool for students to use while researching their final essays or projects. A student whose final project dealt with women's leadership in churches could easily search our database for Paul's references to women, descriptions of gender roles, and accounts of church hierarchy. Another student whose paper concerned the role of violence in Paul's rhetoric drew from tagged passages about slavery, conquest, and pain. They made connections they would not likely have noticed without the class index.

When informally surveyed, my students have highlighted both benefits and challenges of working with social annotation and Perusall. Some aspects of Perusall, particularly when working with PDF files, are still a bit clunky. Because the display makes it easier to work with smaller PDF files, a PDF gospel can be difficult to read. Unless a comment includes a citation, the index of embedded hashtags directs a user to the tagged text and page but not the chapter and verse. Perusall does not (at least at the time of writing) have a mobile app, and students who prefer to work on a phone or

---

30. Chickering and Gamson, "Seven Principles," 3–5.

tablet have reported that the interface is hard for them to navigate. Finally, some students struggle with reading on screens, and so find themselves moving between the annotated online text and their hard copy.

On the positive side, my more inquisitive students have noted the benefit of being able to converse with me online as well as in class and office hours. Many students appreciate learning from others' interpretations by interacting online with their peers. Several have expressed appreciation for the ability to talk back to the text or authors with handles such as @EvangelistFormerlyKnownAsMark, @RealPaul, and @PseudoPaul. They like making notes that connect the biblical text to secondary readings. They consistently agree that the various assignments, especially the practice of tagging, increase their attentiveness to the text, defamiliarizing it and helping them to adopt an academic mindset. Their anecdotal observations underscore research that links the pedagogical effectiveness of social annotation to its text-centered and dynamic interpersonal dialogue.[31]

If we want our biblical studies students to improve their reading, we ought to give them every opportunity for practice. When reading together, we can pause, question, and discuss. When reading apart, we can use online social annotation. It reframes reading to capitalize on students' social nature and penchant for annotation, creating an active learning tool that encourages communication and collaboration among all the members of a learning community. Online social annotation is, in many ways, a natural extension of the social reading and annotation that have long driven biblical scholarship. It can be used to invite students into that time-honored practice while actualizing its democratic potential in diverse and innovative ways. While no tool is perfect, I have found social annotation to be invaluable for extending many of the benefits of reading together to reading together apart.

Bibliography

"About Perusall." Perusall. https://tinyurl.com/SBL03108bd.

"Accessibility Statement." Perusall. https://tinyurl.com/SBL03108be.

---

31. For the perceived learning benefits of social annotation among students, see particularly Gao, "Case Study of Using"; Kalir et al., "When I Saw My Peers"; Novak, Razzouk, and Johnson, "Educational Use."

Brierton, Sara, Elizabeth Wilson, Mark Kistler, Jim Flowers, and David Jones. "A Comparison of Higher Order Thinking Skills Demonstrated in Synchronous and Asynchronous Online College Discussion Posts." *NACTAJ* 60 (2016): 14–21.

Brown, Monica, and Benjamin Croft. "Social Annotation and an Inclusive Praxis for Open Pedagogy in the College Classroom." *JIME* 1 (2020). doi:10.5334/jime.561.

Chickering, Arthur W., and Stephen C. Ehrmann. "Implementing the Seven Principles: Technology as a Lever." *AAHEB* 49.2 (1996): 3–6.

Chickering, Arthur W., and Zelda F. Gamson. "Seven Principles for Good Practice in Undergraduate Education." *AAHEB* 3 (1987): 2–6.

Clarke, Andrew J. "Perusall: Social Learning Platform for Reading and Annotating (Perusall LLC, perusall.com)." *JPSE* (2019). doi:10.1080/15512169.2019.1649151.

Crews, Tena B., Kelly Wilkinson, and Jason K. Neill. "Principles for Good Practice in Undergraduate Education: Effective Online Course Design to Assist Students' Success." *MERLOT* 11 (2015): 87–103.

Gao, Fei. "A Case Study of Using a Social Annotation Tool to Support Collaboratively Learning." *VCTEFP* 21 (2013). https://tinyurl.com/SBL03108bb.

Garcia, Antero, and Remi H. Kalir. *Annotation*. Cambridge, MA: MIT Press Open, 2019.

Geertsma, Anke. "Annotation Tools: A Resource for College Instructors." CUNY Academic Commons. https://annotation.commons.gc.cuny.edu/.

Johnson, Sherryl. "Applying the Seven Principles of Good Practice: Technology as a Lever—in an Online Research Course." *JIOL* 13.2 (2014): 41–50.

Johnson, Steven. "The Fall, and Rise, of Reading." *Chronicle of Higher Education*, 16 April 2019. https://tinyurl.com/SBL03108ay.

Johnson, Tristan E., Thomas N. Archibald, and Gershon Tenenbaum. "Individual and Team Annotation Effects on Students' Reading Comprehension, Critical Thinking, and Meta-cognitive Skills." *CHB* 26.6 (2010). doi:10.1016/j.chb.2010.05.014.

Kalir, Jeremiah H. "Open Web Annotations as Collaborative Learning." *FM* 24 (2019). https://tinyurl.com/SBL03108ba.

Kalir, Jeremiah Holden, Esteban Morales, Alice Fleerackers, and Juan Alperin. "'When I Saw My Peers Annotating:' Student Perceptions of

Social Annotation for Learning in Multiple Courses." *JILS* 121 (2020). doi:10.1108/ILS-122019-0128/full/html.

King, Gary. "Introduction to Perusall." Harvard University, 5 April 2016. https://tinyurl.com/SBL03108bf.

Lee, Seow Chong, and Foong May Yeong. "Fostering Student Engagement Using Online, Collaborative Reading Assignments Mediated by Perusall." *APS* 3.3 (2018): 46–48.

Leibovich, Mark. "An Eyesore in Washington Becomes an Icon." *New York Times*, 10 June 2020. https://tinyurl.com/SBL03108az.

McFarlin, Timothy. "Using Open-Source, Collaborative Online Reading to Teach Property." *SLULJ* 355 (2020). doi:10.2139/ssrn.3558169.

Medine, Carolyn M. Jones. "Through Literacy to Fluency: Reading in the Religious Studies Classroom." *TTR* 19 (2016): 359–77.

Miller, Kelly, Brian Lukoff, Gary King, and Eric Mazur. "Use of a Social Annotation Platform for Pre-class Reading Assignments in a Flipped Introductory Physics Class." *FE* 3 (2018): 1–12.

Novak, Elena, Rim Razzouk, and Tristan E. Johnson. "The Educational Use of Social Annotation Tools in Higher Education: A Literature Review." *IHE* 15 (2012): 39–49.

Perrow, Margaret. "Strengthening the Conversation in Blended and Face-to Face Courses: Connecting Online and In-Person Learning with Crossover Protocols." *CT* 65.3 (2017): 97–105.

Porter-O'Donnell, Carol. "Beyond the Yellow Highlighter: Teaching Annotation Skills to Improve Reading Comprehension." *EJ* 93.5 (2004): 82–89.

Schacht, Paul. "Annotation." Modern Language Association. https://tinyurl.com/SBL03108bc.

Seatter, Lindsey. "Towards Open Annotation: Examples and Experiments." *KULA* 3 (2019). doi:10.5334/kula.49.

"Scientific Research about the Perusall Platform." Perusall. https://perusall.com/research.

Siemens, Ray, Alyssa Arbuckle, Lindsey Seatter, Randa El Khatib, and Tracey El Hajj. "The Value of Plurality in 'The Network with a Thousand Entrances.'" *IJHAC* 11.2 (2017): 153–73.

Sun, Yanyan, and Fei Gao. "Comparing the Use of a Social Annotation Tool and a Threaded Discussion Forum to Support Online Discussions." *IHE* 32 (2017): 72–79.

Information Literacy Assignments for Biblical Studies

Steve Jung

Biblical studies students have access to a plethora of books, articles, and websites that refer to, publish, and interpret the Bible. These resources, however, seldom address the needs of the undergraduates who regularly consult them. For example, one of my students once used a pastor's website as a resource for information about Abraham. Another consulted a denomination's theological perspective for a paper on Jesus. Neither resource was acceptable for use in a university course. The students needed to evaluate their resources. Did they provide information backed by research, or did they state popular beliefs? What was the level of the author's expertise? What method or bias drove their conclusions? The students might have asked these questions if they had learned the principles of information literacy.

Information literacy is the ability to understand and think critically about information creation, information use, and information as a resource. In its Information Literacy Valid Assessment of Learning in Undergraduate Education rubric, the Association of American Colleges and Universities defines information literacy as "the ability to know when there is a need for information" as well as "to be able to identify, locate, evaluate, and effectively and responsibly use and share that information for the problem at hand."[1] The Association of College and Research Libraries, in its "Framework for Information Literacy for Higher Education," defines information literacy as "the set of integrated abilities encompassing the reflective discovery of information, the understanding of how information

---

1. "Information Literacy VALUE Rubric," Association of American Colleges and Universities, https://tinyurl.com/SBL03108bh. The definition originated with the National Forum on Information Literacy, defunct since 2015.

is produced and valued, and the use of information in creating new knowledge and participating ethically in communities of learning."[2] According to the Association of College and Research Libraries, information literacy is a vital skill for a world in which authority depends on context and credentials, human beings intentionally create information with value in the marketplace of ideas, research involves interdependent lines of inquiry and scholarly conversation, and the search for information requires methodological and evaluative skills.[3]

The teaching of information literacy is vital for our students and institutions alike. Students need to know what makes for reliable academic resources and how to find them. This knowledge is important not only for strong academic performance but also for life beyond the academy. Research scientist Alison Head has surveyed college graduates from the classes of 2007–2012 about the skills they still needed to learn after graduation. She discovered that many "found it difficult to stay informed in the rapidly changing digital age." They struggled to "find the time for continued learning (88%), locate affordable sources (73%), and stay current, given the volume of information 'out there' (70%)." Half of them "reported being frustrated by no longer having access to their former instructors and lectures as well as their campus library's databases, such as ProQuest, JSTOR, or EBSCO."[4]

Because students need to learn information literacy, institutions need to teach it. Increasingly, institutions must also document the teaching and learning of information literacy. Many accrediting agencies evaluate the extent of campus information literacy throughout all degree programs and individual courses. The Western Association of Schools and Colleges Senior College and University Commission includes information literacy —along with written and oral communication, quantitative reasoning, and critical thinking—as core competencies for which colleges and universities must submit learning outcomes as well as evidence for student achievement.[5]

---

2. "Framework for Information Literacy for Higher Education," Association of College and Research Libraries, https://tinyurl.com/SBL03108bg.

3. "Framework for Information Literacy."

4. Alison Head, "Staying Smart: How Today's Graduates Continue to Learn Once They Complete College," 9 January 2016, 5, https://tinyurl.com/SBL03108bi.

5. "4: Educational Quality: Student Learning, Core Competencies, and Standards of Performance at Graduation," WASC Senior College and University Commission, Handbook of Accreditation 2013 Revised, 2013, https://tinyurl.com/SBL03108bj.

Once we have taught students (in the words of the American Association of Colleges and Universities's definition) to "identify, locate, evaluate, and effectively and responsibly use and share" information about the Bible, how can we help them practice information literacy and assess the extent to which they have learned it? I suggest eight exercises. Each one can be added to a research project in the form of footnotes, an annotated reference page, an appendix, or a resource evaluation form. These exercises are simple and take little time to grade. When assigned regularly over the course of a student's undergraduate career, they build strong information literacy skills.

Exercise 1: Evaluating Resources

For this assignment, students take advantage of available resource evaluation tools. They include the CRAAP form, which librarians often use to teach students how to evaluate a resource with regard to its currency, relevance, authority, accuracy, and purpose.[6] Currency relates both to the date of the resource and the date of its resources. A source is relevant if it pertains to the research topic. It has authority if its author and resources lay claim to advanced degrees, professional experience, or special knowledge. Accuracy refers to a measure of information, grammar, and quality of resources. It can also involve the evaluation of old or outdated theories. A resource's purpose is the intention behind its production. Is it meant to provide information, education, political opinions, or entertainment? And what about its bias? The question of bias is particularly important for the field of biblical studies.

I developed my own CRAAP form for use with articles and websites (see fig. 3). I recommend that students fill one out for each resource they use. If they answer no to any question on the form, they should defend that answer on the back of the page. Students will quickly develop information literacy skills by completing CRAAP forms and attaching them to any paper or project.

---

6. Another popular framework uses the acronym RADAR (rationale, authority, date, accuracy, and relevance).

Article/Website Evaluation Checklist

Author/Creator – _____

Title – _____

Journal Title – _____ Vol./Issue – _____ pgs. – _____

Database/ - _____

DOI/URL - _____

CURRENCY		
Was it "published" recently enough?	YES	NO
Is the data from a recent enough study?	YES	NO
Was it updated recently enough?	YES	NO
Are all the hyperlinks still working?	YES	NO
RELEVANCE		
Is it directly related to your topic?	YES	NO
Is the academic level of the resource appropriate to your research?	YES	NO
Does it use scholarly or technical language?	YES	NO
Does it assume the reader is well educated in the discipline?	YES	NO
Is this something you would feel comfortable citing in your research?	YES	NO
Does the article provide references that are also useful?	YES	NO
AUTHORITY		
Is there a brief biography (education and work) for the creator? An "about us"?	YES	NO
Are they an authority in this field?	YES	NO
What makes them an authority?		
Is there contact information to verify the information about the creator?	YES	NO
Is the journal an authority in the field?	YES	NO
Is the cite domain appropriate for its content and creator? (.edu, .gov, .mil, .org, .net, or .com)	YES	NO
ACCURACY		
Is the information supported by evidence?	YES	NO
Are there citations or documentation to evidence?	YES	NO
Are there hyperlinks to other sites with evidence?	YES	NO
Is there an explanation of the research methodology?	YES	NO
Has the information been reviewed or refereed by editors or peers?	YES	NO
Is this a "peer reviewed" article?	YES	NO
Is there a way to confirm the information?	YES	NO
All theories are current? No disproven theories present.	YES	NO
Is the article and content free of errors (grammar and spelling)?	YES	NO
Did you verify that this journal is peer reviewed? Did you use the journal or publisher's website?	YES	NO
PURPOSE		
Is there a stated purpose by the creator of the content?	YES	NO
The information is presented as fact. Not as opinion or propaganda?	YES	NO
Are various sides of an issue presented evenly?	YES	NO
The language objective in tone? Not biased language?	YES	NO
No biases present? (political, religious, cultural, ideological or personal)	YES	NO

If your resource fails any of these criteria, then either do not use the resource or be very careful with how you handle it and present its findings in your research.

Fig. 3 CRAAP form

Exercise 2: Searching with Keywords

Searching catalogs and academic databases requires some skill. Students must therefore be taught strategic use of keywords for finding relevant resources. First, they must learn the technical terminology of biblical studies. Next, they move on to finding and using subject headings in catalogs and databases as well as enhancing a search's accuracy and relevance with limiters such as date, resource type, and peer-review status.

Students can then demonstrate the strategies behind their search process by completing a variety of assignments. First-year students can add brief footnotes describing the search strategy used for each resource. The footnote might read, "I used the keywords 'sacrament' and 'baptism' to search for books. I found several appropriate books. I selected the subject heading 'baptism: history' from one of them and found other relevant titles. I then used the subject heading in a 'subject' search in the ATLA Religion Database to find this article."

Sophomores can be expected to explain a strategy for locating one resource. They might write a detailed paragraph, perhaps as an appendix. Juniors and seniors can do the same, adding a second paragraph of critical reflection on their research methodology, describing what worked, what did not, and what might be more effective.

Exercise 3: Searching by Time Period

Students might need to search for a seminal work or the early works of a particular time period. Catalogs and databases often provide a way to perform such a search. Using a time period to limit a search can help students find works on the beginning of the quest for Paul or the second quest for the historical Jesus. Searching within a limited time frame puts a focus on the early conversation of the first generation of scholars researching a specific topic.

First-year students working on a paper or project might reconstruct a scholarly conversation by limiting their search to a specific date range. Their bibliography of resources for the paper or project, drawn from that time period, would serve as evidence of their search. While first-year students might limit that search to the past five or ten years, sophomores might be ready to research the origins of a specific movement such as the second quest for the historical Jesus (1953–1980). Juniors and seniors can take on the more complex task of tracing a scholarly conversation from its origin through its dissemination over a number of years, starting with the seminal work and then searching within a particular timeframe for other works that cite it. They, too, would append a bibliography of resources dated within the relevant time frame.

Exercise 4: Identifying Bias

Biblical studies students should recognize that authors and publishers are biased. They must learn how to identify a bias and know what to expect from a biased resource. They can learn to recognize which publishing companies started as denominational printing houses. They can analyze the biases of books published by academic societies, university presses, and self-publishing companies. They can research the stated aims and missions of academic journals and all kinds of websites. They can differentiate the theological and religious discourse of books and journal articles from the data-based research of government documents.

First-year students learning to identify bias might start with distinct theological perspectives. As they evaluate and use resources for papers and projects, they can assess these biases and describe them in footnotes or an annotated reference page. For example, they might explain that an author belongs to a Baptist group that believes in the cessation of the charismata or that a publisher promotes the teachings of one order within the Roman Catholic Church. Sophomores, juniors, and seniors might be expected to identify and evaluate how a resource's bias influences its perspective.

Exercise 5: Evaluating Media

Different media come with various benefits and drawbacks. For example, an informative book that took years to write might be outdated by the time it is published. An informative academic journal article takes less time to write, but it offers a narrower focus. A magazine article takes even less time, but it often lacks critical analysis. An academic blog post may feature keen analysis, but it lacks peer review and bias control.

First-year students can practice evaluating media by incorporating and assessing various types while researching papers and projects. For every book, article, encyclopedia entry, website, or other medium, they might write footnotes or an annotated reference page describing its currency, accuracy, depth, and/or authority as related to its medium. Sophomores might use an appendix to relate the currency, accuracy, depth, and/or authority of each medium to the value of the information it conveys. The result might read something like this:

> The book on African American interpretation was detailed and thorough, but most of the ideas were a little outdated. On the other hand, the articles I read were completely up to date, but not as detailed as to the relationships between some of the main actors and their denominations. Book-length treatments offer depth, but at the cost of currency. The opposite is true for journal articles.
>
> I also checked out the blog of one of my authors. The blog was up to date, with posts from the week before this assignment was due, but the writer was slightly biased against one denominational group. That same author wrote a very balanced article. They were both "current," but the peer review process for the article seems to have removed the blatant bias of the blog.

Juniors and seniors can turn the lens on themselves, using an appendix to critically evaluate their own project or paper as a medium for information.

Exercise 6: Evaluating Licensing and Equity

Upper-division students might be especially interested in the legal and licensing aspects of publishing as well as the equity and distribution of information. They can learn about the licensing (or not) of open-access journals, open educational resources, creative-commons resources, and copyrighted works. They can identify and assess the cost and equity of database access. Instructors might invite librarians to teach their students on these topics.

For assignments, students could reflect on the value copyright versus creative-commons licensing, assessing how that value affects access to important information. In an appendix to a paper or project, they can describe the legal issues, cost, and distribution methods of each information resource. They can then argue the pros and cons of the various licensing agreements, focusing on the legal and ethical use and distribution of resources.

Exercise 7: Creating a Reference Page

Students need to learn that reference pages do more than prevent plagiarism. According to the 2016 edition of the Modern Language Association of America style guide, "Good writers understand why they create citations. The reasons include demonstrating the thoroughness of the writer's research, giving credit to original sources, and ensuring that readers can find the sources consulted in order to draw their own conclusions about the writer's argument."[7] Since information has value, scholars and students alike must avoid appropriating others' ideas without attribution. Since scholarship is a conversation, each participant takes on a moral obligation to name all other cited voices.

First-year students can exercise this obligation and demonstrate that information has value by constructing a reference page that includes all resources used for a given paper or project. Citations can be copied from auto-generators used in a library catalog or electronic databases, then formatted in accordance with an appropriate style manual. Sophomores, juniors, and seniors might do the same while checking the auto-generated citations against the publisher's information and making the necessary corrections.

Exercise 8: Reflecting on the Writing Process

Most student work is based on primary and secondary sources. It serves as tertiary commentary on the state of research. In this way, all biblical studies students contribute to the academic field. Juniors and seniors are in a position to regard themselves as successors to the scholars whose works they have read. Like the authors of Mishnah, Hadith, and the four canonical gospels, they are standing on the shoulders of giants. Therefore, they might conclude a paper or project with an appendix reflecting on their work as tertiary (or perhaps even secondary) participation in the scholarly conversation. They can reflect on how others researched their topic, how they researched their topic, and how they relied on the ideas of others to formulate their own. They can show how their work contributes to current scholarship in the field.

---

7. Modern Language Association of America, *MLA Handbook*, 8th ed. (New York: Modern Language Association of America, 2016), 4.

Finding Other Information Literacy Assignments

In 2017, I constructed a website to house and model practical information literacy assignments for a presentation to the Teaching Biblical Studies in a Liberal Arts Context Program Unit at the Annual Meeting of the American Academy of Religion/Society of Biblical Literature.[8] I designed it so that attendees could return to their institutions and access these assignments, share them with colleagues, and discuss them with their librarians. It features tabs for assignments designed to match the 2017 information literacy standards promoted in the American Association of Colleges and Universities's Valid Assessment of Learning in Undergraduate Education rubric, the Association of College and Research Libraries's Standards and its frameworks, and various other repositories of information literacy assignments.

Other relevant websites include PRIMO, Project CORA, LOEX, and the Association of College and Research Libraries Sandbox. PRIMO, the Peer-Reviewed Instructional Materials Online Database, is a searchable collection of assignments and tutorials hosted and reviewed by members of the Instruction Section of the Association of College and Research Libraries.[9] Project CORA (Community of Online Research Assignments) offers another searchable collection of assignments, this one developed by a group of California librarians.[10] Each assignment is clearly tagged to relevant academic disciplines (including theology) and principles of information literacy. Similarly, users can search LOEX (Library Orientation Exchange) for assignments and tutorials collected by a team of instruction librarians.[11] Finally, the Association of College and Research Libraries Framework for Information Literacy Sandbox curates a searchable and growing list of open-sourced assignments.[12]

Bibliography

"4: Educational Quality: Student Learning, Core Competencies, and Standards of Performance at Graduation." WASC Senior College and University Commission. https://tinyurl.com/SBL03108bj.

---

8. Steve Jung, "Practical Information Literacy Assignments," https://sites.google.com/view/practical-information-literacy/.

9. PRIMO, https://primodb.org/.

10. Project CORA, https://www.projectcora.org/.

11. LOEX, https://www.loex.org/.

12. ACRL Framework for Information Literacy Sandbox, https://sandbox.acrl.org/.

ACRL Framework for Information Literacy Sandbox. https://sandbox.acrl.org/.

"Framework for Information Literacy for Higher Education." Association of College and Research Libraries. https://tinyurl.com/SBL03108bg.

Head, Alison. "Staying Smart: How Today's Graduates Continue to Learn Once They Complete College." 9 January 2016. https://tinyurl.com/SBL03108bi.

"Information Literacy VALUE Rubric." Association of American Colleges and Universities. https://tinyurl.com/SBL03108bh.

Jung, Steve. "Practical Information Literacy Assignments for Biblical and Religious Studies." https://sites.google.com/view/practical-information-literacy/.

LOEX. https://www.loex.org/.

Modern Language Association of America. *MLA Handbook*. 8th ed. New York: Modern Language Association of America, 2016.

PRIMO. https://primodb.org/.

Project CORA. https://www.projectcora.org/.

Quick Tip

Bite-Sized Expertise:
Bible Dictionary Article Abstracts
and Presentations

KARA J. LYONS-PARDUE

The Bible dictionary article abstract is an assignment that combines writing and presentation, allowing students to explore various subconcepts within a particular area of biblical studies. The assignment requires the student to summarize a particular Bible dictionary entry chosen from a list of instructor-approved options. In less than a single typed page, distributed or posted for their classmates and accompanied by a presentation or video of no longer than five minutes, the students contribute bit by bit to course instruction. The assignment instills confidence, generates student-to-student interaction, and cultivates a respect for scholarly sources. The Bible dictionary article abstract assignment is a mainstay of my upper-division biblical literature courses. The key to its success lies in the planning.

In the planning stage, I first brainstorm a variety of topics relevant to the course but tangential or supplemental to its central subject. I then align those topics (two to four per week, depending on class size) with the texts or subjects covered in an individual class session. For example, when my course on the gospels focused on Mark 4–8, Bible dictionary article options included "parable," the titles "Son of Man" and "Messiah," and "Galilee." One of our sessions on Romans in a Pauline epistles class might feature articles on "faith," "righteousness," and "Israel."

After brainstorming but still in the syllabus-design phase, I pair potential topics with articles available in the Bible dictionaries on reference in the university library. Most of my assigned articles are found in either the *New Interpreter's Dictionary of the Bible* or the *Anchor Bible Dictionary*. I compare article length for consistency and make sure that undergraduates can understand them. The articles often coordinate with online entries available from the Society of Biblical Literature's Bible Odyssey.

A third step sets expectations for the students. Early in the semester, I provide an example of a written abstract. I also enact a timed, live presentation example. I coordinate this example with an introductory course topic, thus using class time to convey relevant information while modeling the assignment. It is a challenge to provide accurate summaries in an engaging manner, especially with strict time constraints. It lifts class morale when it becomes obvious that the instructor struggles with this challenge!

Students then select the article topic that grabs their interest—one per student, with due dates staggered throughout the semester. Sometimes I need to provide simple explanations for more specialized topics (e.g., apocalypticism, Diatessaron, apocryphal gospels). Usually, I allow students to choose their assigned articles in descending order of academic rank, starting with seniors. When I used this assignment in the online environment, I streamlined the process with a discussion board listing all the topics and dates from the syllabus and requesting that students comment with their first and second choices.

The students' preparatory work involves reading their assigned article in the approved Bible dictionary, citing responsibly and summarizing the main concepts in no more than three hundred words. The word limit reinforces that the goal is to demonstrate understanding by highlighting the article's most important aspects. At the same time, I encourage students to note examples that illustrate the main points they have selected. If they need to say more, they can do so during their four- to five-minute presentation.

Before their presentations, students distribute their abstract to classmates, who add it to their growing collection for further reference. Afterward, their classmates can ask questions. The effort of research, even confined to one Bible dictionary article, seems to increase students' investment in the subject matter. I have heard students explaining Q, historical Jesus research, and the Feast of Unleavened Bread to one another with surprising levels of enthusiasm.

Beyond supplementing their learning about topics related to the Bible, the assignment challenges students to communicate a complex subject in a comprehensible, concise, and compelling fashion. The pressure of educating their peers encourages them to invest additional effort. The students tend to ask questions that they might not ask to their professor. Overall, we end up covering far more topics—and at a higher level—than could fit into a regular lecture or planned discussion.

Quick Tip
Constructing a House Church to Hear Romans

TIMOTHY A. GABRIELSON

Perhaps the greatest struggle in teaching the Bible to undergraduates lies in giving them a dynamic encounter with the ancient writings. The two-fold pedagogical goal, as I see it, is to situate the Scriptures historically and to engage the minds, emotions, and values of modern students who might not care much about the past. One solution is to immerse students in the lived realities of the ancient world. Doing so preserves the historical component of the course while also inviting students to participate in history through their imaginations.

In a small, upper-level course on Romans populated by majors and minors in the theology department, I led my students to form a house church with Jewish and gentile characters. From the perspectives of those personae, students then read and reacted to Paul's letter. The semester-long activity worked in tandem with a traditional exegetical approach. We began by placing the epistle in the contexts of Paul's biography and the process of letter writing in antiquity. We also learned about gentiles, Jews, and Jewish sympathizers in Rome.[1]

My thanks go to the Society of Biblical Literature Teaching Biblical Studies in an Undergraduate Liberal Arts Context Program Unit for accepting a prior version of this paper (fall 2020). Two attendees, David Howell and Adam Porter, suggested a similar concept, that of a "reacting pedagogy," which I would also commend. See "Reacting to the Past," Barnard College, https://reacting.barnard.edu/. I would especially like to thank the members of my Romans course for engaging so well and providing invaluable feedback.

1. To set this up, I relied particularly on Peter Lampe, *From Paul to Valentinus: Christians at Rome in the First Two Centuries*, trans. Michael Steinhauser, ed. Marshall D. Johnson (Minneapolis: Fortress, 2003); and Peter Oakes, *Reading Romans in Pompeii: Paul's Letter at Ground Level* (Minneapolis: Fortress, 2009).

Against this background, we formed a house church. Each student fashioned one gentile and one Jewish or Jewish-affiliated character.[2] They drew notecards for

- *ethnicity:* Egyptian, Ethiopian, Galatian, Greek, Jewish, Latin, Persian, Syrian[3]
- *relation to Jewishness* (for Jewish or Jewish-affiliated characters): strictly observant, loosely observant, proselyte, Godfearer
- *social role/occupation:* retired military officer, shop owner's widow, merchant's wife, secondborn son to a trader, artisan's daughter, skilled laborer, unskilled laborer, skilled freedman, disabled person

They rolled a die for

- *economic status:* moderate surplus, stable income, subsistence, impoverished[4]
- *years as a Christian:* 1 = sympathizer, 2–3 = five years; 4–5 = 10 years; 6 = 15 years
- *years affiliated with Jewishness* (for proselytes/Godfearers): five times the roll of the die (if reasonable)

Students then had to perform two or more hours of research on each of their characters, using reputable sources and at least one print encyclopedia.[5] In subsequent class periods, they each submitted a one-page description of their gentile and Jewish characters, which included the following:

- name
- age

---

2. Students had some precedent for this activity. They had already read chapter 2 of Sylvia C. Keesmaat and Brian J. Walsh, *Romans Disarmed: Resisting Empire, Demanding Justice* (Grand Rapids: Brazos, 2019).

3. I had two Greek and two Jewish notecards, and one each for the other ethnicities.

4. Each of the social-role notecards included a range of economic statuses. For example, the unskilled laborer role might receive "stable income," "subsistence," or "impoverished," but not "moderate surplus."

5. I did not impose a set list of sources, but we discussed how to discern trustworthy online content and in books. We also have a particular section of our library with common resources in biblical studies, such as the *Anchor Bible Dictionary*, so I directed my students there for the print encyclopedia.

+ precise city/cities of background
+ precise occupation
+ major life events before hearing Romans

After students had finished this work, we formed the house church as follows:

+ *moderate surplus* (6): Onomaris (Galatian widow of shop owner), the patron, and five children;
+ *stable* (5): Brutus Gallus (Latin ex-military officer); Tychikos Aigyptiotes (Egyptian dock worker), with wife and child; one other character;
+ *subsistence* (10): Nympha (Syrian Godfearer, daughter of textile worker), Persis (Persian nursemaid), Dionysios of Sparta (Greek freedman, blacksmith, Jewish proselyte), seven other personae (including Onomaris's freedman);
+ *impoverished* (9): Mary (observant Jew, disabled widow, patronized by Onomaris), Nikodemos (semiobservant Jew, second-born son to glassworker), and seven other characters.

We added the unnamed characters to reach a church of thirty persons.

Finally, students were prepared to hear Romans in their characters. Most days followed a traditional class format, in which we read individual sections of Romans (e.g., Rom 1:1–17; 18–32) and traced Paul's logic. Four times in the semester, we paused and "heard" Romans through our house-church characters instead. We did this for Romans 1–4; 5–8; 9–11; and 12–16, respectively. Students wrote one page apiece on how their gentile and Jewish characters were hearing Romans. They also wrote a third page about how they themselves were hearing the letter.[6] In each of these four class periods, I reserved the time for discussion.

The activity fulfilled both components of my goal. For one, it engaged students. One student said she felt like she was playing the board game Life as we drew cards and rolled the dice, and some remarked on how personal the letter had become to them. At the same time, it brought the

---

6. I gave guidelines for length, formatting, and submission matters, but the prompt was simply, "How are your gentile character, your Jewish character, and you yourself 'hearing' this section of Romans?" Since we had already discussed Paul's meaning with some depth before we "heard" our larger units of Romans in character, students were well equipped to answer this open-ended prompt.

historical context to the forefront. Students regularly saw details in the text that they had never noticed before. They scoured Romans 16 when constructing their characters. The Jewish proselyte grew frustrated with Paul's depreciation of circumcision, a slave was unsettled by Paul's metaphor of "slavery to righteousness," and the church's patron felt called out by the apostle's plea for generosity. Students also engaged with Paul's reasoning at an evaluative level. One student, a devout Christian, noted that she felt "freed" to assess Paul's arguments rather than begin with the presumption that he was right. Doing so deepened her appreciation for Romans.

One aspect of this activity requires special comment. We cannot ignore the cruel legacy of slavery in antebellum America and other Western nations as we reconstruct the ancient world. It is critical to avoid assigning the role of slave or freedperson to someone who, given the racialized history of American slavery, might view the role as a stigma. I decided not to include "slave" as a role, and I rigged it to make sure the African American student in my class did not receive a freedman role either. In some contexts, having students pick the cards at random may be unwise.

The exercise required considerable forethought, but it was well worth the time invested. Students both learned more and cared more than in any other classes I have taught. They enjoyed being immersed in the lived realities of first-century Roman Christianity. The exercise also sharpened their analysis of the epistle and helped them attend to a wide array of concerns—not only theology but food, money, ethnicity, and class. Forming a house church generated student enthusiasm and prompted a more historical and holistic reading of Romans.

Bibliography

Keesmaat, Sylvia C., and Brian J. Walsh. *Romans Disarmed: Resisting Empire, Demanding Justice.* Grand Rapids: Brazos, 2019.

Lampe, Peter. *From Paul to Valentinus: Christians at Rome in the First Two Centuries.* Translated by Michael Steinhauser. Edited by Marshall D. Johnson. Minneapolis: Fortress, 2003.

Oakes, Peter. *Reading Romans in Pompeii: Paul's Letter at Ground Level.* Minneapolis: Fortress, 2009.

"Reacting to the Past." Barnard College. https://reacting.barnard.edu/.

PART 3
ENGAGING GEN Z

LA BIBLIA EN ACENTO LATINO:
BIBLICAL STUDIES FOR FIRST-GENERATION
LATINX STUDENTS

MELANIE A. HOWARD

As a part of the largest minoritized group in the United States today, Latinx students have been the subject of a growing body of research related to questions of best practices for matters of both pedagogy and student affairs.[1] Yet while Latinx students are growing in number, they nonetheless trail behind their white, black, and Asian peers in terms of their likelihood of obtaining a four-year college degree.[2] This statistic, while sobering,

---

1. Here I follow Shaun Harper in the choice of *minoritized* rather than *minority* language. As Harper notes, "Persons are not born into a minority status nor are they minoritized in every social context (e.g., their families, racially homogeneous friendship groups, or places of worship). Instead, they are rendered minorities in particular situations and institutional environments that sustain an overrepresentation of Whiteness." See Harper, "Race without Racism: How Higher Education Researchers Minimize Racist Institutional Norms," *RHE* 36 (Fall 2012): 9 n. 1. I am grateful to my colleague Dr. Kizzy Lopez for bringing Harper's work to my attention. I also use the term *Latinx* both because of its potential to be inclusive of nonbinary gender identities and because of its emergence as an increasingly common term especially within higher education. In using it, I also recognize my own position of privilege as a white educator. For a discussion of the term's use in higher education settings as well as its indication of privilege, see Cristobal Salinas, "The Complexity of the 'x' in Latinx: How Latinx/a/o Students Relate to, Identify With, and Understand the Term Latinx," *JHHE* 19 (2020): 149–68.

2. Jens Miguel Krogstad, "5 Facts about Latinos and Education," Pew Research Center, 28 July 2016, https://tinyurl.com/SBL03108bk. According to Krogstad, research from 2014 indicated that at that time, only 15 percent of Hispanics in the 25–29-year-old bracket had completed a four-year college degree, compared to 22 percent of Blacks, 41 percent of whites, and 63 percent of Asians. This statistic notwithstanding, Latinx students rank highly in their motivation to complete college.

promotes a deficit-based view of first-generation Latinx students.[3] Recent research suggests that an asset-based view is more appropriate to student success since it recognizes the cultural capital and support structures that students bring with them.[4] Thus, despite some data that suggest a lag in the completion of four-year degrees, other data point to significant sources of cultural wealth that first-generation Latinx students bring to their studies.

Much recent research on pedagogy and student development focuses on the needs of first-generation Latinx students. In general, scholars are attending to issues of student diversity and the opportunities that diversity presents to college educators and administrators.[5] Much of this

---

According to Ruffalo Noel Levitz's "2018 National Freshman Motivation to Complete College Report," students who identified as "Hispanic/Latino" outranked students of all other ethnicities in their positive answer to the prompt "Strong desire to continue my education." See Levitz, "2018 National Freshman Motivation to Complete College Report," 2018, https://tinyurl.com/SBL03108d3.

3. The combination of the characteristic "first-generation" and "Latinx" reflects my own teaching setting at Fresno Pacific University, where 42 percent of traditional undergraduate students are the first in their family to attend college. Roughly the same percentage of this student population identifies as Hispanic or Latino. While not all the first-generation students are Latinx and not all the Latinx students are first generation, my own setting displays a significant overlap between these populations. However, I recognize that these student demographic characteristics are different and that the presence of one such characteristic does not necessitate the presence of the other.

4. For example, Tara Yosso proposes that students of color bring with them several elements of cultural capital that serve them well as students. See Yosso, "Whose Culture Has Capital? A Critical Race Theory Discussion of Community Cultural Wealth," *REE* 8 (2005): 69–91. Likewise, drawing on Yosso's work, a 2017 study of first- and second-generation Latinx students revealed that despite challenges, students reported having an equal number of support systems, including family and their own self-determination, among others. See Claudia Kouyoumdjian et al., "A Community Cultural Wealth Examination of Sources of Support and Challenges among Latino First- and Second-Generation College Students at a Hispanic Serving Institution," *JHHE* 16 (2017): 61–76. Earlier work by Kenneth González, Carla Stoner, and Jennifer Jovel also suggests that social and familial capital can be instrumental in creating pathways to higher education, specifically for Latina students. See González, Stoner, and Jovel, "Examining the Role of Social Capital in Access to College for Latinas: Toward a College Opportunity Framework," *JHHE* 2 (2003): 146–70.

5. See, e.g., Karen Longman, *Diversity Matters: Race, Ethnicity, and the Future of Christian Higher Education* (Abilene, TX: Abilene Christian University Press, 2017); Ann Intili Morey and Margie K. Kitano, *Multicultural Course Transformation in Higher Education: A Broader Truth* (Needham Heights, MA: Allyn & Bacon, 1997);

scholarship highlights research-based pedagogical strategies.[6] I do not intend to duplicate any of the work that has already been done in this area. Rather, I wish to show how teaching within the discipline of biblical studies might support and engage first-generation Latinx students. I have discovered that attention to the areas of translation between linguistic worlds (both ancient and modern), identity formation, and family provide helpful points of connection between the experiences of first-generation Latinx students and the field of biblical studies.

Bridging the Gap: From First-Generation Latinx Students to Biblical Studies

Scholarship on Latinx student success suggests useful first steps toward welcoming first-generation Latinx students to the discipline of biblical studies. Applying Latinx perspectives to biblical studies serves as a strong second step. Biblical scholars and theologians such as Justo González, Miguel De La Torre, Elsa Tamez, Francisco Lozada Jr., Fernando Segovia, and Jean-Pierre Ruiz have related biblical themes to the lived experiences of Latinx readers.[7] Other scholars have addressed best

---

Daryl G. Smith, ed., *Diversity and Inclusion in Higher Education: Emerging Perspectives on Institutional Transformation* (New York: Routledge, 2014).

6. For example, Kathleen Ross's volume offers practical pedagogical tips for instructors to capitalize on the strengths of all students, especially first-generation Latinx students. See Ross, *Breakthrough Strategies: Classroom-Based Practices to Support New Majority College Students* (Cambridge: Harvard Education Press, 2016). Similarly, Alicia Chávez and Susan Longerbeam offer guidelines for capitalizing on the cultural gifts that students bring to the classroom. See Chávez and Longerbeam, *Teaching across Cultural Strengths: A Guide to Balancing Integrated and Individuated Cultural Frameworks in College Teaching* (Sterling, VA: Stylus, 2016). Given that the support of first-generation Latinx students continues even beyond the classroom, Edward Delgado-Romero and Carlos Hernandez's work on the competencies needed for faculty advisers of Hispanic student organizations is equally important. See Delgado-Romero and Hernandez, "Empowering Hispanic Students through Student Organizations: Competencies for Faculty Advisors," *JHHE* 1 (2002): 144–57.

7. See Efrain Agosto, "Social Analysis of the New Testament and Hispanic Theology: A Case Study," *JHLT* 5.4 (1998): 6–29; Efrain Agosto and Jacqueline M. Hidalgo, *Latinxs, the Bible, and Migration* (London: Palgrave Macmillan, 2018); Edwin David Aponte and Miguel A. De La Torre, eds., *Handbook of Latina/o Theologies* (St. Louis: Chalice, 2006); Francisco García-Treto, "Crossing the Line: Three Scenes of Divine-Human Engagement in the Hebrew Bible," in *Teaching the Bible: The Discourses and*

practices for pedagogy in the field of biblical studies.[8] At the time of this writing, however, I could find no widely available and sustained treatments of the implications of Latinx biblical scholarship for teaching biblical interpretation. How can biblical studies instructors capitalize on the theological and hermeneutical emphases of Latinx scholars in order to teach all students, especially first-generation Latinx students? The area of convergence for biblical scholarship, pedagogy, and Latinx perspectives remains open for exploration.[9]

Politics of Biblical Pedagogy, ed. Fernando F. Segovia and Mary Ann Tolbert (Eugene, OR: Wipf & Stock, 1998), 105–16; Justo L. González, *Santa Biblia: The Bible through Hispanic Eyes* (Nashville: Abingdon, 2010); Pablo A. Jimenez, "In Search of a Hispanic Model of Biblical Interpretation," *JHLT* 3.2 (1995): 44–64; Francisco Lozada Jr., *Toward a Latino/a Biblical Interpretation* (Atlanta: SBL Press, 2017); Francisco Lozada Jr. and Fernando F. Segovia, eds., *Latino/a Biblical Hermeneutics: Problematics, Objectives, Strategies* (Atlanta: SBL Press, 2014); Harold J. Recinos and Hugo Magallanes, eds., *Jesus in the Hispanic Community: Images of Christ from Theology to Popular Religion* (Louisville: Westminster John Knox, 2009); Pablo Richard, "The Hermeneutics of Liberation: Theoretical Grounding for the Communitarian Reading of the Bible," in Segovia and Tolbert, *Teaching the Bible*, 272–82; Jean-Pierre Ruiz, "Beginning to Read the Bible in Spanish: An Initial Assessment," *JHLT* 1.2 (1994): 28–50; Ruiz, "Four Faces of Theology: Four Johannine Conversations," in Segovia and Tolbert, *Teaching the Bible*, 86–101; Ruiz, *Readings from the Edges: The Bible and People on the Move* (Maryknoll, NY: Orbis, 2011); Fernando F. Segovia, *Decolonizing Biblical Studies: A View from the Margins* (Maryknoll, NY: Orbis, 2000); Elsa Tamez, *Bible of the Oppressed* (Eugene, OR: Wipf & Stock, 2006); Miguel De La Torre, *The Politics of Jesús: A Hispanic Political Theology* (Lanham, MD: Rowman & Littlefield, 2015). Despite this work on Latinx biblical criticism, Aquiles Ernesto Martínez nonetheless laments that at least as of 2011, Latinx biblical studies lag behind theological works as he writes, "Hispanic/Latino theology has reached maturity. Two decades after its inception, current literature is numerous, diverse, and insightful. Sadly, we cannot make the same enthusiastic claim about the work of our 'biblistas' in helping us articulate our Latino/a biblical interpretation." See Martinez, "U.S. Hispanic/Latino Biblical Interpretation: A Critique from Within," *ThTo* 68 (2011): 134.

8. See David J. A. Clines, "Learning, Teaching, and Researching Biblical Studies, Today and Tomorrow," *JBL* 129 (2010): 5–29; Dale B. Martin, *Pedagogy of the Bible: An Analysis and Proposal* (Louisville: Westminster John Knox, 2008); Mark Roncace and Patrick Gray, eds., *Teaching the Bible: Practical Strategies for Classroom Instruction* (Atlanta: Society of Biblical Literature, 2005); Segovia and Tolbert, *Teaching the Bible*.

9. I have previously made only an initial foray into this question in "What Does Athens Have to Do with the Classroom? Looking to Paul in Teaching and Learning with Latino, First-Generation College Students," *Didaktikos* (2020): 33–35.

My own white identity makes me enter this area with caution. I run the risks of imposing white savior-ism on students, colonizing the work of Latinx colleagues in the field, and offering paternalistic strategies for teaching. Because of my own power and privilege, I am susceptible to blind spots that might cause me to participate in the recolonizing, oppression, and marginalization of the very communities to whom I seek to listen and from whom I seek to learn. I do not want to minimize the seriousness of any of these risks.

At the same time, I hope that I can serve as a responsible co-conspirator in this work. I also seek to capitalize on my white identity by enjoining white faculty colleagues to attend to the development of culturally sustaining pedagogical practices that contribute to first-generation Latinx student success.[10] Data from the Society of Biblical Literature suggest that at the time of this writing, over 86 percent of members of the society who hold faculty status in the United States identify as white.[11] Given the likelihood of a cultural distance between Bible instructors and first-generation Latinx students, introducing those students to the discipline of biblical studies requires that faculty adopt culturally sustaining pedagogical practices. The opportunity to contribute to the development of those practices is worth the risks.

My assessment of these risks illustrates a fundamental assumption that underlies this essay: namely, that effective teaching of first-generation Latinx students may have far more to do with the abilities of instructors to learn from their students than with interpretive prowess. I agree with Robert W. Pazmiño that "to move Latino/a values and insights from the margin or periphery of curricular and extracurricular concerns to the center of theological education requires more than awareness and analysis of cultural differences. It requires the relinquishment of power to shift structural and curricular arrangements to support educational equity."[12] I

---

10. I use the language of *co-conspirator* rather than *ally*, following Bettina Love's use of the term to convey the risks that co-conspirators assume. See Love, *We Want to Do More than Survive: Abolitionist Teaching and the Pursuit of Educational Freedom* (Boston: Beacon, 2019). I also follow Django Paris in the use of the term "culturally sustaining pedagogy." As Paris describes it, this term "supports the value of our multiethnic and multilingual present and future." See Paris, "Culturally Sustaining Pedagogy: A Needed Change in Stance, Terminology, and Practice," *ER* 41 (2012): 95.

11. "Member Data Report, 2019," Society of Biblical Literature, 2019, https://tinyurl.com/SBL03108bl.

12. Robert W. Pazmiño, "Theological Education with Hispanic Persons: Teaching Distinctiveness," *TTR* 6 (2003): 138.

am interested in practical ways for educators to follow Pazmiño in the call to relinquish power in order to center Latinx insights. Relinquishing power does not necessitate abandoning exegetical techniques. It may, however, require refocused attention. I suggest particular attention to three phenomena common to Latinx culture: translation, identity formation, and family.

Translation

Biblical scholars and many Latinx students are familiar with the process of translation. Scholars navigate between ancient and modern languages; students navigate between English and Spanish. To be sure, not all first-generation Latinx students are heritage speakers of Spanish. Still, many maintain familiarity, if not fluency. Code-switching between home and school environments thus often involves shifting between a heritage language and a second language.[13]

Code-switching is a daily reality for several of my students. Many of them commute to campus. They begin their mornings at home speaking Spanish with their families, switch to English throughout the school day, use one or both languages in a part-time job, and then switch back to Spanish in the evening at home, often while doing their homework in English. They translate daily.

Because of this, my students can readily understand a fundamental element of academic biblical studies: translating the biblical texts from their original languages into the vernacular. Bible instructors are well acquainted with the struggles of drawing out the nuances of a text trans-

---

13. The term *code-switching* is itself a complex term that assumes different meanings including the use of multiple languages in a single utterance (intrasentential), in multiple utterances (intersentential), or in different contexts (situational). While navigating the nuances of code-switching goes beyond the scope of this essay, I simply note that I am primarily considering situational code-switching here even as other forms of code-switching may also be present. I am grateful to Dr. Kristina Lewis for directing me to literature on this topic, including Dean Schmeltz, "Code Switch at an Alternative High School," *WPEL* 34 (2019): 103–16; Vershawn Ashanti Young, *Other People's English: Code-Meshing, Code-Switching, and African American Literacy* (Anderson, SC: Parlor, 2018); Rebecca S. Wheeler and Rachel Swords, *Code-Switching: Teaching Standard English in Urban Classrooms* (Urbana, IL: National Council of Teachers of English, 2006).

lated from Hebrew or Greek into English. I suspect that many instructors have tried to explain how the semantic range of מִשְׁפָּט or λόγος provides a far richer understanding of a text than what can be conveyed in the English translation alone. For monolingual students, this point might be difficult to convey. In contrast, multilingual students readily understand the differing semantic worlds of various languages. They more easily recognize that the biblical text in its original language may contain nuances absent in English translation.

I have leveraged my students' attention to nuance in translation, hoping to bridge the gap between my discipline and my students. As I revised a course on the Gospel of Matthew, I asked myself, "How can this course be more accessible to first-generation Latinx students?" It seemed that one of the easiest ways would be to assign readings by Latinx authors.[14] This led me to Francisco Lozada's essay "Matthew 6:9b–13 (The Lord's Prayer): Explorations into a Latino/a Optic on Language and Translation."[15] In this essay, Lozada explores the twin issues of the context of the reader and the context of the text. Examining his own ambivalent relationship to both English and Spanish, Lozada examines the Lord's Prayer (Matt 6:9b–13) while asking questions about how the act of translating that prayer from Greek affects the interpretation of the prayer. Impressed by Lozada's deft moves from autobiography to a nuanced discussion of translating ὀφειλήματα (and with my fingers crossed that it was not only my own *gringa* identity that led me to find Lozada's essay useful), I assigned it.

I was a little nervous on the day that students were scheduled to discuss Lozada's essay. I asked, "So, what did you think? Did Lozada's essay match up with any of your own experiences?" The response: several vigorous nods and an enthusiastic "Yes!" from the back of the classroom. In the discussion that followed, several students shared anecdotes about their own language acquisition and how their encounters with the biblical text in their first language differed from encounters with the same text in another language.

---

14. Pazmiño supports this impulse in his recommendation that "faculty make use of required writings of Hispanic theologians and scholars writing for the Hispanic community" ("Theological Education with Hispanic Persons," 144).

15. Francisco Lozada Jr., "Matthew 6:9b–13 (The Lord's Prayer): Explorations into a Latino/a Optic on Language and Translation," in *Matthew*, ed. Nicole Wilkinson Duran and James P. Grimshaw, T@C (Minneapolis: Fortress, 2013), 271–85.

In this classroom discussion, my multilingual students demonstrated growth in their understanding of biblical texts and their confidence in the ability to interpret those texts. They made progress toward one of the course's two goals: to defamiliarize and to (re)familiarize students with the Bible. For students who are familiar with the Bible from nonacademic settings, I hope to defamiliarize the text by demonstrating that it originated in a distant past in a far-off land with an unfamiliar culture and foreign language. In contrast, students who find the Bible utterly unfamiliar approach biblical studies with apprehension and anxiety. They fear that their lack of previous knowledge places them at a disadvantage. I seek to (re)familiarize them with the text.

First-generation Latinx students often fall into the latter category. For some of them, commitments to Catholic faith and their sense of deference to interpretation by its clergy complicate their approach to biblical studies. In order to familiarize these students with the Bible, I have encouraged them to capitalize on their experience with translation. In the process, I have witnessed students gaining confidence and proficiency as they recognize their own familiarity with translation processes as an asset for interpreting biblical texts. By capitalizing on their experiences of translation, code-switching, and navigating complex social and semantic worlds, first-generation Latinx students can better relate to the Bible and grow in their understanding of it.

Identity Formation

Code-switching among languages, cultures, and groups of differing privilege constitutes an important identity marker for first-generation Latinx students. The process of code-switching aids students in understanding the Bible across language divides. Likewise, a focus on identity formation not only connects to the experience of my students but also highlights ways in which biblical texts themselves contribute to the identity formation of minoritized populations.

The formation of Latinx identity is complex. Identity signifiers can include national origin, generational status, Spanish-language use, racial/ethnic identity, and religious identity.[16] Not all Latinx students share in

---

16. Aida I. Ramos, "The Complexities of Latinx Identity" (paper presented at the Council for Christian Colleges and Universities' Latin American Studies Program, San Jose, Costa Rica, 25 May 2017).

these identity markers, as demonstrated by the differences between first-generation, Mexican Catholic students whose first language was Spanish and third-generation, Brazilian Pentecostal students whose first language was English.

Latinx theologians and biblical scholars have addressed the intricacies of Latinx identity. In 1983, Virgilio Elizondo considered how the *mestizaje* ("mixed") identity of Mexican Americans could shed light on the similarly *mestizaje* identity of Jesus.[17] Since then, Jacqueline Hidalgo has also recognized the hybridity of identity and the ambivalence that such hybridity can bring to the process of biblical interpretation.[18] She understands the questions she brings to the biblical text and her use of interdisciplinary methods as responses to recognizing hybridity.

The complexity of Latinx identity formation invites instructors to adopt constructive identity formation practices for their students. For many of my first-generation Latinx students, I must also consider Vasti Torres's and Ebelia Hernandez's observation that "for the commuter students, the college experience is primarily felt within the classroom. There is a need for ... faculty [to] understand how the classroom experiences influence ethnic identity."[19] Attention to ethnic identity development in the context of classroom experiences can be particularly effective not only for holistic student development but also for the acquisition of desired student learning outcomes.

Biblical studies classrooms provide an ideal environment for identity development. Here, the primary course texts explore the formation of national identity, the experience of diaspora, conflicts among groups of differing religions, and a host of other issues that relate to identity formation. According to Steffano Montano, "Theological educators must develop learning outcomes and reflective projects that challenge students

---

17. Virgilio Elizondo, *Galilean Journey: The Mexican-American Promise* (Maryknoll, NY: Orbis, 1983).

18. Jacqueline M. Hidalgo, "Reading from No Place: Toward a Hybrid and Ambivalent Study of Scriptures," in Lozada and Segovia, *Latino/a Biblical Hermeneutics*, 165–86. Immediately following Hidalgo's essay in the same volume, Francisco Lozada Jr. reflects on similar issues related to the complexity of Latinx identity in relationship to biblical studies. See Lozada, "Toward a Latino/a Biblical Studies: Foregrounding Identities and Transforming Communities," in Lozada and Segovia, *Latino/a Biblical Hermeneutics*, 187–202.

19. Vasti Torres and Ebelia Hernandez, "The Influence of Ethnic Identity on Self-Authorship: A Longitudinal Study of Latino/a College Students," *JCSD* 48 (2007): 572.

to understand their own identities and the identities of others around them as being socially inscribed with either privileged (for white students) or oppressive (for students of color) stereotypes so that they are better ready to resist those inscriptions in themselves and others."[20] Montano maintains that "theological educators must engage in processes that take a critical look at our teaching methods."[21] This kind of engagement could include explicit attention to code-switching, both in the biblical text and in the lives of students.

For many bicultural or multicultural students who are forming their cultural identity, navigating between cultures and code-switching is a familiar practice. Within their families, they may be juggling dual identities as children to their parents and caregivers to their younger siblings. Within campus communities, they may be juggling even more identities as a friend, roommate, student, peer leader, or student worker. Students may therefore engage in code-switching as means of highlighting different identity features for different situations. Jack K. Chambers and Natalie Schilling-Estes note, "Even an individual who identifies as having a single 'ethnicity' must construct an identity at the confluence of a multitude of other social communities.... Code-switching (as well as other mixed varieties) can provide a particularly effective way of signaling the complexities of minority ethnic identity."[22] Code-switching and identity formation are intimately linked.

Biblical texts demonstrate the connection between code-switching and identity formation. For example, early Christians were navigating a new religious identity in contexts where Jewish, Greek, and Roman dynamics competed for influence. As a diaspora Jew, Paul shares his individual Jew/gentile code-switching behavior in becoming like a Jew to Jews and like one outside the law to those outside the law (1 Cor 9:20–22). The Bible also addresses group identity formation. Throughout the first chapters of

---

20. Steffano Montano, "Addressing White Supremacy on Campus: Anti-racist Pedagogy and Theological Education," *RelEd* 114 (2019): 280.

21. Montano, "Addressing White Supremacy," 280.

22. Jack K. Chambers and Natalie Schilling-Estes, *The Handbook of Language Variation and Change* (Hoboken, NJ: Wiley-Blackwell, 2013), 393. Highlighting a similar idea in relation to bilingual speakers of English and Spanish, Manuel Diaz-Campos observes, "Various styles of bilingualism, some self-consciously artful, are becoming important elements in the reconstruction of the Latino or Hispanic identity in the United States." See Diaz-Campos, *The Handbook of Hispanic Sociolinguistics* (Oxford: Wiley-Blackwell, 2011), 742.

Hosea, for example, the prophet chastises the people of Israel for failing to live out their proper identity as God's people. Hosea's remarks are then repurposed by the author of 1 Peter, who invites his marginalized audience to recognize and embrace their identity as God's people (1 Pet 2:10).[23] Both biblical authors are attempting to contribute to the identity formation of their audiences with regard to the divine rather than to the mighty empires around them.

In an exercise designed to bring students' own identity formation to bear on biblical interpretation, I used the experience of immigration to illustrate how 1 Peter attempts to form the Christian identity of its audience. I asked students to work in groups on the following scenario:

> Imagine that you have been asked to preach to a congregation where there is a high population of undocumented immigrants and their families. Many of them are feeling nervous about recent decisions regarding Deferred Action for Childhood Arrivals (DACA). The pastor of the congregation has asked that you preach on 1 Peter 2. What will be the main points of your sermon? Which portions of the text will you focus on most closely? What do you want your sermon to accomplish? Be prepared to share a brief outline and the key points of your sermon with the class.

Although this situation was framed as a hypothetical one, I knew that, for some students, the scenario was quite real. Their identities were entangled not only with their ethnicity and spirituality but also with their nationality. These issues pressed on them as they engaged with a text that calls on a persecuted minority to live as exiles (1 Pet 2:11), accepting government authority (2:13–14), and enduring suffering (2:20) while identifying as God's people (2:10).

This exercise was fraught with complications for students for whom these questions cut to the heart of their experience.[24] Regardless, their sermon outlines demonstrated a growing awareness of their identity forma-

---

23. Justo González also points to this text as an important one because of the ways in which it encourages solidarity, one of the key paradigms for Hispanic perspectives on the Bible that he identifies (*Santa Biblia*, 104–5).

24. As part of a trauma-informed classroom, such activities should be approached with care and situated within best practices for trauma-informed teaching. For a further discussion of appropriate engagement with trauma in the classroom, see Janice Carello and Lisa D. Butler, "Potentially Perilous Pedagogies: Teaching Trauma Is Not

tion in relation to ethnicity, spirituality, and nationality. Students leveraged this personal connection to relate to the kind of identity development that the author of 1 Peter advocates for a persecuted religious minority.

Family

Identity formation includes family ties. Vasti Torres explores this relationship as it affects student success. She has concluded that the degree to which a student's family is acculturated will affect the student's formation of identity.[25] This is especially true for first-year Latinx college students. For example, a Latina student whose parents encourage an English-language education may be more likely to persist than a similar student whose parents promote more traditional gender roles that dissuade women from higher education.

The close family ties so important to Latinx culture can support the education of Latinx college students. Tara Yosso counts "familial capital" among the assets that students of color bring to their college experiences. She defines it as "those cultural knowledges nurtured among *familia* (kin) that carry a sense of community history, memory and cultural intuition.... This form of cultural wealth engages a commitment to community well being and expands the concept of family to include a more broad understanding of kinship."[26] In Yosso's formulation, families do not distract. Instead, they strengthen. Timothy Baldwin and Martin Avila Jr. concur as they identify four key values permeating several Latinx cultures: *colectivismo* (and specifically *familismo*), *personalismo*, *respeto*, and *confianza*.[27] I

---

the Same as Trauma-Informed Teaching," *JTD* 15 (2014): 153–68. See also Kathleen Gallagher Elkins's chapter in this volume.

25. Vasti Torres, "Familial Influences on the Identity Development of Latino First-Year Students," *JCSD* 45 (2004): 457–69. In an earlier study, Torres also found that parents especially influence the ethnic identity development of their children: "All of the students credited their parents for their views on ethnicity and its role in their life. They also talked about their Latino ethnicity in a positive manner and attributed this positive meaning of ethnicity to their parents." See Torres, "Influences on Ethnic Identity Development of Latino College Students in the First Two Years of College," *JCSD* 44 (2003): 538.

26. Yosso, "Whose Culture Has Capital?," 79.

27. Timothy Baldwin and Martin Avila Jr., "'Culture Is Sneaky': How Culture Shapes the Ways Latin@ Undergraduates Communicate, Relate, and Learn," *Advance*

have found that *familismo* performs particularly well in connecting biblical studies to first-generation Latinx student experience.[28]

The Hebrew Bible and the New Testament place a high value on family. In the Deuteronomic teachings, parents are encouraged to teach their children about the law (Deut 11:19; 32:46). Likewise, Proverbs enjoins the proper training of children (Prov 22:6), recognizing the family as a primary venue for the transmission of cultural and religious values. As Christopher Wright observes, "A most important aspect of the role of the family in ancient Israel was as the vehicle of continuity for the faith, history, law, and traditions of the nation."[29] Family, as depicted in the Hebrew Bible, serves as an important bearer of culture.

Likewise, in New Testament formulations, family functions as a primary metaphor for understanding relationships among Christians. Jesus defines his followers in familial terms (Matt 12:46–50; Mark 3:31–35; Luke 8:19–21). Similarly, the household codes found in the New Testament epistolary literature (Eph 5:22–6:9; Col 3:18–4:1; Titus 2:1–10; 1 Pet 3:1–6) suggest that early Christians continued to value the institution of the family.

I have capitalized on the Latinx cultural value of close family ties when teaching about Jesus's call for disciples and what that call entails in terms of the disruption of established family structures. Jesus's redefinition of the family as those who do the will of God (Matt 12:46–50; Mark 3:31–35; Luke 8:19–21) seems to scorn the strong family ties valued by many first-generation Latinx students.

I ask students to imagine a time when their family has asked them to babysit a younger sibling or take an elderly relative to a doctor's appointment. What if they simply said no and went off with a stranger instead?

(2017): 31–36. These four values may be roughly translated as collectivist orientation (or family orientation), personal orientation, respect, and trust.

28. Justo González highlights this value of family as being particularly emblematic of Hispanic Christian perspectives (*Santa Biblia*, 103–13). Pazmiño also emphasizes this cultural value of family for what it means in terms of establishing student-teacher relationships: "Teaching itself can then be seen through Hispanic eyes as a form of godparenting that supports the emergence of inexperienced persons. In theological education, teachers can serve as godparents for their students as they introduce them into various faith families" ("Theological Education with Hispanic Persons," 142). This relational aspect of contributing to first-generation Latinx student success should not be diminished.

29. Christopher Wright, "Family," *ABD* 2:764.

My students are often horrified by this thought experiment. They imagine the consequences they would face as a result of such disrespect to their family. This horror tends to stay with them throughout the semester as they grapple with Jesus's radical demands and their potential to strain familial relationships. They frequently discuss the conflict between familial and religious commitments on their final exams.

Conclusion

Both the literature on student needs and my own experience suggest that we can develop strategic and successful ways to teach biblical studies to first-generation Latinx students. Focusing on issues of translation helps students to appreciate the Bible as a product of a language and culture that differs from that of North American English speakers. Attention to students' processes of identity formation helps them to recognize similar processes among ancient audiences. Finally, highlighting culturally valued family ties can aid students in finding resonance and dissonance between their experiences and biblical texts.

Areas of resonance and dissonance may vary among first-generation Latinx students, who hail from a wide range of backgrounds. Students enter the classroom with differing language fluencies, immigration statuses, and socioeconomic statuses. Attending to these personal differences promotes student success.[30] Yet despite these differences, nearly all students can relate to finding the right expression, constructing personal identity, and fulfilling obligations to family. Biblical studies instructors must therefore learn from their students' experiences and make connections between the values of their students and the texts that they teach.

Bibliography

Agosto, Efrain. "Social Analysis of the New Testament and Hispanic Theology: A Case Study." *JHLT* 5.4 (1998): 6–29.

Agosto, Efrain, and Jacqueline M. Hidalgo. *Latinxs, the Bible, and Migration*. London: Palgrave Macmillan, 2018.

---

30. Vasti Torres notes, "By understanding individual differences, practitioners can create more welcoming environments." See Torres, "Validation of a Bicultural Orientation Model for Hispanic College Students," *JCSD* 40 (1999): 295.

Aponte, Edwin David, and Miguel A. De La Torre, eds. *Handbook of Latina/o Theologies*. St. Louis: Chalice, 2006.

Baldwin, Timothy, and Martin Avila Jr. "'Culture Is Sneaky': How Culture Shapes the Ways Latin@ Undergraduates Communicate, Relate, and Learn." *Advance* (Fall 2017): 31–36.

Carello, Janice, and Lisa D. Butler. "Potentially Perilous Pedagogies: Teaching Trauma Is Not the Same as Trauma-Informed Teaching." *JTD* 15 (2014): 153–68.

Chambers, Jack K., and Natalie Schilling-Estes. *The Handbook of Language Variation and Change*. Hoboken, NJ: Wiley-Blackwell, 2013.

Chávez, Alicia, and Susan Longerbeam. *Teaching across Cultural Strengths: A Guide to Balancing Integrated and Individuated Cultural Frameworks in College Teaching*. Sterling, VA: Stylus, 2016.

Clines, David J. A. "Learning, Teaching, and Researching Biblical Studies, Today and Tomorrow." *JBL* 129 (2010): 5–29.

De La Torre, Miguel A. *The Politics of Jesús: A Hispanic Political Theology*. Lanham, MD: Rowman & Littlefield, 2015.

Delgado-Romero, Edward, and Carlos Hernandez. "Empowering Hispanic Students through Student Organizations: Competencies for Faculty Advisors." *JHHE* 1 (2002): 144–57.

Diaz-Campos, Manuel. *The Handbook of Hispanic Sociolinguistics*. Oxford: Wiley-Blackwell, 2011.

Elizondo, Virgilio. *Galilean Journey: The Mexican-American Promise*. Maryknoll, NY: Orbis, 1983.

García-Treto, Francisco. "Crossing the Line: Three Scenes of Divine-Human Engagement in the Hebrew Bible." Pages 105–16 in *Teaching the Bible: The Discourses and Politics of Biblical Pedagogy*. Edited by Fernando F. Segovia and Mary Ann Tolbert. Eugene, OR: Wipf & Stock, 1998.

González, Justo L. *Santa Biblia: The Bible through Hispanic Eyes*. Nashville: Abingdon, 2010.

González, Kenneth, Carla Stoner, and Jennifer Jovel. "Examining the Role of Social Capital in Access to College for Latinas: Toward a College Opportunity Framework." *JHHE* 2 (2003): 146–70.

Harper, Shaun. "Race without Racism: How Higher Education Researchers Minimize Racist Institutional Norms." *RHE* 36 (Fall 2012): 9–29.

Hidalgo, Jacqueline M. "Reading from No Place: Toward a Hybrid and Ambivalent Study of Scriptures." Pages 165–86 in *Latino/a Biblical*

Hermeneutics: Problematics, Objectives, Strategies. Edited by Francisco Lozada Jr. and Fernando F. Segovia. Atlanta: SBL Press, 2014.

Howard, Melanie. "What Does Athens Have to Do with the Classroom? Looking to Paul in Teaching and Learning with Latino, First-Generation College Students." *Didaktikos: Journal of Theological Education* (November 2020): 33–35.

Jimenez, Pablo A. "In Search of a Hispanic Model of Biblical Interpretation." *JHLT* 3.2 (1995): 44–64.

Kouyoumdjian, Claudia, Bianca L. Guzmán, Nichole M. Garcia, and Valerie Talavera-Bustillos. "A Community Cultural Wealth Examination of Sources of Support and Challenges among Latino First- and Second-Generation College Students at a Hispanic Serving Institution." *JHHE* 16 (2017): 61–76.

Krogstad, Jens Miguel. "5 Facts about Latinos and Education." Pew Research Center, 28 July 2016. https://tinyurl.com/SBL03108bk.

Levitz, Ruffalo Noel. "2018 National Freshman Motivation to Complete College Report." 2018. https://tinyurl.com/SBL03108d3.

Longman, Karen. *Diversity Matters: Race, Ethnicity, and the Future of Christian Higher Education.* Abilene, TX: Abilene Christian University Press, 2017.

Love, Bettina. *We Want to Do More than Survive: Abolitionist Teaching and the Pursuit of Educational Freedom.* Boston: Beacon, 2019.

Lozada, Francisco, Jr. "Matthew 6:9b–13 (The Lord's Prayer): Explorations into a Latino/a Optic on Language and Translation." Pages 271–85 in *Matthew.* Edited by Nicole Wilkinson Duran and James P. Grimshaw. T@C. Minneapolis: Fortress, 2013.

———. *Toward a Latino/a Biblical Interpretation.* Atlanta: SBL Press, 2017.

———. "Toward a Latino/a Biblical Studies: Foregrounding Identities and Transforming Communities." Pages 187–202 in *Latino/a Biblical Hermeneutics: Problematics, Objectives, Strategies.* Edited by Francisco Lozada Jr. and Fernando F. Segovia. Atlanta: SBL Press, 2014.

Lozada, Francisco, Jr., and Fernando F. Segovia, eds. *Latino/a Biblical Hermeneutics: Problematics, Objectives, Strategies.* Atlanta: SBL Press, 2014.

Martin, Dale B. *Pedagogy of the Bible: An Analysis and Proposal.* Louisville: Westminster John Knox, 2008.

Martínez, Aquiles Ernesto. "U.S. Hispanic/Latino Biblical Interpretation: A Critique from Within." *ThTo* 68 (2011): 134–48.

"Member Data Report, 2019." Society of Biblical Literature, 2019. https://tinyurl.com/SBL03108bl.

Montano, Steffano. "Addressing White Supremacy on Campus: Anti-racist Pedagogy and Theological Education." *RelEd* 114 (2019): 274–86.

Morey, Ann Intil, and Margie K. Kitano. *Multicultural Course Transformation in Higher Education: A Broader Truth.* Needham Heights, MA: Allyn & Bacon, 1997.

Paris, Django. "Culturally Sustaining Pedagogy: A Needed Change in Stance, Terminology, and Practice." *ER* 41 (2012): 93–97.

Pazmiño, Robert W. "Theological Education with Hispanic Persons: Teaching Distinctiveness." *TTR* 6 (2003): 138–45.

Ramos, Aida I. "The Complexities of Latinx Identity." Paper presented at the Council for Christian Colleges and Universities' Latin American Studies Program. San Jose, Costa Rica, 25 May 2017.

Recinos, Harold J., and Hugo Magallanes, eds. *Jesus in the Hispanic Community: Images of Christ from Theology to Popular Religion.* Louisville: Westminster John Knox, 2009.

Richard, Pablo. "The Hermeneutics of Liberation: Theoretical Grounding for the Communitarian Reading of the Bible." Pages 272–82 in *Teaching the Bible: The Discourses and Politics of Biblical Pedagogy.* Edited by Fernando F. Segovia and Mary Ann Tolbert. Eugene, OR: Wipf & Stock, 1998.

Roncace, Mark, and Patrick Gray, eds. *Teaching the Bible: Practical Strategies for Classroom Instruction.* RBS 49. Atlanta: Society of Biblical Literature, 2005.

Ross, Kathleen. *Breakthrough Strategies: Classroom-Based Practices to Support New Majority College Students.* Cambridge: Harvard Education Press, 2016.

Ruiz, Jean-Pierre. "Beginning to Read the Bible in Spanish: An Initial Assessment." *JHLT* 1.2 (1994): 28–50.

———. "Four Faces of Theology: Four Johannine Conversations." Pages 86–101 in *Teaching the Bible: The Discourses and Politics of Biblical Pedagogy.* Edited by Fernando F. Segovia and Mary Ann Tolbert. Eugene, OR: Wipf & Stock, 1998.

———. *Readings from the Edges: The Bible and People on the Move.* Maryknoll, NY: Orbis, 2011.

Salinas, Cristobal. "The Complexity of the 'x' in Latinx: How Latinx/a/o Students Relate to, Identify With, and Understand the Term Latinx." *JHHE* 19 (2020): 149–68.

Schmeltz, Dean. "Code Switch at an Alternative High School." *WPEL* 34 (2019): 103–16.

Segovia, Fernando F. *Decolonizing Biblical Studies: A View from the Margins.* Maryknoll, NY: Orbis, 2000.

Segovia, Fernando F., and Mary Ann Tolbert, eds. *Teaching the Bible: The Discourses and Politics of Biblical Pedagogy.* Eugene, OR: Wipf & Stock, 1998.

Smith, Daryl G., ed. *Diversity and Inclusion in Higher Education: Emerging Perspectives on Institutional Transformation.* New York: Routledge, 2014.

Tamez, Elsa. *Bible of the Oppressed.* Eugene, OR: Wipf & Stock, 2006.

Torres, Vasti. "Familial Influences on the Identity Development of Latino First-Year Students." *JCSD* 45 (2004): 457–69.

———. "Influences on Ethnic Identity Development of Latino College Students in the First Two Years of College." *JCSD* 44 (2003): 532–47.

———. "Validation of a Bicultural Orientation Model for Hispanic College Students." *JCSD* 40 (1999): 285–98.

Torres, Vasti, and Ebelia Hernandez. "The Influence of Ethnic Identity on Self-Authorship: A Longitudinal Study of Latino/a College Students." *JCSD* 48 (2007): 558–73.

Wheeler, Rebecca S., and Rachel Swords. *Code-Switching: Teaching Standard English in Urban Classrooms.* Urbana, IL: National Council of Teachers of English, 2006.

Wright, Christopher. "Family." *ABD* 2:761–69.

Yosso, Tara. "Whose Culture Has Capital? A Critical Race Theory Discussion of Community Cultural Wealth." *REE* 8 (2005): 69–91.

Young, Vershawn Ashanti. *Other People's English: Code-Meshing, Code-Switching, and African American Literacy.* Anderson, SC: Parlor, 2018.

Becoming a Trauma-Informed Bible Professor

Kathleen Gallagher Elkins

College professors often do their work in the context of uncertain or difficult times. My current students, for example, are living through a global pandemic and the ongoing Black Lives Matter protests in the midst of a US election year. Yet even apart from these pressing concerns, I often teach about trauma. Anyone who teaches the Bible does. The Bible speaks of traumatic experiences such as war, famine, forced migration, sexual assault, child abuse, and crucifixion. When we teach our students about the Bible, therefore, we must also consider their emotional well-being in response to these topics. This is even more crucial when we are living in difficult times.

My interest in this topic began in 2015, when the teaching blogosphere lit up with arguments about trigger warnings. Some professors said we should (or at least, they do) use trigger warnings about topics and texts that might trigger posttraumatic stress. Others responded by arguing that trigger warnings coddle our students and treat them as if they cannot handle difficult topics when in fact life requires handling such topics.

In my research that summer and since, I have become convinced that arguments about trigger warnings miss the point. We are not coddling or protecting students if we decide to give trigger warnings. We are instead giving them information about what they will encounter. For a student

In the summer of 2016, I was awarded a grant to research the pedagogy of traumatized students. Thank you to the Wabash Center for Teaching and Learning in Theology and Religion for that grant and to my cohort of pretenure participants for their input and friendship. I am also grateful to the organizers and panelists of the Teaching Biblical Studies in an Undergraduate Liberal Arts Context program unit at the Annual Meeting of the Society of Biblical Literature in Denver in November 2018. My thanks to Jennifer Kaalund and Peter Anthony Mena for their invaluable feedback on earlier drafts.

who has experienced trauma, a trigger warning gives them power, the very thing that their traumatizing experience took away. At minimum, this power consists of a choice for how and when to engage with the material. Students can choose a time when they feel safe and have an opportunity to process the experience afterwards. A professor who decides to give trigger warnings does students a favor.

Using a trigger warning, however, does not address the entirety of the problem. One of the challenges inherent in teaching traumatized students is their detachment. Psychologically speaking, we might call this emotional numbness or dissociation.[1] Even without the presence of overt triggers, a traumatized student may not be able to pay attention in class. A colleague of mine related a story in which the class was considering a troubling biblical text and discussing the idea of being triggered by it. A student shared that, although this was a well-intentioned conversation, it was off the mark. For her, a trigger to a traumatic incident in her life was a certain shade of blue. Another student agreed and shared that the trigger for her (one that no one could warn her about or protect her from) was a popular cologne that her rapist had used.[2] Herein lies a problem with arguing over whether to give students a trigger warning. We cannot know or anticipate a traumatized person's triggers. We might label certain incidents as likely triggers, but we will sometimes get it wrong. And so, rather than arguing for or against trigger warnings, I propose that we commit to becoming trauma-informed teachers in trauma-informed classrooms.

A trauma-informed college professor aims to support all students. As Heather McCauley and Adam Calser write in their call for trauma-informed college counselors,

> A trauma-informed approach does not necessarily seek disclosure, rather it shifts our frame of reference so that we are mindful of the myriad of

---

1. Victims of trauma often distance themselves emotionally from the traumatic experience by "dissociation" or emotional numbness in order to "make the unbearable bearable." See Peter A. Levine, *In an Unspoken Voice: How the Body Releases Trauma and Restores Goodness* (Berkeley, CA: North Atlantic Books, 2010), 50. For a general discussion of dissociation, see Judith L. Herman, *Trauma and Recovery: The Aftermath of Violence; From Domestic Abuse to Political Terror* (New York: Basic Books, 1992), 1–2, 34–35, passim.

2. My thanks to Jill Peterfeso and other Wabash Center colleagues who shared these and other examples with me. My thinking in this piece is shaped by my Wabash Center cohort in more ways that I can properly cite.

experiences that may influence our students. It also equips us with language to normalize conversations about violence, an important step in shifting the culture on campuses from one plagued by silence to one that challenges the misconception that sexual assault is normal or acceptable.[3]

In certain ways, the goal of becoming trauma-informed is like the goal of universal design.[4] It really cannot hurt anyone and in fact it helps people who may experience significant barriers to learning. It is one way of creating a student- and learning-centered classroom. Trauma-informed professors recognize and mitigate barriers to learning for traumatized students. Doing so just takes some deliberate awareness and work on our part.

I will focus my argument on how we teach students who have experienced trauma, especially when our topics in biblical studies remind them of that trauma. In my Women in the Bible class, for example, we read Judg 19, the horrifying story of the rape and abuse of the Levite's concubine. The text might trigger posttraumatic stress in a student who has experienced sexual assault or whose family history includes intimate-partner violence. How might instructors support such students in a way that minimizes psychological harm?

I will also discuss the way students respond to new information about the Bible and religion in a way that seems to mimic a trauma response. They are not traumatized by the information, though they may react as if learning the material is a shattering, traumatic event. I have recognized these reactions in students who consider the Bible inerrant, infallible, or foundational for their religious beliefs. A devout Christian student who learns about the Synoptic problem may respond as if they have been traumatized by this information. Likewise, white students entering a discussion about racism and religion for the first time may react with anger, outrage, or disbelief.[5] These and similar experiences, however disorienting and distressing, do not reach the level of trauma.

---

3. Heather L. McCauley and Adam W. Casler, "College Sexual Assault: A Call for Trauma-Informed Prevention," *JAH* 56 (2015): 585.

4. Universal design increases accessibility by reducing barriers for people who might otherwise be excluded. For Universal Design for Learning guidelines, see "The UDL Guidelines," CAST, https://tinyurl.com/SBL03108bm.

5. Robin J. DiAngelo, *White Fragility: Why It's So Hard for White People to Talk about Racism* (Boston: Beacon, 2018).

Defining Trauma

The term *trauma* is increasingly used to describe all manner of not-actu-ally-traumatizing experiences. For example, students describe themselves as "traumatized" by a TV show ending or call a bad test grade "traumatic." These are, of course, inappropriate uses of the word. Still, trauma is a sub-jective experience.[6] An incident that traumatizes one person does not necessarily traumatize another. This phenomenon adds to the difficulty of defining trauma.

Trauma, as any New Testament scholar could tell you, comes from the Greek noun meaning "wound" (τραῦμα). In English, however, the word *trauma* connotes an injury far more serious than a physical or even psychological wound.[7] Trauma goes beyond a commonplace experience of suffering or pain to an experience that transforms and disrupts. The titles of groundbreaking studies indicate the shattering nature of traumatic experiences. They include expressions such as "unsayable," "unspoken," "damaged," "unclaimed experience," and "aftermath."[8] All of these terms point to the catastrophic nature of trauma. A traumatizing experience causes feelings of terror and helplessness. It damages a person's sense of self.[9] As Judith Herman writes, traumatic events "shatter the construction of the self that is formed and sustained in relation to others."[10]

In addition to isolated experiences of violence and loss such as war or sexual assault, students may also have survived living conditions that often lead to posttraumatic stress disorder. Researchers in psychology and

---

6. For reflection on an individual's subjective assessment of a traumatic experi-ence, see Maria P. P. Root, "Reconstructing the Impact of Trauma on Personality," in *Personality and Psychopathology: Feminist Reappraisals*, ed. Laura S. Brown and Mary Ballou (New York: Guilford, 1992), 237.

7. LSJ indicates that the semantic range for this word encompasses "a wound, hurt, damage." See LSJ, s.v. "τραῦμα."

8. Annie Rogers, *The Unsayable: The Hidden Language of Trauma* (New York: Random House, 2006); Levine, *In an Unspoken Voice*; Hilde Lindemann, *Damaged Identities, Narrative Repair* (Ithaca, NY: Cornell University Press, 2001); Cathy Caruth, *Unclaimed Experience: Trauma, Narrative, and History* (Baltimore: Johns Hopkins University Press, 1996); Herman, *Trauma and Recovery*.

9. As Caruth argues, "The wound of the mind—the breach in the mind's experi-ence of time, self, and the world—is not, like the wound of the body, a simple and healable event" (*Unclaimed Experience*, 3).

10. Herman, *Trauma and Recovery*, 51.

social work have shown that toxic stress in early childhood can have long-reaching consequences. Ileen Schwartz-Henderson, who directs a national program focused on play spaces for traumatized children, writes:

> A landmark study, begun in the late 1990s with continuing results today, examined the long-term consequences of what we now call toxic stress, as well as its cause: ACEs (Adverse Childhood Experiences). The negative experiences that happen in the early years have been shown to have a serious detrimental impact on physical and emotional health throughout life and into adulthood and have been shown to cause early death. These experiences continue today in the form of abuse, neglect, or violence in the family and in the community, and they are on the rise.[11]

"Traumatic stress," a different but related phenomenon, "occurs when a person experiences an event that is overwhelming, usually life-threatening, terrifying, or horrifying" and is helpless to stop it.[12] Students who have survived a childhood with many or severe adverse experiences (such as physical violence, sexual abuse, or having an alcoholic parent) bring those experiences into our classrooms. Even with our society's increasing attention to mental health, they may not have received any treatment or therapy to deal with those experiences.

Many psychological studies of trauma focus on individuals and their experiences of traumatic loss. Other researchers point to the effects of trauma on groups—in particular, marginalized groups with a history of large-scale suffering. Perhaps the most famous example is that of Holocaust survivors, who have been the subject of much psychological and neuroscientific research.[13] The study of "historical trauma," otherwise known as "insidious trauma," is crucial for understanding factors that may affect our students. Maria Yellow Horse Brave Heart and her colleagues define historical trauma as "cumulative emotional and psychological wounding across generations, including the lifespan, which emanates from massive group

---

11. Ileen Schwartz-Henderson, "Trauma-Informed Teaching and Design Strategies: A New Paradigm," *Exchange* 231 (2016): 36.

12. Sandra L. Bloom and Brian J. Farragher, *Restoring Sanctuary: A New Operating System for Trauma-Informed Systems of Care* (Oxford: Oxford University Press, 2013), 10.

13. Rachel Yehuda's work is especially well known here. See Rachel Yehuda and Amy Lehrner, "Intergenerational Transmission of Trauma Effects: Putative Role of Epigenetic Mechanisms," *WP* 17 (2018): 243–57.

trauma."[14] Their research focuses on indigenous peoples of the Americas, although they also refer to other indigenous groups and survivors of other massive group traumas such as the Nazi genocide of the Jews or the transatlantic slave trade. In these situations, a group's identity is radically changed, and their traditional beliefs and practices are disrupted. They might also suffer displacement from traditional homelands.[15] Maria Root describes the effects of insidious trauma as "cumulative and directed toward a community of people. In effect, it encompasses some very 'normative,' yet nevertheless traumatic, experiences of groups of people."[16] Students dealing with the effects of these traumatic experiences populate our classrooms, too.

A trauma-informed professor should thus be mindful of the possibility of traumatic stress in an individual student's life. A trauma-informed professor should also consider the influence of historical or insidious trauma, especially in those students whose communities have survived massive group trauma. It is crucial to emphasize that acknowledging traumatic stress in an individual or large-scale trauma for a group does not mean seeing a person or group as weak, damaged, or pathological. It does, however, acknowledge their woundedness.

What Does It Mean to Be Trauma-Informed?

A growing body of literature addresses the need for trauma-informed care. The contexts for trauma-informed practices include law, social work, primary and secondary education, and medicine.[17] Practitioners in these settings frequently encounter people who have experienced trauma. In order to create the conditions for effective interaction, these practitioners must understand how trauma affects a person. Janice Carello and Lisa Butler, social work professors at the University of Buffalo, have written about the need for trauma-informed professionals:

---

14. Maria Yellow Horse Brave Heart et al., "Historical Trauma among Indigenous Peoples of the Americas: Concepts, Research, and Clinical Considerations," *JPD* 43 (2011): 283.

15. All of these themes are relevant to the study of the Bible, which includes narratives and memories of exile, forced migration, enslavement, siege warfare, and conquest.

16. Root, "Reconstructing the Impact," 240.

17. Sarah Katz and Deeya Haldar, "The Pedagogy of Trauma-Informed Lawyering," *CLR* 22 (Spring 2016): 359–93; Frederick Streets, "Social Work and a Trauma-Informed Ministry and Pastoral Care: A Collaborative Agenda," *SWC* 42 (2015): 470–87.

To be trauma-informed, in any context, is to understand the ways in which violence, victimization, and other traumatic experiences may have impacted the lives of the individuals involved and to apply that understanding to the design of systems and provision of services so they accommodate trauma survivors' needs and are consonant with healing and recovery.... [The five principles of trauma-informed work are] ensuring safety, establishing trustworthiness, maximizing choice, maximizing collaboration, and prioritizing empowerment.[18]

Unlike lawyers and social workers, biblical scholars do not work with people in contexts where a person's trauma is the focus of discussion. Our work is like that of other educators who teach knowledge and skills, sometimes to traumatized students. The data bear this out. Carello and Butler cite studies in psychology that show that "66%–94% of college students report exposure to one or more traumatic events, approximately 9%–12% of [first-year college students] meet criteria for post-traumatic stress disorder, and many more may suffer subsyndromal symptoms."[19] Given these statistics, college professors must become trauma-informed. Having heeded Carello and Butler's information and having been convinced of the necessity to make our syllabi and educational practices trauma informed, we might wonder how to do that. What would a trauma-informed Bible class look like? What might a trauma-informed professor do?

Carello and Butler list eight initial steps to reduce risk and make educational practices more trauma informed. I will focus on four of them. These four seem most pressing in my own work and would, I hope, transfer to other contexts outside my own. First, they argue, professors must "identify learning as the primary goal and student emotional safety as a necessary condition for it."[20] It behooves us to remember that we are not therapists.

---

18. Janice Carello and Lisa D. Butler, "Practicing What We Teach: Trauma-Informed Educational Practice," *JTSW* 35 (2015): 264.

19. Carello and Butler, "Practicing What We Teach," 263. For a discussion of what is "outside the range" and the statistical frequency with which people, especially women, experience trauma, see Laura S. Brown, "Not Outside the Range: One Feminist Perspective on Psychic Trauma," in *Trauma: Explorations in Memory*, ed. Cathy Caruth (Baltimore: Johns Hopkins University Press, 1995), 100–112.

20. In full, they are "(a) Identify learning as the primary goal and student emotional safety as a necessary condition for it; (b) recognize that many students have trauma histories that may make them vulnerable to exploitation by authority figures and highly susceptible to symptom recrudescence, and integrate that knowledge into your educational practice; (c) be prepared to provide referrals to your institution's

As a female professor, I frequently have students (often, but not exclusively, women) share personal and painful details of their lives with me. But my job is to teach! That is why I was hired and what I am trained to do. I can listen compassionately, but I am not a therapist. Carello and Butler, however, remind us that student safety is the precondition for learning. I can therefore utilize strategies that enhance students' emotional safety. I can give them time to write before discussing a difficult biblical text. My attendance policy can allow for a certain number of missed classes without documentation or explanation. Sometimes, the only thing I can do is to follow another of Carello and Butler's steps: "Be prepared to provide referrals to your institution's counseling services or emergency care if needed." This means I need to know what student distress looks like and know how to get a student in touch with the professionals who can help. I can take advantage of training in mental health first aid.[21]

Two of Carello and Butler's other steps are worth considering in brief. The authors remind us that we should "appreciate how a trauma history may impact [our] students' academic performance, even without trauma being a topic in the classroom." As someone who teaches about religious violence, the Holocaust, and women in the Bible, trauma is often my topic. But even on days when the topic is much more benign, I must remember that a student who has experienced trauma may still be affected. Last, Carello and Butler recommend that we "check any assumptions that trauma is good (or even romantic), even though some good may be found by those who successfully adapt to the fallout of such experiences."[22]

---

counseling services or emergency care if needed …; (d) appreciate how a trauma history may impact your students' academic performance, even without trauma being a topic in the classroom; (e) become familiar with the scientific research on trauma, retraumatization, and secondary traumatization, and note the serious psychosocial and educational sequelae associated with each; (f) become familiar with the clinical literature on traumatic transference and countertransference … to better understand your students' and your own reactions to traumatic material; (g) understand the limitations and potential pitfalls of generalizing laboratory research to other contexts; and (h) check any assumptions that trauma is good (or even romantic), even though some good may be found by those who successfully adapt to the fallout of such experiences."

21. Mental health first aid training is the CPR of mental health. It trains participants to care for someone in a mental health emergency until professional help can intervene. See "Mental Health First Aid," mentalhealthfirstaid.org.

22. Janice Carello and Lisa D. Butler, "Potentially Perilous Pedagogies: Teaching Trauma Is Not the Same as Trauma-Informed Teaching," *JTD* 15 (2014): 163–64.

Although I have learned much from relating trauma theory to biblical studies, I sometimes worry that certain studies of trauma make it seem secretly beautiful.[23] Trauma—even trauma in the Bible—is not beautiful to traumatized persons. We must heed Carello's and Butler's reminder.[24]

These concrete steps of prioritizing learning and safety, providing referrals, appreciating how trauma histories affect students, and resisting the temptation to romanticize trauma were helpful for me as I worked toward the goal of being a trauma-informed Bible professor. But what do we do with students for whom studying the Bible in an academic setting seems to provoke a traumatic response?

The Oatmeal Comic as a Trauma-Informed Tool

As is surely true of every Bible professor, I have taught students who feel threatened by a critical approach to biblical texts and religion. Some of those students behave as if they are traumatized by ideas that seem to challenge biblical inerrancy. Students react with disbelief, shock, and even anger. Even if students are physically and emotionally secure, they may feel intellectually, spiritually, and personally insecure. Although we sometimes present critical issues as "just an idea" or "a theory," the emotional impact is real.

Because I teach a required introductory theology course every semester, I think about first-year college students in particular. They start college,

---

23. For some recent works on biblical studies and trauma theory, see Eve-Marie Becker, Jan Dochhorn, and Else K. Holt, eds., *Trauma and Traumatization in Individual and Collective Dimensions: Insights from Biblical Studies and Beyond* (Göttingen: Vandenhoeck & Ruprecht, 2014); David Carr, *Holy Resilience: The Bible's Traumatic Origins* (New Haven: Yale University Press, 2014); Elizabeth Boase and Christopher G. Frechette, eds., *Bible through the Lens of Trauma*, SemeiaSt 86 (Atlanta: SBL Press, 2016). According to Elizabeth Johnson, Johann Baptist Metz's idea that God suffers with us "eternalizes suffering by placing it in God; it gives suffering a certain splendor, making it secretly beautiful." See Johnson, *Quest for the Living God: Mapping Frontiers in the Theology of God* (New York: Continuum, 2011), 65.

24. My thanks to Peter Mena, who pointed me to Gloria Anzaldúa's conception of the United States–Mexico border as "*una herida abierta* [an open wound] where the Third World grates against the first and bleeds." See Gloria Anzaldúa, *Borderlands/La Frontera: The New Mestiza* (San Francisco: Aunt Lute, 1987), 3. Anzaldúa's description of the wound as productive but not noble offers a way to think about the tensions involved in trauma-informed teaching.

many of them having read the Bible in church and Catholic school, and then learn of perspectives on the Bible that they have never imagined. They are not fragile (and certainly not "snowflakes"), but they are being confronted with intellectually and epistemologically threatening ideas. The experience does indeed undo them, at least for a time. It is not a traumatizing experience, but it might feel threatening in some of the same ways.

In class periods when I know that many students might feel threatened by a theory or concept, I turn to an online comic called *The Oatmeal*. The entry "You're Not Going to Believe What I'm about to Tell You" focuses on the amygdala and how it can lead us to dismiss new information that threatens our worldview.[25] I display the comic and encourage students to think about how it might help them to consider new theological ideas.

This activity works for a few reasons. First of all, the cartoon is very funny. There is always some giggling in the room while we consider it. Laughter at George Washington's teeth ("the petting zoo of nightmares") or an amygdala sword-fighting a new idea lowers the emotional temperature of the room. One of my favorite frames depicts the amygdala as a pinky toe that yells irrational warnings at us. This image has helped students distance themselves from their shock and anger. Also helpful are drawings of the human brain building and protecting its worldview.

These ideas from *The Oatmeal* come in handy when I teach black theology to my predominantly white students.[26] I begin the unit by asking them to describe first their feelings and then their thoughts about white privilege and racism. After they spend a few minutes free-writing, they pull up *The Oatmeal* on their phones and read the comic through. I then give these instructions: "Using what you learned in the comic, look at your felt and thought response. Are there aspects of this topic that activate a strong emotional and/or intellectual response? Why is that? Is the response connected to your worldview (or the consistent 'house' that our brain builds, according to the comic)?"

---

25. Matthew Inman, "You're Not Going to Believe What I'm about to Tell You," *The Oatmeal*, https://tinyurl.com/SBL03108bn.

26. I wonder whether white students react emotionally to the topic of systemic racism due to moral injury, which "comes from having transgressed one's basic moral identity and violated core moral beliefs." See Rita Nakashima Brock and Gabriella Lettini, *Soul Repair: Recovering from Moral Injury after War* (Boston: Beacon, 2013), xiii–xiv. See also Sheila Wise Rowe, *Healing Racial Trauma: The Road to Resilience* (Downers Grove, IL: IVP Books, 2020); DiAngelo, *White Fragility*.

Our discussions after this activity are often quite lively. Some students continue to sidestep the concept of black theology. They might reject the existence of systemic racism, thereby proving the comic's theory that we avoid ideas that threaten our carefully constructed worldviews. Others, however, acknowledge the challenge. For example, they admit that they have a hard time discussing systemic racism because their "pinky toe is yelling at them" so loudly!

Even though *The Oatmeal* cartoon activity does not address trauma or traumatized students, it shows how trauma-informed teaching can address other student needs. Students enter a class with diverse backgrounds and assumptions, making certain new ideas easier to encounter than others. *The Oatmeal* comic shows this beautifully. An idea interests or destabilizes us depending on how it coheres with our worldview (as the comic says, the stable "house" that we build over time). If it seems like the idea might burn my house down, I panic. If not, it seems interesting. Thinking about the effects of trauma helps me teach those students for whom ideas about systemic racism or gospel authorship threaten to burn their stable house down. And it helps me to consider how I can enable them to see an academic approach to the Bible less as a threat and more as an opportunity to learn.

Conclusion

The Oatmeal comic activity does not suit every occasion for teaching traumatized students. I would not use it with topics that would likely trigger traumatic memories. It is too light-hearted for that. It also does not accurately frame a discussion about a traumatic event, since it instead concerns challenging ideas. Regardless, the activity is based on a few principles that do lead to a more trauma-informed pedagogy. First, it gives students some agency in how they encounter the ideas. They spend time writing at the beginning of class, then reading and thinking about an idea before we discuss it as a group. Second, the activity acknowledges difficult feelings that might arise. It demonstrates the instructor's recognition of student commitments that go beyond a dispassionate, free exchange of ideas. Third, it uses humor and reflection to lower the emotional temperature in the room before the class wrestles with a challenging idea, thus making discussion feel a little safer.

In the case of students who have experienced trauma, we can support them by prioritizing learning and safety, providing referrals, appreciating how trauma histories affect students, and resisting the temptation to romanticize trauma. We can be attentive, sensitive, and responsive to classroom dynamics. Who is speaking? Who is not speaking? What are students really asking? What is unsayable and silenced? The task of becoming trauma informed is ongoing and, from what I have learned, never complete. But by committing to the process and attempting to create trauma-sensitive classrooms, we can respond to and effectively teach diverse groups of students. In an era where the effects of various kinds of trauma are increasingly recognized, trauma-informed teaching is a necessity.

Bibliography

Anzaldúa, Gloria. *Borderlands/La Frontera: The New Mestiza*. San Francisco: Aunt Lute, 1987.

Becker, Eve-Marie, Jan Dochhorn, and Else K. Holt, eds. *Trauma and Traumatization in Individual and Collective Dimensions: Insights from Biblical Studies and Beyond*. Göttingen: Vandenhoeck & Ruprecht, 2014.

Bloom, Sandra L., and Brian J. Farragher. *Restoring Sanctuary: A New Operating System for Trauma-Informed Systems of Care*. Oxford: Oxford University Press, 2013.

Boase, Elizabeth, and Christopher G. Frechette, eds. *Bible through the Lens of Trauma*. SemeiaSt 86. Atlanta: SBL Press, 2016.

Brock, Rita Nakashima, and Gabriella Lettini. *Soul Repair: Recovering from Moral Injury after War*. Boston: Beacon, 2013.

Brown, Laura S. "Not Outside the Range: One Feminist Perspective on Psychic Trauma." Pages 100–112 in *Trauma: Explorations in Memory*. Edited by Cathy Caruth. Baltimore: Johns Hopkins University Press, 1995.

Carello, Janice, and Lisa D. Butler. "Potentially Perilous Pedagogies: Teaching Trauma Is Not the Same as Trauma-Informed Teaching." *JTD* 15 (2014): 153–68.

———. "Practicing What We Teach: Trauma-Informed Educational Practice." *JTSW* 35 (2015): 262–78.

Carr, David. *Holy Resilience: The Bible's Traumatic Origins*. New Haven: Yale University Press, 2014.

Caruth, Cathy. *Unclaimed Experience: Trauma, Narrative, and History*. Baltimore: Johns Hopkins University Press, 1996.

DiAngelo, Robin J. *White Fragility: Why It's So Hard for White People to Talk about Racism*. Boston: Beacon, 2018.

Herman, Judith L. *Trauma and Recovery: The Aftermath of Violence; From Domestic Abuse to Political Terror*. New York: Basic Books, 1992.

Inman, Matthew. "You're Not Going to Believe What I'm about to Tell You." *The Oatmeal*. https://tinyurl.com/SBL03108bn.

Johnson, Elizabeth A. *Quest for the Living God: Mapping Frontiers in the Theology of God*. New York: Continuum, 2011.

Katz, Sarah, and Deeya Haldar. "The Pedagogy of Trauma-Informed Lawyering." *CLR* 22 (Spring 2016): 359–93.

Levine, Peter A. *In an Unspoken Voice: How the Body Releases Trauma and Restores Goodness*. Berkeley, CA: North Atlantic Books, 2010.

Lindemann, Hilde. *Damaged Identities, Narrative Repair*. Ithaca, NY: Cornell University Press, 2001.

McCauley, Heather L., and Adam W. Casler. "College Sexual Assault: A Call for Trauma-Informed Prevention." *JAH* 56 (2015): 584–85.

Rogers, Annie. *The Unsayable: The Hidden Language of Trauma*. New York: Random House, 2006.

Root, Maria P. P. "Reconstructing the Impact of Trauma on Personality." Pages 229–65 in *Personality and Psychopathology: Feminist Reappraisals*. Edited by Laura S. Brown and Mary Ballou. New York: Guilford, 1992.

Rowe, Sheila Wise. *Healing Racial Trauma: The Road to Resilience*. Downers Grove, IL: IVP Books, 2020.

Schwartz-Henderson, Ileen. "Trauma-Informed Teaching and Design Strategies: A New Paradigm." *Exchange* 231 (2016): 36–40.

Streets, Frederick. "Social Work and a Trauma-Informed Ministry and Pastoral Care: A Collaborative Agenda." *SWC* 42 (2015): 470–87.

"The UDL Guidelines." CAST. https://tinyurl.com/SBL03108bm.

Yehuda, Rachel, and Amy Lehrner. "Intergenerational Transmission of Trauma Effects: Putative Role of Epigenetic Mechanisms." *WP* 17 (2018): 243–57.

Yellow Horse Brave Heart, Maria, Josephine Chase, Jennifer Elkins, and Deborah B. Altschul. "Historical Trauma among Indigenous Peoples of the Americas: Concepts, Research, and Clinical Considerations." *JPD* 43 (2011): 282–90.

Food, Hunger, and the Bible: Experiential Learning in the Core Curriculum

LESLEY DIFRANSICO

As educators, we endeavor to engage our students and encourage active learning. Though we might go about achieving these goals in different ways, they all involve significant work on course design, including development of assignments and classroom activities. Faced with the challenge of engaging disinterested and indifferent students in core undergraduate courses, I sought an approach to course design and development that might enhance the active learning tools I was already using in every class. My goals revolved around these central questions: How might this course and its pedagogical approach fully engage each student in the classroom? How do I design courses that challenge and motivate students who are excited and interested while at the same time appealing to the students who are bored or even hostile to ideas of faith? How do I cultivate a lasting and significant learning experience for all students?

In an attempt to address these concerns, I endeavored to design and offer a course with my specific students in mind. Since I teach Bible courses at a private Catholic liberal arts university, many of them are undergraduates taking required core curriculum courses. Some students sign up for a core course because they are excited about the subject, yet others register because it is a requirement. A few do so begrudgingly. I sought to propose a course that would fulfill a core requirement while bringing the Bible into conversation with modern issues and concerns. I wanted to invite my students to engage through experiential activities and reflections. I imagined that if I designed a course that intersected with students' experiences—a course that would draw students before they even entered the classroom— then those students would be primed and ready when they walked through the door. I hoped that student enthusiasm would lay a solid foundation for significant learning experiences for the rest of the semester. I sought to combat the problem of student apathy with creative teaching techniques and assignments, thereby fostering a successful learning community. With this in mind, I designed a course called Food, Hunger, and the Bible. I employed a model that imagines, designs, and offers content suited specifically to student interests and supports significant learning through experiences inside and outside the classroom.

In this essay, I will summarize how I conceived and designed this course in order to achieve student learning goals in the context of my institutional setting and student population. I will then offer a brief overview of the scholarship on experiential learning that inspired core components of this course. Drawing primarily on the concept of significant learning presented by L. Dee Fink, I will share strategies and examples of experiential learning activities, and consider how they contribute to the goal of fostering student engagement and student ownership of learning.[1]

Designing the Course:
The Story of Food, Hunger, and the Bible

In a biblical studies course, instructors consider how to set and support learning goals in light of the student population and institutional mission. In the undergraduate liberal arts setting at Loyola University Maryland—a Jesuit institution—all of my students are required to take two core classes in theology. Many of my courses focus on the Bible with goals of improving biblical literacy and interpretive skills while inviting students to connect biblical concepts and themes to their own lives. I want my students not only to think critically about the biblical texts and their worlds but also to understand how issues presented in the Bible relate to modern concerns. I want to make the concepts and questions of biblical studies real and relevant.

I therefore surveyed students about potential course ideas to see what might attract and inspire them. My students are diverse. They come from various backgrounds and represent a range of experiences with the Bible. Some have been raised in religious households and received religious

---

1. L. Dee Fink, *Creating Significant Learning Experiences: An Integrated Approach to Designing College Courses* (San Francisco: Jossey-Bass, 2013), 68–70. Fink proposes an integrated approach to course design in which student learning goals are supported by teaching and learning activities, and tracked with feedback and assessment.

education, while others have no religious background or experience. Some demonstrate foundational biblical literacy, while others know little to nothing about the Bible. Some are excited or interested to learn about the Bible, while others remain apathetic or even hostile to required Bible courses. Because of these differences among my students, I wondered how one course might address their various interests and motivate them to learn, regardless of their backgrounds and preconceived notions.

I conducted informal conversations with students in all my classes (along with some students I encountered outside the classroom), asking them what theology courses they would like to take. I asked, "What would you want to study that is not already offered? What do you think other students here at Loyola would want to study? Why?" I received a variety of suggestions, some of which proved impractical. One concept, however, came up repeatedly: my students wanted courses that brought the Bible into conversation with current social justice issues and concerns. I was encouraged by this feedback. Social justice is a core focus within the mission of a Jesuit institution, and my students wanted to learn about it and practice it. I gravitated to the theme of social justice and the Bible, so I sought ways to design a related interdisciplinary course.

I also contemplated how to offer course content that would be relevant to a variety of academic majors. I want biology and business majors to be able to appreciate how biblical studies connects to their academic areas and interests. Moreover, I wanted my new course to appeal to everyone on a personal and intellectual level. These reflections led me to the idea of a course on food, hunger, and the Bible. Such a course, I hoped, would be directly and immediately relevant to my students. Many of them were interested in food justice and topics such as ethical food production, agribusiness, and genetically modified organisms. They often followed food issues online and would be able to connect their learning in my course to their learning in other courses.[2] And students uninterested in food issues are still interested in food. Food is a relevant topic for everyone.[3]

---

2. Food justice involves establishing equity in all aspects of the food sphere, including the food system, food production and labor, and food access and availability. Founded on the principle that all people have a right to nutritious food, food justice attempts to address perceived inequities on social, economic, racial, and structural levels.

3. I recognize that some of my students struggle with issues about food. I want to be sensitive to their concerns when I ask them to share experiences or discuss food in

As I developed the course, I realized that there is no shortage of Bible texts about food. The topic invites study and discussion of themes such as ethical food production, methods of preparation, consumption, communal eating, eating rituals, food in relation to ethnic or religious identity, food as a vehicle to foster relationships and create unity, food and memory, and food as religious symbol or sacrament. Each of these themes connects directly to contemporary issues that interested my students.

As I taught the course, I found that it fosters biblical literacy. Students learn about the structure and composition of the Bible as well as the historical and cultural contexts of various texts. They track common themes, tensions, and intertextual connections. Students also read secondary sources that interpret passages about food. They work on analyzing these interpretations, learning how various scholars and religious practitioners interpret and apply biblical passages and principles. In addition, they read current literature about modern systems of food production, agribusiness and industrial agriculture, and food justice issues on a local, national, and global level. The course exposes students to a broad array of biblical texts, themes, and applications. They are often surprised by the array and diversity of the texts, and are fascinated by the questions and themes that connect food in the Bible to food issues today. Students do not get bogged down by overemphasis on one passage or concept because every class session presents something new and offers different questions and topics for discussion.

Significant Learning Experiences

Food, Hunger, and the Bible consistently invites students to share in experiential learning. I ask my students to draw on prior experiences as a bridge to new learning, to connect their experiences to biblical concepts and themes, and to take ownership of their learning by relating the course to their daily lives. Experiential learning fosters the development of academic skills and the retention of knowledge. Studies have demonstrated that student retention of information drops significantly after one week

---

class. Though I invite students to give examples and reflect on their personal experiences, I often direct them to do so only to the extent they are comfortable. They are not required to share every detail, though many students will willingly and transparently reflect on eating disorders or traumatic experiences with food insecurity.

of study and even more over the course of time.[4] I have come to realize that students develop skills and retain information when they participate directly in the making of meaning and construction of knowledge, and I designed my course accordingly.[5] I have drawn inspiration from Fink's concept of cultivating a "significant learning experience": one that results in "something that is truly significant in terms of our students' lives."[6] I want to challenge my students to extend their learning beyond content and present them with opportunities for acquiring new knowledge that might affect how they think or live. I want to let them consider how biblical concepts and passages might apply to situations, tensions, and dilemmas in their own lives. As John C. Bean explains, inviting students to connect course concepts to personal experience grabs their attention. It can "help students assimilate new concepts by connecting the concepts to personal experiences."[7] They retain new knowledge and learn new skills.[8]

My course design was also inspired by the idea of encouraging student ownership of the learning process. Ken Bain suggests asking and then expecting students to commit to the course's goals and assignments. He notes that asking works better than requiring. Effective teachers, he says, "approach each class as if they expect students to listen, think, and respond."[9] Their requests and expectations help students own the learning process. They feel invited to share in the construction of knowledge

---

4. See Phillip Saunders, "The Lasting Effects of Introductory Economics Courses," *JEE* 12 (1980): 1–14. Saunders's influential study on course-information retention rates demonstrated that student knowledge from a course they had taken five years previously was about the same as that of students who had never taken the course. See also John Van Maaren's and Hanna Tervanotko's essay in this volume.

5. See James Pelech, *The Comprehensive Handbook of Constructivist Teaching: From Theory to Practice* (Charlotte, NC: Information Age, 2010); Rajendra Kumar Shah, "Effective Constructivist Teaching Learning in the Classroom," *SIJE* 7 (2019): 1–13. Shah presents a thoughtful analysis of constructivist approaches to teaching and highlights the importance of using active learning approaches that suit the students at hand.

6. Fink, *Creating Significant Learning Experiences*, 6–7.

7. John C. Bean, *Engaging Ideas: The Professor's Guide to Integrating Writing, Critical Thinking, and Active Learning in the Classroom* (San Francisco: Jossey-Bass, 2001), 123.

8. Bean, *Engaging Ideas*, 123. See also Elizabeth F. Barkley, K. Patricia Cross, and Claire Howell Major, *Collaborative Learning Techniques: A Handbook for College Faculty* (San Francisco: Jossey-Bass, 2014), 15.

9. Ken Bain, *What the Best College Teachers Do* (Cambridge: Harvard University Press, 2004), 113–14.

through participation in classroom discussion, focused preparation, and peer teaching. Allowing students to choose approaches to their assignments grants them a sense of autonomy.[10] Inviting them to engage in activities or reflect on relevant experiences also contributes to student agency. Students bring their observations to the classroom, where they analyze them and integrate knowledge together with their peers. They become active agents in the learning process as they discover new experiences and relate them in new ways to prior knowledge and course content.

Constructive conversation like this builds a respectful, collaborative community that enables group learning and active discussion. Students come to class ready to share their own experiences. They know that their voices and perspectives matter. According to Elizabeth F. Barkley, K. Patricia Cross, and Claire Howell Major, working collaboratively with their peers motivates students to acquire deeper levels of understanding.[11] Students appreciate collaborative learning and invest in the process as they relate the Bible to their own concerns. As Fink notes, "In a powerful learning experience, students will be engaged in their own learning, there will be a high energy level associated with it, and the whole process will have important outcomes or results."[12]

When considering the experiential component of Food, Hunger, and the Bible, I recognize that while each student has different experiences, views, and thoughts about food, they all have some foundational experience of it. On day one, they might not be able to talk on an academic level about how food functions in relationships, community, or tradition. Students can, however, tell a story about how a meal with their host family in a foreign country really made them feel at home after a long trip, or about how their grandma always makes awesome lasagna when the whole family gets together, or that it is just not Thanksgiving without Uncle Joe's smoked turkey. When they connect their memories to the shared class discussion, they build a community that makes each student feel invested in learning.[13]

---

10. Elizabeth F. Barkley, *Student Engagement Techniques: A Handbook for College Faculty* (San Francisco: Jossey-Bass, 2010), 81–82.

11. Barkley, Cross, and Major, *Collaborative Learning Techniques*, 14–33. They define collaborative learning as "interactive group work that has three essential elements: intentional design, co-laboring, and meaningful learning" (13).

12. Fink, *Creating Significant Learning Experiences*, 8.

13. See Barkley, *Student Engagement Techniques*, 122–23. "To be a true learning community," says Barkley, "*all* members must exchange information, ideas, opinions.

One of the first exercises for students in Food, Hunger, and the Bible involves sharing a personal memory. Students consider this prompt: "Think about the best thing you ever ate and try to remember the setting and experience. Where were you? With whom? What did it taste/smell/ look/feel like? Why was this eating experience so memorable?" Students are then asked to free-write, partner up and discuss with a classmate, and report back to the whole class. In sharing their answers, students will often tell stories. The class begins to uncover the profound implications and significance of food, eating, and meals. A straightforward, low-pressure exercise gets everyone talking and sets the stage for a collaborative learning community. For the next class, students are tasked with composing their own philosophy of food. This exercise provides a baseline against which they can track their learning over the course of the semester.

From this point on, students connect course concepts with prior experience and engage in new experiences designed to foster learning. Pairing such activities with reflective writing not only allows students to ponder and analyze what they are learning but also prepares them for class discussion and collaborative learning.[14] "Having students engage in an experiential exercise," notes Fink, "becomes much more potent when it is linked with reflective dialogue."[15] Beyond the acquisition of foundational knowledge, the application and integration of that knowledge in their own lives promote significant learning.[16]

Reading Assignments and Experiential Learning Activities

I designed Food, Hunger, and the Bible to encourage students to relate the biblical text to their own lives. I ask students to

---

If you do not take steps to ensure all students participate, only a few students will speak up while the majority remain quiet.... It is also important to help students feel comfortable in speaking up and saying what they truly think, believe, and feel."

14. Bean, *Engaging Ideas*, 174. Bean notes that "out-of-class exploratory writing" serves to "prime the pump for class discussions."

15. Fink, *Creating Significant Learning Experiences*, xiii.

16. Fink, *Creating Significant Learning Experiences*, 43. See also Ann Burlein, "Learning to Drink Deeply from Books: Using Experiential Assignments to Teach Concepts," *TTR* 14 (2011): 137–55.

1. read Gen 1–3 alongside excerpts from Ellen Davis's agrarian read-
    ing of the Bible and consider how agriculture and food play into a
    biblical theology of creation;[17]
2. read Norman Wirzba's *Food and Faith: A Theology of Eating* and
    reflect on the significance of a Christian theology of food as it
    relates to a theology of creation;[18]
3. consider how the communal meal relates to memory as they read
    about exodus events and the Passover;[19]
4. discuss the theology of divine providence in the manna story of
    Exodus as well as concepts of food access in the desert wanderings;[20]
5. study Levitical food laws and discuss food practices in ancient
    Israel along with food as a marker of ethnic and religious identity
    in the past and present;
6. study biblical laws on just labor and wages for agricultural work-
    ers, just treatment of animals in agriculture, and a Sabbath for
    the land; then discuss how these principles relate to the modern
    world;[21]
7. read about communal meals and hospitality in the ancient Near
    East, the sacrificial system in ancient Israel, and food rituals in the
    ancient world as they consider their own food rituals today;
8. read the book of Ruth from the perspective of food insecurity
    and power dynamics and consider food security for the foreigner
    while learning about food-access priority areas in Baltimore;[22]

---

17. Ellen Davis, *Scripture, Culture, and Agriculture: An Agrarian Reading of the Bible* (New York: Cambridge University Press, 2009).

18. Norman Wirzba, *Food and Faith: A Theology of Eating* (New York: Cambridge University Press, 2011).

19. Razia Parveen, "Food to Remember: Culinary Practice and Diasporic Identity," *OralHist* 44 (2016): 47–56; Jordan D. Troisi et al., "Threatened Belonging and Preference for Comfort Food among the Securely Attached," *Appetite* 90 (2015): 58–64.

20. Susan Hylen, "Seeing Jesus John's Way: Manna from Heaven," *WW* 33 (2013): 341–48.

21. Students sometimes read "What Is Sustainable Agriculture?," University of California, Davis, https://tinyurl.com/SBL03108bo.

22. Secondary sources include Gale A. Yee, "'She Stood in Tears amid the Alien Corn': Ruth, the Perpetual Foreigner and Model Minority," in *They Were All Together in One Place? Toward Minority Biblical Criticism*, ed. Fernando Segovia, Tat-siong Benny Liew, and Randall C. Bailey (Atlanta: Society of Biblical Literature, 2009), 119–40.

9. read the Prophets and portions of Lamentations while studying famine, military conflict and food scarcity, and food symbols and metaphors;[23]

10. study Jesus's teachings on food, how New Testament teaching and practice conform to and depart from Levitical food laws, and the communal and sacramental aspects of the Last Supper as they consider how food fosters communal identity;

11. consider how communal eating forged unity in the New Testament church (according to the experiences of Peter in Acts and writings of Paul) as they reflect on food and relationships in their own lives and communities;

12. contemplate how food functions in symbols and metaphors both in the Bible (for example, Jesus as the bread of life) and in the modern world.[24]

Students complete these assignments outside class by reading, reflecting, and recording their reflections.

For some assignments, I want them to think critically about their prior knowledge, beliefs, or daily practices, thus interrogating foundational assumptions and knowledge. For others, I ask them to reflect on the activity and connect the experience to biblical material and modern food issues. I compose prompts with specific learning outcomes in mind. Early in the course, for example, I tell students, "Track everything you consume for two to three days. Include comments on when, where, and with whom you are eating. Note any observations about your habits and experience." I ask students to submit a log and a personal reflection about eating habits, what they expected from the exercise, and what surprised them. I also ask them to evaluate their eating habits if they feel comfortable doing so. I do not grade the log, but I do grade the reflection, providing feedback on how the student connected the experience to the course content or relevant

---

23. Students browse and read various resources offered by the United Nations Refugee Agency, https://www.unhcr.org/en-us/. When locusts were in the news (November 2020), students read the book of Joel along with David Njagi, "The Biblical Locust Plagues of 2020," *BBC*, 6 August 2020, https://tinyurl.com/SBL03108bp.

24. Relevant secondary sources include Carol Baker Wilson, *For I Was Hungry and You Gave Me Food: Pragmatics of Food Access in the Gospel of Matthew* (Eugene, OR: Pickwick, 2014); Jane S. Webster, "That One Might Not Fall: A New Testament Theology of Food," *Int* 67 (2013): 363–73.

Bible passages. Students, most of whom live on campus, often note their surprise at how many times a meal consists of a rushed granola bar while walking to class, or how rarely they sit down with friends to share lunch or dinner. The exercise establishes students' awareness of their eating habits. It also serves as a reference point as we begin to study Bible passages related to food along with modern food concerns.

In another exercise, I ask students to try tracking where their food is grown, processed, and packaged as well as to note when they cannot find that information. This exercise encourages them to contemplate the physical distance from farm to table, the environmental impact of the food system, and the processes involved in industrial agriculture. At this point in the course, students have read the Genesis creation narratives and have considered the first humans as gardeners. They have also studied the agrarian realities of ancient Israel.[25] These activities confront them with their own distance (physical and otherwise) from the growth and production of what they consume. Students also recognize the distance between their own experience and that of the biblical authors. They start to understand the importance of considering the authors' historical and cultural contexts.

Later in the course, when we read the book of Ruth and discuss food insecurity as related to social, cultural, and economic power dynamics, I ask students to research federal SNAP benefits and to attempt to live for twenty-four hours within the daily SNAP allowance ($7.80 for a single adult as of January 2021).[26] Students track what they spend and how they spend it, then detail how they had to change their food habits to stay within their budget. If they exceed the limit, they must explain why. Because many of my students enjoy food security, they have not contemplated the reality or experience of food insecurity. To live within such a restricted budget requires them to make tough choices and sacrifice nutritious options. They experience, though in an artificial way, some Bible concepts that relate to today's concerns. Students often report how difficult it was to spend so little, how hungry they were when they had to sacrifice a meal, or how outraged they felt about the insufficiency of the daily SNAP benefit to provide reliable, nutritious food.

---

25. Students read chapter 3, "The Means of Existence," in Philip J. King and Lawrence E. Stager, *Life in Biblical Israel* (Louisville: Westminster John Knox, 2001), along with select essays by Wendell Berry.

26. SNAP stands for Supplemental Nutrition Assistance Program.

Other prompts ask students to go meatless or vegan for a day and to eat only if they can share the meal with others. These exercises require personal and intentional practice along with thoughtful reflection and integration with course content discussions. The activities aid students in "looking backwards," learning from their experiences and applying new knowledge to future practice and understanding.[27] Further, the activities prompt them to consider important questions and issues, thus preparing them to come to class ready to share, discuss, and relate the activity to assigned readings. The work of engaging with the course questions and applying new knowledge to their own lives fosters significant and lasting learning as well as a deeper appreciation of the Bible.

What Students Learn

Having now taught Food, Hunger, and the Bible to six groups over three successive spring semesters, I have been able to assess its effectiveness in achieving my student learning goals. I have gathered evidence from student work such as projects, written reflections, and essay exams; formal student feedback on university course evaluations; and informal student feedback during, immediately after, and as much as a year after the course. In graded assignments, especially in the comprehensive final essay exam, many students demonstrate thorough knowledge of and critical thinking about the Bible and food issues. In formal and informal feedback, most students report a greater understanding of the Bible and its relevance. Most also indicate a greater awareness of food issues and our food system as well as how biblical themes might be applied to these modern concerns. Some students express a desire to change personal habits and practice ethical eating. They note the importance of meals in building relationships and commit to eating more often with family and friends. Some decide to purchase reusable water bottles and coffee mugs. A few say that they are going meatless because the meat industry troubles them in many ways.

Certain students become passionate about food justice issues. They not only change personal habits but also get involved in community service. While I do not intend for these exercises to change my students' habits, I do appreciate the impact that the resulting knowledge has on their lives. I

---

27. See Tony Ghaye, *Teaching and Learning through Reflective Practice: A Practical Guide for Positive Action* (New York: Routledge, 2011), 1.

want my students to understand that the course content is not abstract or theoretical. It has real-life implications for themselves and others. The biblical authors were reflecting on, writing about, and even legislating about numerous concerns about food and hunger. Those concerns mattered then, and they matter today.

I often question whether I have made a difference. Did they really learn? Will they ever think of these issues again? Am I contributing to the mission of my university in helping my students become broadly educated, socially responsible citizens of a global community? These questions drive my focus on designing courses, classroom approaches, and experiential activities that actively engage students, foster ownership of and investment in the learning process, and result in significant learning. These strategies have worked with my course Food, Hunger, and the Bible. Students are eager to attend class, engage in discussions and activities, and demonstrate significant learning. Other courses might implement the same strategies by bringing the Bible into conversation with the modern world and especially with student experiences and concerns. Whether in a course on food, hunger, and the Bible, on the Bible and migration, or on the Bible and popular culture, instructors can develop and offer exciting courses that will enable students to connect personally with academic study of the Bible and experience significant and lasting learning.

Bibliography

Bain, Ken. *What the Best College Teachers Do.* Cambridge: Harvard University Press, 2004.

Barkley, Elizabeth F. *Student Engagement Techniques: A Handbook for College Faculty.* San Francisco: Jossey-Bass, 2010.

Barkley, Elizabeth F., K. Patricia Cross, and Claire Howell Major, *Collaborative Learning Techniques: A Handbook for College Faculty.* San Francisco: Jossey-Bass, 2014.

Bean, John C. *Engaging Ideas: The Professor's Guide to Integrating Writing, Critical Thinking, and Active Learning in the Classroom.* San Francisco: Jossey-Bass, 2001.

Burlein, Ann. "Learning to Drink Deeply from Books: Using Experiential Assignments to Teach Concepts." *TTR* 14 (2011): 137–55.

Davis, Ellen. *Scripture, Culture, and Agriculture: An Agrarian Reading of the Bible.* New York: Cambridge University Press, 2009.

Fink, L. Dee. *Creating Significant Learning Experiences: An Integrated Approach to Designing College Courses.* San Francisco: Jossey-Bass, 2013.

Ghaye, Tony. *Teaching and Learning through Reflective Practice: A Practical Guide for Positive Action.* New York: Routledge, 2011.

Hylen, Susan. "Seeing Jesus John's Way: Manna from Heaven." *WW* 33 (2013): 341–48.

King, Philip J., and Lawrence E. Stager. "The Means of Existence." Pages 85–86 in *Life in Biblical Israel.* Louisville: Westminster John Knox, 2001.

Njagi, David. "The Biblical Locust Plagues of 2020." *BBC.* https://tinyurl.com/SBL03108bp.

Parveen, Razia. "Food to Remember: Culinary Practice and Diasporic Identity." *OralHist* 44 (2016): 47–56.

Pelech, James. *The Comprehensive Handbook of Constructivist Teaching: From Theory to Practice.* Charlotte, NC: Information Age, 2010.

Saunders, Phillip. "The Lasting Effects of Introductory Economics Courses." *JEE* 12 (1980): 1–14.

Shah, Rajendra Kumar. "Effective Constructivist Teaching Learning in the Classroom." *SIJE* 7 (2019): 1–13.

Troisi, Jordan D., Shira Gabriel, Jaye L. Derrick, and Alyssa Geisler. "Threatened Belonging and Preference for Comfort Food among the Securely Attached." *Appetite* 90 (2015): 58–64.

United Nations Refugee Agency. https://www.unhcr.org/en-us/.

Webster, Jane S. "That One Might Not Fall: A New Testament Theology of Food." *Int* 67 (2013): 363–73.

"What Is Sustainable Agriculture?" University of California, Davis. https://tinyurl.com/SBL03108bo.

Wilson, Carol Baker. *For I Was Hungry and You Gave Me Food: Pragmatics of Food Access in the Gospel of Matthew.* Eugene, OR: Pickwick, 2014.

Wirzba, Norman. *Food and Faith: A Theology of Eating.* New York: Cambridge University Press, 2011.

Yee, Gale A. "'She Stood in Tears amid the Alien Corn': Ruth, the Perpetual Foreigner and Model Minority." Pages 119–40 in *They Were All Together in One Place? Toward Minority Biblical Criticism.* Edited by Fernando Segovia, Tat-siong Benny Liew, and Randall C. Bailey. Atlanta: Society of Biblical Literature, 2009.

Visiting the Dead: Connecting Ancient Text with Modern Practice

John Van Maaren and Hanna Tervanotko

Experiential learning has taken its place as a leading pedagogy for enhancing student learning. With roots in the theory of John Dewey and driven by David Kolb's seminal work *Experiential Learning: Experience as the Source of Learning and Development*, the most comprehensive bibliography as of 2019 included 4,418 "important contributions" to experiential learning theory.[1] Experiential learning has been labeled a "high-impact practice" by the American Association of Colleges and Universities and has been promoted by the Ontario Ministry of Education for its potential to "strengthen the sense of engagement and motivation to learn that are foundational to all students' success."[2] The importance of experiential

Hanna Tervanotko is grateful for Dr. Helen Dixon for her help in planning this course. Conversations with her were an important source of inspiration when the visit to the local cemetery was planned. Funding for this project was provided by McMaster University as part of the PALAT Grant supported by the Paul R. MacPherson Institute for Leadership, Innovation & Excellence in Teaching.

1. These are selected out of more than one hundred thousand citations in Google Scholar and ResearchGate between 1971 and 2019. Alice Y. Kolb and David A. Kolb, "Experiential Learning Theory (ELT) Bibliography," Experience Based Learning Systems, https://learningfromexperience.com/research-library/#rl-bibliography; John Dewey, *Experience and Education*, KDPLS (New York: Macmillan, 1938); David A. Kolb, *Experiential Learning: Experience as the Source of Learning and Development* (Englewood Cliffs, NJ: Prentice Hall, 1984).

2. Jane E. Brownell and Lynn E. Swaner, *Five High-Impact Practices: Research on Learning Outcomes, Completion, and Quality* (Washington, DC: Association of American Colleges and Universities, 2010); Ontario Ministry of Education, "Community-Connected Experiential Learning: A Policy Framework for Ontario Schools, Kindergarten to Grade 12," 2016, 5.

learning for nursing or education students is self-evident, since practicums and student teaching provide direct and guided experience in future vocational roles. Its importance for the humanities is less obvious. The challenge of implementing experiential learning is especially acute in undergraduate biblical studies, where direct experience of ancient texts is less easily available. Nevertheless, biblical studies students can benefit from experiential learning that increases deep understanding, critical thinking, and lifelong learning—all learning goals associated with a liberal education and linked to experiential learning strategies elsewhere in this volume.[3]

This essay advocates for undergraduate experiential learning by summarizing its implementation and impact in a religious studies course titled Death and Afterlife in Early Judaism and Christianity, taught by coauthor Hanna Tervanotko at McMaster University in Hamilton, Ontario. In this class, students read texts from the Hebrew Bible, New Testament, and other early Jewish literature to consider practices and beliefs associated with death among ancient Jews and early Christ-followers. In order to connect the ancient texts to modern practice, students visited a nearby Christian cemetery and met with a local rabbi. Student survey responses were overwhelmingly positive and indicated that the experiential learning prompted transformed understandings of the discipline of religious studies, increased peer interaction, and led to a greater appreciation of the impact of ancient texts on modern-day practices.

The following discussion first introduces experiential learning theory, outlines best practices for classroom implementation, and summarizes the results of empirical research on experiential learning's impact. It then outlines the integration of the two experiential learning activities and summarizes data on the students' perceived experience, collected through a questionnaire. This data provides fodder for discussing the place of experiential learning in student conceptual development, disciplinary understanding, mental health and well-being, and retention in the religious studies classroom. We conclude that experiential learning may have the greatest impact in an introductory course on religious studies and especially for students who have little if any experience with the academic study of religion. Our results also suggest experiential learning may serve as an effective strategy for increasing student enrollment in religious stud-

---

3. Janet Eyler, "The Power of Experiential Education," *LE* 95 (2009): 26. See Lesley DiFransico's essay in this volume.

ies courses and reaffirming the place of religious studies in the university context, one that prepares students for personal, professional, and civic life by prompting the "curious and sympathetic imagination" capable of "recognizing humanity in strange costumes."[4]

Definition of Experiential Learning

Karen Lovett provides a practical definition for those looking to implement experiential learning in the university classroom. She describes experiential learning as "a process that involves active engagement and self-guided learning in a purposeful, immersive experience, as well as reflection and sense-making about that experience in order to transform it into knowledge that can be applied in subsequent experiences and contexts."[5] In contrast to classroom lectures, documentaries, or reading assignments through which students learn indirectly from the experiences of others, experiential learning activities allow students to learn from direct encounters. These experiences are much more intense, memorable, and likely to influence behavior.[6] In contrast to the myriad of other daily student experiences (e.g., eating breakfast, socializing with friends, and traveling to school), many of which are habitual and automatic, experiential learning includes strategic reflection on a new experience in order to prompt a transformation in the understanding of the subject matter. In a classroom setting, discussions and writing assignments often structure the reflection, positioning experiential learning as a complement to, rather than replacement for, traditional classroom activities. Accordingly, it is experiential learning's combination of a fresh (sometimes disruptive) experience and structured (ideally integrative) reflection on that experience that distinguishes experiential learning from other types of experiencing and learning.[7]

---

4. Martha C. Nussbaum, *The New Religious Intolerance* (Cambridge: Harvard University Press, 2012), 21, 142.

5. Karen Lovett, "Introduction: Listening and Learning from Experiential Learning Educators," in *Diverse Pedagogical Approaches to Experiential Learning: Multidisciplinary Case Studies, Reflections, and Strategies*, ed. Karen Lovett (London: Palgrave Macmillan, 2020), 2. For a list of other, similar definitions, see Colin Beard and John P. Wilson, *Experiential Learning: A Handbook for Education, Training and Coaching*, 3rd ed. (London: Kogan Page, 2013), 24–26.

6. Beard and Wilson, *Experiential Learning*, 20.

7. Alice Y. Kolb and David A. Kolb, "Eight Important Things to Know about The Experiential Learning Cycle," *AEL* 40 (2018): 9.

Types of Experiential Learning

Experiential learning encompasses a broad range of undergraduate experiences that break down into two basic categories: cocurricular and course-based experiential learning. Many types of experiential learning are curricular yet unattached to individual courses. These include service learning, adventure education, study abroad, internships, undergraduate research, and capstone projects. Cocurricular experiential learning (e.g., a semester-long internship) tends to take longer than course-based experiential learning (e.g., a two-hour field trip), and many options are coordinated by a specific university office rather than an individual faculty member. Cocurricular experiential learning often focuses on professional skill acquisition, not course objectives, and usually includes external incentives associated with getting the job done as opposed to earning good grades or pleasing the course instructor.[8]

Experiential learning components can also be integrated into individual courses. Within a course, experiential learning may be confined to the classroom or take place live and out in the community.[9] Classroom-confined experiential learning differs from lecturing by its emphasis on active learning and structured reflection on that learning. It employs many active learning pedagogies, including problem-based learning, flipped classrooms, simulation and gaming, and role-play insofar as these involve open-ended problems that place the burden of analysis and decision-making on the student.[10] Live experiential learning is most associated with excursions that allow students direct and often new experience of themes studied in the classroom. This exposure learning is more emotive and

---

8. Eyler, "Experiential Education," 29.

9. I. Georgiou, C. Zahn, and B. J. Meira, "A Systemic Framework for Case-Based Classroom Experiential Learning," *SRBS* 25 (2008): 808.

10. Franz Böcker, "Is Case Teaching More Effective than Lecture Teaching in Business Administration? An Exploratory Analysis," *Interfaces* 17 (1987): 64. See Sally Bethell and Kevin Morgan, "Problem-Based and Experiential Learning: Engaging Students in an Undergraduate Physical Education Module," *JHLSTE* 10 (2011): 128–34; Anna-Sofia Alklind Taylor, Per Backlund, and Lars Niklasson, "The Coaching Cycle," *SG* 43 (2012): 648–72. These methods correspond with a student-centered/conceptual-change approach to teaching and contrast with a teacher-centered/information-transfer approach. Keith Trigwell and Michael Prosser, "Development and Use of the Approaches to Teaching Inventory," *EPR* 16 (2004): 409–24; Kolb and Kolb, "Eight Important Things," 8.

therefore more effective in challenging preconceived notions and stereotypes.[11] Exposure learning can also happen within the classroom through direct encounter with visiting practitioners who discuss or demonstrate their expertise. Our case study includes two exposure experiential learning components. One was part of a class excursion, and the other was classroom confined.

Implementation of Experiential Learning

Instructors looking to implement experiential learning can access a variety of models, including Alice Y. Kolb and David A. Kolb's much-used experiential learning cycle. It provides a simple and actionable structure for implementing experiential learning.[12] Their four-stage recursive circle is based on the dual dialectics of experience/conceptualization and action/reflection (see fig. 4).[13] On the one hand, concrete experience must be balanced with abstract conceptualization, as new experiences are integrated into existing frames of meaning in order to create new connections that lead to deep understanding. In the best case, the particularity and immediacy of the learner's concrete experience refine their abstract conceptualization, providing generalized ways to order the past and a framework for approaching future experiences. On the other hand, active experimentation must be balanced with reflective observation on that experimentation. Active experimentation normally leads to confusion; reflective observation prompts learning that lasts. In addition, dialogue with others allows students to make explicit, and thereby better retain, the new knowledge that emerges as they work through their confusion. Imbalance in either of these poles (experience/conceptualization, action/reflection) inhibits learning. Without abstract conceptualization or reflective observation, students do not learn from the new experience, and their knowledge lacks clarity. Without new, concrete experience or active experimentation, reflection and conceptualization remain abstract and are not refined and challenged by real-world data.

---

11. Rik Scarce, "Field Trips as Short-Term Experiential Education," *TS* 25 (1997): 220.

12. Alice Y. Kolb and David A. Kolb, "Experiential Learning Theory as a Guide for Experiential Educators in Higher Education," *ELTHE* 1 (2017): 9.

13. Kolb and Kolb, "Eight Important Things," 11.

The experiential learning cycle (fig. 4) integrates these two dialectics into an endless cycle of continuous exchange between the learner's internal world and the external environment. At the top of the circle, the learner encounters a new experience. While all stages are experiences in a broad sense, the immediacy and newness of concrete experience sets it apart from the other stages and from everyday experience. Concrete experience should be followed by reflective observation on new data. This reflection may be guided by an expert who has already integrated the given experience into their internal world and who is able to point out inconsistencies between the new experience and the learner's current understanding. Depending on the type of experiential learning, this expert may be a course instructor, internship supervisor, or professional practitioner. Expert guidance can take the form of moderating a group discussion or providing a targeted essay prompt for personal reflection in a written response or student journal. It is important that the expert distinguishes reflection (which leads to learning something new) from opinion (a matter of agreeing or disagreeing).

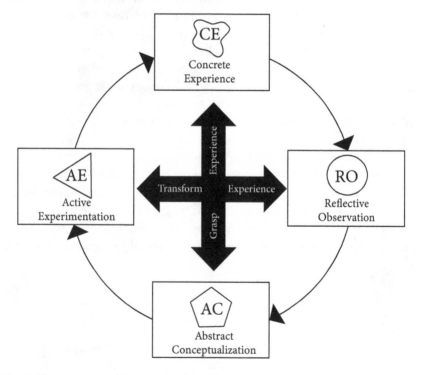

Fig. 4. The experiential learning cycle

Reflection in turn leads to abstract conceptualization as reflection prompts new ideas or modifications to existing conceptual schema. At this stage, students move beyond describing their experience to making connections between their reflection and existing knowledge. These conceptual advancements are then applied to the learner's world through active experimentation. The application allows for further refinement as new understanding is tested through the immediacy of new problems and situations that may demonstrate its practical limits or wider applications. Learners then bring the resulting knowledge to another concrete experience. When part of a structured internship or university course, the next journey around the experiential learning cycle should expand in complexity and application, prompting deeper learning.

The Impact of Experiential Learning

The impact of experiential learning on long-term success, course satisfaction, and specific learning outcomes is well documented. For example, a study of the long-term impact of student participation in a Model United Nations course and a judicial internship program at a California State University campus found that participants were more likely than their peers to graduate, finish in four years, attend graduate school, and be employed after graduation.[14] A multiyear study of a peace-and-conflict course at Uppsala University collected student performance and self-perception data during the year before and the two years after implementing multiple classroom-confined experiential learning components. The final exam failure rate fell from 22 percent (2010) to 11 percent (2011) to 5 percent (2012), and the rate of students passing with distinction jumped from 27 percent (2010) to 42 percent (2011) to 52 percent (2012). Students also self-reported higher learning outcomes as the percentage of course evaluation responses that indicated a "high" ability to identify central course concepts rose from 29 percent (2010) to 49 percent (2011) and 39 percent (2012; lower than in 2011 but still significantly higher than before implementing experiential learning in 2010).[15]

---

14. Leigh A. Bradberry and Jennifer De Maio, "Learning by Doing: The Long-Term Impact of Experiential Learning Programs on Student Success," *JPSE* 15 (2019): 102–5.

15. Roxanna Sjöstedt, "Assessing a Broad Teaching Approach: The Impact of Combining Active Learning Methods on Student Performance in Undergraduate Peace and Conflict Studies," *JPSE* 11 (2015): 212–16.

Participation in experiential learning is associated not only with degree completion and course success but also with developing ways of thinking that are foundational to a liberal arts education. These learning outcomes include deep learning, critical thinking, knowledge transfer to new situations, and engagement in lifelong learning.[16] Cocurricular experiential learning is better studied than course-based experiential learning, and while not fully transferable to course-based experiential learning, the results of these studies are still useful for framing our discussion. A large study of high-impact practices by the Association of American Colleges and Universities examined 25,336 responses to the National Survey of Student Engagement from thirty-eight higher-education institutions in California, Oregon, and Wisconsin. It found significant perceived gains on a standardized scale (1–100) in deep learning activities for students who participated in service learning (+8.5), study abroad (+4.3), internships (+5.2), student/faculty research (+8.1), and senior capstone projects (+6.1). The study found that participation in multiple "high-impact practices" led to even higher perceived engagement in deep learning: +6.3 for 1–2 high-impact practices, +12.8 for 3–4 high-impact practices, and +19.8 for 5–6 high-impact practices. Similarly, students reported gains in their general education (1–2 high-impact practices: +4.6; 3–4 high-impact practices: +9.9; 5–6 high-impact practices: +14), practical competence (1–2 high-impact practices: +6.7; 3–4 high-impact practices: +12.5; 5–6 high-impact practices: +18.1), and personal and social development (1–2 high-impact practices: +7.2; 3–4 high-impact practices: +14.1; 5–6 high-impact practices: +14.1).[17]

Marc Behrendt and Teresa Franklin provide a useful literature review of excursion experiential learning in primary and secondary school.[18] They emphasize the dual cognitive and emotive impact of direct encounter with subject material previously studied in the classroom. First, they note cognitive gains as students make connections between theoretical concepts and experience. These cognitive gains lead to enhanced observation, perception, curiosity, and motivation and also prompt student-led investigations.

---

16. Eyler, "Experiential Education," 26.

17. Ashley Finley and Tia McNair, *Assessing Underserved Students' Engagement in High-Impact Practices* (Washington, DC: Association of American Colleges and Universities, 2013), 9–10.

18. Marc Behrendt and Teresa Franklin, "A Review of Research on School Field Trips and Their Value in Education," *IJESE* 9 (2014): 238.

Second, Behrendt and Franklin emphasize the emotive impact of direct encounter. Personal connections with the subject material lead to greater care and passion, future civic engagement, and appreciation for diversity. In addition, Behrendt and Franklin highlight indirect benefits of field trips, including social growth and positive interactions among participants.

Janete Eyler notes that in postsecondary education, "field-based pedagogies have struggled to gain legitimacy in the liberal arts."[19] Significant work has been done in the field of geography, where class excursions have been associated with increased affective and cognitive growth.[20] Individual studies from other disciplines have found similar results.[21] Only a few examine experiential learning in religious studies.[22] Most of these are descriptive rather than data driven.[23] To our knowledge, the only study to include data collection on impact addresses the integration of social justice into the religious studies classroom.[24] This study, conducted by Fred

---

19. Eyler, "Experiential Education," 26.

20. Max Hope, "The Importance of Direct Experience: A Philosophical Defence of Fieldwork in Human Geography," *JGHE* 33 (2009): 169–71. See also Mick Healey and Alan Jenkins, "Kolb's Experiential Learning Theory and Its Application in Geography in Higher Education," *JG* 99 (2000): 185–95.

21. E.g., Cara M. Djonko-Moore and Nicole M. Joseph, "Out of the Classroom and into the City: The Use of Field Trips as an Experiential Learning Tool in Teacher Education," *SAGE Open* 6 (2016), https://tinyurl.com/SBL03108bq; see also Laurence Pattacini, "Experiential Learning: The Field Study Trip, a Student-Centred Curriculum," *Compass* 11 (2018): 2.

22. Alice Kolb and David Kolb do not include religious studies in their list of thirty disciplines using experiential learning. See Kolb and Kolb, *The Kolb Learning Style Inventory 4.0: A Comprehensive Guide to the Theory, Psychometrics, Research on Validity and Educational Applications* (Boston: Hay Resources Direct, 2013), 91–140. Other case studies address experiential learning activities without framing them as experiential learning. See Harold Morales and Mark Barnes, "The Baltimore Mural Project: An Approach to Threshold Concepts in Religious Studies," *TTR* 21 (2018): 185–96.

23. Pamela Jean Owens, "Experiencing the Other as the Self: Cultural Diversity Courses as Liberating Praxis," *TTR* 8 (2005): 245–52; Joyce Ann Mercer, "Red Light Means Stop! Teaching Theology through Exposure Learning in Manila's Red Light District," *TTR* 5 (2002): 90–100; Jeffrey Carlson, "From Site Unseen to Experiential Learning: Religious Studies in the 'Discover Chicago' Model," *TTR* 1 (1998): 120–27. See also Barbara A. B. Patterson, "Ethnography as Pedagogy: Learning and Teaching in a Religion Department Internship Class," *TTR* 6 (2003): 24–34.

24. Fred Glennon, "Experiential Learning and Social Justice Action: An Experiment in the Scholarship of Teaching and Learning," *TTR* 7 (2004): 30–37.

Glennon, evaluated the impact of a project in a senior seminar titled Ethics from the Perspective of the Oppressed. In this project, students completed ten hours of active engagement with a social justice issue of their choice. The active engagement was preceded by research and followed by reflection. Data was collected from document analysis of student assignments and responses to a follow-up survey. According to document analysis, 70 percent of students whose preproject essays demonstrated a narrow view of social justice demonstrated a more sophisticated understanding of social justice in their postproject paper. Further, 85 percent of students reported some change in their understanding of social justice, 80 percent reported a greater sense of moral agency, and 50 percent reported that they were still engaged with the issue four months after the course. The evidence for experiential learning impact is undeniable, yet more discipline-specific research needs to be done. Our case study, then, contributes to the small body of religious studies experiential learning literature by considering the impact of exposure experiential learning focused on the acquisition of discipline-specific content in a general education religious studies course.

Experiential Learning in the Religious Studies Classroom: A Small-Scale Case Study

Our study collected student perception data about two exposure experiential learning components in a religious studies course at McMaster University, a research-intensive university in Hamilton, Ontario. The course addressed ancient Jewish and Christian portrayals of death and the afterlife, including leading causes of death, preparation for death, rituals related to death, belief in the afterlife, the concept of a soul, and communication with the dead. Part of the course's stated purpose was to "gain new insights on our own contemporary culture and its view on mortality."

In order to relate ancient customs to modern practice, students participated in two experiential learning activities, led by local religious practitioners, about Christian and Jewish customs and beliefs surrounding death. During the introductory class period, instructor Hanna Tervanotko explained that the course included experiential learning activities that emphasized active learning and reflection. During the class period immediately preceding each experiential learning activity, she encouraged students to consider continuities and discontinuities between the practices of ancient and contemporary communities. After conversing in small groups about what they were most interested to learn, her students prepared questions for the experts.

The experiential learning began in the fourth week of class with a concrete experience (the category located atop Kolb and Kolb's experiential learning cycle). The students visited a prominent Roman Catholic cemetery where many of the bishops, priests, and religious sisters of the Diocese of Hamilton, along with a number of politicians and other famous citizens, are buried.[25] The visit was facilitated by a cemetery administrator, who led a walking tour while discussing the cemetery's history. He recounted the evolving understandings of who could be buried there (e.g., members of interdenominational families and persons with questionable reputations), identified prominent Hamiltonians and their relation to the Roman Catholic Church, and led students to the burial chapel, where they learned about changing attitudes toward cremation. Reflective observation began at the end of the visit, while students discussed their experience with the guide, a local expert on contemporary Roman Catholic practice. During the following class period, students were able to further reflect on the visit in a discussion led by the course instructor, an expert on ancient Christian practice.

The first of two writing assignments sought to foster abstract conceptualization by providing students with an opportunity to integrate new knowledge into their existing frame of meaning. This assignment, due a few weeks after the visit, asked students to discuss how contemporary practice at the cemetery reflected biblical laws and practices. Many of the essays showed that students had developed independent questions and observations that integrated the cemetery visit with course material and their own experience in and with religious communities. Students also suggested a new title for the final written assignment based on their cemetery visit and written response. Their creativity and engagement beyond the grading requirements of the course suggest that the visit prompted internal motivation for some.

The second experiential learning activity included a second concrete experience along with elements of active experimentation. It took place in the tenth week of class, when a rabbi from a local synagogue visited the class to discuss the customs and beliefs in his Jewish community. He

---

25. For another summary of the cemetery visit, see Hanna Tervanotko, "Materiality of Death and Afterlife: Visit to Local Cemetery," *Ancient Jew Review*, 10 August 2020, https://tinyurl.com/SBL03108br.

discussed burial practices, beliefs about the dead, the afterlife, mourning practices, and the role of the rabbi as officiant. The visit enabled active experimentation as students relied on their previous cemetery visit to formulate questions and discuss differences. As with the Christian cemetery tour, students had the opportunity for reflective observation both during the visit with the rabbi, an expert on contemporary Jewish practice, and in the following class period with the course instructor, an expert on ancient Jewish practice. The second writing assignment, due four weeks after the visit, asked students to compare contemporary Jewish and Christian practice with one ancient practice covered in the course. The assignment gave students an opportunity for abstract conceptualization as well as comparative reflection on Jewish and Christian burial customs. It asked students to draw on course material related to ancient practice and belief in addition to their encounters with contemporary communities.

The choice to include a second experiential learning activity had two purposes. First, it provided the necessary balance for a course addressing Jewish and Christian approaches to death. The inclusion of experiential learning activities from two different religious traditions that share some sacred texts enabled a distinctive comparison. Second, it provided the closest approximation to active experimentation that was possible for course-based experiential learning. Students were able to bring their new conceptualization, developed after the Christian cemetery tour, to their visit with the rabbi, further refining and testing their new conceptualization. Further active experimentation will take place in students' day-to-day lives as they encounter other religious practices related to death. We hope that the habits of guided reflection and conceptualization learned in the course will allow students to continue moving around the experiential learning cycle as future experiences refine their understanding of death and its rituals.

Student Perceptions of Visiting the Dead

Two weeks after the second experiential learning activity (but before the final writing assignment), we invited students to complete a voluntary questionnaire about their perception of the course's experiential learning activities. The questionnaire, created by instructor Hanna Tervanotko, appears in appendix 1. Nine out of twenty-six students responded (35 percent). These responses provide material for driving more and better conversations about experiential learning in religious studies.[26] Due to the small number and self-selected nature of respondents, the results are not easily generalized to exposure experiential learning.

All respondents indicated that the experiential learning activity was "very valuable" (rather than "somewhat valuable" or "not valuable at all"), and all but one respondent indicated they were "very likely" to take another religious studies course. This latter result is noteworthy, as most enrolled students were not completing a major or minor in religious studies and had no incentive apart from personal interest for taking additional religious studies courses. It suggests that departments facing decreased enrollment and budget cuts might improve their numbers by incorporating experiential learning into their courses in order to appeal to a wider student demographic that is especially interested in acquiring skills and perspectives that they can apply in their future careers. The appeal of experiential learning as a way for students to relate course content to their personal lives finds confirmation in short-answer responses, in which many indicated that the most valuable part of experiential learning involved making the course material real and connecting ancient texts to modern practice.

For some, the experiential learning activities were transformative. Nearly half of the respondents (four out of nine) indicated that the experiences changed their perspective on the discipline of religious studies. It seems that a student's first experiential learning experience may be most transformative. No respondents with past course-based experiential learning participation indicated a changed perspective, while all but one without past participation indicated a changed perspective. Student short answers confirm the importance of the first experiential learning participation. One student explained that the experience did not change their perspective because they were already familiar with religious studies methods.[27] The transformative potential of initial experiential learning participation suggests that exposure experiential learning, by asking stu-

---

26. For an outline of how student responses can drive better conversations, see Katarina Mårtensson, Torgny Roxå, and Thomas Olsson, "Developing a Quality Culture through the Scholarship of Teaching and Learning," *HERD* 30 (2011): 51–62. See Torgny Roxå et al., "Reconceptualizing Student Ratings of Teaching to Support Quality Discourse on Student Learning: A Systems Perspective," *HE* 83 (2022): 35–55.

27. Student response: "Religious Studies has a diverse range of methods to approach the study of religion. The experiential learning feels in line with how some scholars study religion."

dents to directly observe, then describe and reflect on their observations, may be uniquely useful for helping students to grasp the descriptive and empirical emphasis in much of religious studies. It may similarly help students differentiate between religious studies and religious instruction, theological education, or the discipline of history. Further, all second- and third-year students indicated changed perspectives, while only a single fourth-year student did. This correlation may be related to student cognitive development during an undergraduate program, as students move from an understanding of knowledge as true or false to an understanding of knowledge as constructed and contextual.[28] In our context, this suggests that students in their fourth year have already developed the cognitive framework for empirical approaches to religious phenomena. Accordingly, exposure experiential learning may be especially transformative in a first-year introductory religious studies course insofar as it increases interest and understanding of the discipline. Their additional interest and understanding may prompt students to take more religion courses or add a religious studies minor.

Two questions concerned the role of course-based experiential learning in the classroom learning environment. When asked to select their preferred learning methods (apart from experiential learning) from a list, all nine respondents selected "attending lecture" and seven of nine indicated "independent study," while no other answer was selected by more than three respondents. This preference for traditional learning approaches over more active learning components (e.g., problem-based learning and role-play) is an important reminder that experiential learning is part of a learning cycle that includes information transfer and therefore supplements rather than replaces other modes of instruction. Student perceptions confirm this perspective, as seven of nine respondents preferred a combination of experiential learning and lecture components, while none preferred a strictly lecture format.

Two open-ended questions allowed respondents to give more detail about their experience by asking them to list elements that enhanced their learning and to indicate their favorite part of the experiential learning activities.[29] As expected, many respondents noted the importance of

---

28. Marcia B. Baxter Magolda, *Knowing and Reasoning in College: Gender-Related Patterns in Students' Intellectual Development* (San Francisco: Jossey-Bass, 1992).

29. The complete list of anonymized student responses to the open-ended questions is included at the end of this essay. Further, two responses to question 7 were too

direct experience (seven of nine) and the chance to hear from an outside expert who was also a practitioner (five of nine).[30] Individual respondents also highlighted the importance of readings that framed the experiential learning, the opportunity to apply what was learned in the classroom, and the value of experiential learning for different learning styles—all aspects of the experiential learning cycle.[31] In addition, seven out of nine respondents noted the importance of getting out of the classroom. One student wrote, "[I] enjoyed getting away from the classroom setting; actually seeing what was being discussed; discussions with someone who works in that field." Students also contrasted their enjoyment of the field trip with the stress of classroom learning. Respondents described the "change of scenery" as "a break," "fun," "a nice way to learn in a more relaxed, informal setting," and something that "didn't feel like learning." The change of scenery also allowed students to interact with each other in a new space. Three respondents noted the importance of getting to know their classmates. In addition, two students reported that the new setting led to informal conversations about course material. Anecdotally, instructor Hanna Tervanotko observed that these unprompted conversations continued on the way back to campus. They provide supporting evidence that exposure experiential learning encourages internal motivation. The importance of the change of scenery can also be seen in the frequent references to the cemetery visit in student short answers. Six of the seven respondents noted the cemetery visit as their favorite part of experiential learning. The two

---

general for inclusion (e.g., "everything") and so we counted the number of responses for "your favorite part" out of seven. Further, some students' favorite element included multiple aspects and so the total number is more than seven.

30. Since responses to question 7 (favorite aspect) overlap with question 6 (beneficial aspects), we focus on student responses rather than number of responses. For example, we count a student who lists direct experience for both question 6 and question 7 as one student who listed direct experience rather than two answers of direct experience.

31. Readings: "Particularly useful is the essay to give context to modern practices, even if not explicitly written about (and materials provided there, i.e., on cremation)." Application: "Being able to go outside the classroom to apply what we learn in the lecture is what I found most engaging." Learning styles: "I am a more visual learner so seeing how things work in person helps me understand more than just reading about it." For a summary of learning styles in relation to the experiential learning cycle, see Kolb and Kolb, "Experiential Learning Theory as a Guide," 21–24. See also Kolb and Kolb, *Kolb Learning Style Inventory 4.0.*

students who explicitly noted the visit by the rabbi also mentioned the cemetery visit.

Conclusion

The student responses make a strong case for integrating experiential learning into religious studies, including biblical studies, classrooms, whether at the curricular or course level. While this small-scale case study did not collect data on student success, it did find overwhelmingly positive student perceptions of exposure experiential learning. An overarching explanation for why all respondents described the exposure experiential learning as "very valuable" was its ability to connect ancient texts to modern practice and thereby contribute to students' personal meaning making. In particular, students repeatedly highlighted the importance of encountering contemporary practices and the value of interacting with practitioners who regularly facilitate rituals related to death. These direct experiences prompted students to consider how religious communities use ancient authoritative texts in contemporary practice as well as to compare practices between Jewish and Roman Catholic communities with overlapping authoritative texts. These exercises allowed students to then reflect on related practices within their own communities, whether religious or otherwise. They also prepared students, through guided reflection, with the critical faculty to make sense of the practices and beliefs of those whom they will encounter throughout their personal and professional lives.

In addition to the long-term learning benefits, students' immediate enthusiasm for experiential learning has important implications for departmental strategic planning. In an atmosphere where the content of religious studies is called into question and many departments face declining enrollment, exposure experiential learning may play an important role in securing the study of religion as a distinct discipline within undergraduate education by reaffirming its contemporary relevance. In particular, exposure experiential learning may play a crucial role in first-year introductory religious studies courses. These high-enrollment courses introduce students from across the university to the academic study of religion, and students often take them because of personal interest. Experiential learning activities may help students grasp the academic study of religion at an early stage as they make decisions about academic programs, leading more students to consider a religious studies major or minor. Further, the emotive and memorable nature of exposure experiential learning inspires informal course endorsements by students in conversations with friends. These endorsements prompt students from across the university to use remaining general-education requirements to explore what the academic study of religion can contribute to their personal meaning making.

Bibliography

Alklind Taylor, Anna-Sofia, Per Backlund, and Lars Niklasson. "The Coaching Cycle." *SG* 43 (2012): 648–72.

Baxter Magolda, Marcia B. *Knowing and Reasoning in College: Gender-Related Patterns in Students' Intellectual Development.* San Francisco: Jossey-Bass, 1992.

Beard, Colin, and John P. Wilson. *Experiential Learning: A Handbook for Education, Training and Coaching.* 3rd ed. London: Kogan Page, 2013.

Behrendt, Marc, and Teresa Franklin. "A Review of Research on School Field Trips and Their Value in Education." *IJESE* 9 (2014): 235–45.

Bethell, Sally, and Kevin Morgan. "Problem-Based and Experiential Learning: Engaging Students in an Undergraduate Physical Education Module." *JHLSTE* 10 (2011): 128–34.

Böcker, Franz. "Is Case Teaching More Effective than Lecture Teaching in Business Administration? An Exploratory Analysis." *Interfaces* 17 (1987): 64–71.

Bradberry, Leigh A., and Jennifer De Maio. "Learning by Doing: The Long-Term Impact of Experiential Learning Programs on Student Success." *JPSE* 15 (2019): 94–111.

Brownell, Jane E., and Lynn E. Swaner. *Five High-Impact Practices: Research on Learning Outcomes, Completion, and Quality.* Washington, DC: Association of American Colleges and Universities, 2010.

Carlson, Jeffrey. "From Site Unseen to Experiential Learning: Religious Studies in the 'Discover Chicago' Model." *TTR* 1 (1998): 120–27.

Dewey, John. *Experience and Education.* KDPLS. New York: Macmillan, 1938.

Djonko-Moore, Cara M., and Nicole M. Joseph. "Out of the Classroom and into the City: The Use of Field Trips as an Experiential Learning Tool in Teacher Education." *SAGE Open* 6 (2016). https://tinyurl.com/SBL03108bq.

Eyler, Janet. "The Power of Experiential Education." *LE* 95 (2009): 24–31.

Finley, Ashley, and Tia McNair. *Assessing Underserved Students' Engagement in High-Impact Practices*. Washington, DC: Association of American Colleges and Universities, 2013.

Georgiou, I., C. Zahn, and B. J. Meira. "A Systemic Framework for Case-Based Classroom Experiential Learning." *SRBS* 25 (2008): 807–19.

Glennon, Fred. "Experiential Learning and Social Justice Action: An Experiment in the Scholarship of Teaching and Learning." *TTR* 7 (2004): 30–37.

Healey, Mick, and Alan Jenkins. "Kolb's Experiential Learning Theory and Its Application in Geography in Higher Education." *JG* 99 (2000): 185–95.

Hope, Max. "The Importance of Direct Experience: A Philosophical Defence of Fieldwork in Human Geography." *JGHE* 33 (2009): 169–82.

Kolb, Alice Y., and David A. Kolb. "Eight Important Things to Know about the Experiential Learning Cycle." *AEL* 40 (2018): 8–14.

———. "Experiential Learning Theory as a Guide for Experiential Educators in Higher Education." *ELTHE* 1 (2017): 7–44.

———. "Experiential Learning Theory (ELT) Bibliography." Experience Based Learning Systems. https://learningfromexperience.com/research-library/#rl-bibliography.

———. *The Kolb Learning Style Inventory 4.0: A Comprehensive Guide to the Theory, Psychometrics, Research on Validity and Educational Applications*. Boston: Hay Resources Direct, 2013.

Kolb, David A. *Experiential Learning: Experience as the Source of Learning and Development*. Englewood Cliffs, NJ: Prentice Hall, 1984.

Lovett, Karen. "Introduction: Listening and Learning from Experiential Learning Educators." Pages 1–12 in *Diverse Pedagogical Approaches to Experiential Learning: Multidisciplinary Case Studies, Reflections, and Strategies*. Edited by Karen Lovett. London: Palgrave Macmillan, 2020.

Mårtensson, Katarina, Torgny Roxå, and Thomas Olsson. "Developing a Quality Culture through the Scholarship of Teaching and Learning." *HERD* 30 (2011): 51–62.

Mercer, Joyce Ann. "Red Light Means Stop! Teaching Theology through Exposure Learning in Manila's Red Light District." *TTR* 5 (2002): 90–100.

Morales, Harold, and Mark Barnes. "The Baltimore Mural Project: An Approach to Threshold Concepts in Religious Studies." *TTR* 21 (2018): 185–96.

Nussbaum, Martha C. *The New Religious Intolerance*. Cambridge: Harvard University Press, 2012.

Ontario Ministry of Education. "Community-Connected Experiential Learning: A Policy Framework for Ontario Schools, Kindergarten to Grade 12." 2016.

Owens, Pamela Jean. "Experiencing the Other as the Self: Cultural Diversity Courses as Liberating Praxis." *TTR* 8 (2005): 245–52.

Pattacini, Laurence. "Experiential Learning: The Field Study Trip, a Student-Centred Curriculum." *Compass* 11 (2018): 1–16.

Patterson, Barbara A. B. "Ethnography as Pedagogy: Learning and Teaching in a Religion Department Internship Class." *TTR* 6 (2003): 24–34.

Roxå, Torgny, Arshad Ahmad, Janette Barrington, John Van Maaren, and Robert Cassidy. "Reconceptualizing Student Ratings of Teaching to Support Quality Discourse on Student Learning: A Systems Perspective." *HE* 83 (2022): 35–55.

Scarce, Rik. "Field Trips as Short-Term Experiential Education." *TS* 25 (1997): 219–26.

Sjöstedt, Roxanna. "Assessing a Broad Teaching Approach: The Impact of Combining Active Learning Methods on Student Performance in Undergraduate Peace and Conflict Studies." *JPSE* 11 (2015): 204–20.

Tervanotko, Hanna. "Materiality of Death and Afterlife: Visit to Local Cemetery." *Ancient Jew Review*, 10 August 2020. https://tinyurl.com/SBL03108br.

Trigwell, Keith, and Michael Prosser. "Development and Use of the Approaches to Teaching Inventory." *EPR* 16 (2004): 409–24.

Appendix 1
Experiential Learning Questionnaire

1. What year are you in?
    a. 2nd
    b. 3rd
    c. 4th
    d. 5th

2. What are your preferred methods to learn? (choose all that apply)
    a. Independent study
    b. Group study
    c. Attending a lecture
    d. Questions and answers
    e. Making my own notes
    f. Discussing the given topic with peers in a tutorial
    g. Other?

3. Have you had experiential learning experiences before this course?
    a. Yes
    b. No
    c. If yes, in which context? (Which course?)

4. How valuable was the experiential learning opportunity in this course?
    a. Very valuable
    b. Somewhat valuable
    c. Not valuable at all

5. In your opinion, how do experiential learning methods compare with a more traditional learning setting (i.e., classroom setting where a teacher lectures)?
    a. I learn better in a traditional setting.
    b. I learn better through experiential learning methods.
    c. I learn best when a course incorporates both methods.
    d. There is no difference between the methods.
    e. Something else?

6. Which elements specifically, of the experiential learning opportunity in this course, enhanced your learning? (You can include as many

aspects as you wish: e.g., being outside the classroom, engaging with material artifacts, comparison between ancient and contemporary practices, informal discussions with your peers, etc.)

7. What was your favorite part of the experiential learning experience?

8. Did this experiential learning opportunity change your perspectives on Religious Studies?
   a. Yes
   b. No
   c. If yes, how?

9. How likely are you to take more courses on Religious Studies?
   a. Very likely
   b. Somewhat likely
   c. Very unlikely
   d. Undecided

Student Responses to Open-Ended Questions

Question 6: Which elements specifically, of the experiential learning opportunity in this course, enhanced your learning? (You can include as many aspects as you wish: e.g., being outside the classroom, engaging with material artifacts, comparison between ancient and contemporary practices, informal discussions with your peers, etc.)

- Cemetery → better understanding of contemporary [indecipherable] and historical developments → better comparison; Change of scenery!!; Observing graves and changes in graves and mausoleums.

- Enjoyed getting away from the classroom setting; actually seeing what was being discussed; discussions with someone who works in that field.

- Hearing from professional in the realm (ex., the man who gave the tour of Holy Sepulchre); immersing physically to receive a better understanding; a break from the classroom setting; getting to know my peers better and talking about the material.

- I am a more visual learner so seeing how things work in person helps me understand more than just reading about it.

- I enjoyed and learned a lot from [the cemetery] & [the rabbi's visit]. I found the information easier to retain and more interesting as I was able to get a first-hand experience and account.

- The field trip allowed me to better understand the topic.

- Being able to go outside the classroom to apply what we learn in the lecture is what I found most engaging.

- For the graveyard visit, I think it enhanced our learning by being able to go and physically look at aspects we had been reading about, such as the tombstones. For both the gravesite visit and [the rabbi's] guest lecture, it was helpful and interesting to have someone give an insider's perspective, that we could listen to and ask questions from.

- Engaging with material artifacts; opportunity to hear from an expert outside the class; informal discussion with peers; comparing ancient and modern practices.

Question 7: What was your favorite part of the experiential learning experience?

- Visiting the cemetery → particularly useful is the essay to give context to modern practices, even if not explicitly written about (and materials provided there, i.e., on cremation).

- Possibly the trip itself. The idea of getting out of the classroom. The fact that we were actually experiencing what was being said.

- Going to Holy Sepulchre, learning about the history and practices of burials; gives a break from the classroom setting.

- My favorite part of experiential learning was how it made what we study feel so much more real as sometimes it can just feel like reading a catalogue.

- My favorite part of the experiential learning experience was the field trip to the cemetery. It was fun and educational and didn't feel like learning.

- I enjoyed every part of it.

- I liked the cemetery visit and the guest lecture from the Rabbi.

- My favorite part was going to the graveyard visit. The director was very happy to show us around, and it was a nice way to learn in a more relaxed, informal setting with my peers.

- Getting to see some elements of modern burials in person & discuss changing practices in modern burials.

QUICK TIP
THE THREE LITTLE PIGS AND THE SYNOPTIC PROBLEM

ROBBY WADDELL

"What could the story of the Three Little Pigs possibly have to do with the Synoptic problem?" Students wonder, too, when I start our class session on the Synoptic problem with an activity involving a fairy tale. Like fairy tales, all stories accumulate variations as storytellers adapt the details to suit their own circumstances. In this activity, I introduce my students to this concept in order to address their concerns about variations in the gospel accounts of Jesus.

Prior to the class session in which I use the Three Little Pigs activity, students read about the Synoptic problem and its proposed solutions. To begin the class session, I follow Wilbert McKeachie's advice: "If students know what they are expected to learn from a lecture, they learn more of that material."[1] I explain that we will engage in a comparative analysis of the oral reception of the Three Little Pigs and the literary interdependence of the gospels. Already, some students feel uneasy. The concept that the gospels have such a complex history of formation creates cognitive dissonance. For some, it generates emotional anxiety. By using a fairy tale, I seek to calm students' anxieties, disarming any unnecessary concerns that might preoccupy a student. My aim is to help them focus on the texts and keep an open mind about scholarly solutions for the Synoptic problem.

I begin by asking the students to write a brief summary of the story of the Three Little Pigs. Inevitably, students complain that they have forgotten the details or lack familiarity with the story. I tell them to do the best they can. It will not affect the outcome of the activity if a student gets the

---

1. Wilbert J. McKeachie and Marilla D. Svinicki, *McKeachie's Teaching Tips: Strategies, Research, and Theory for College and University Teachers* (Belmont, CA: Wadsworth Cengage Learning, 2014), 63.

details wrong. In fact, differences in the retellings of the story will help. When at least half the class has stopped writing, I ask everyone to stop writing. It helps if some students run out of time because unfinished stories serve as a parallel to the shorter ending of Mark.

I then solicit four volunteers (or more if time permits) to read their summary. With four accounts of the story, I can draw a nice parallel to the canonical gospels, comparing the shortest one to Mark and the most original one to John. With more than four examples, I take the opportunity to discuss the existence of noncanonical gospels.

As the volunteers read their synopsis, I quickly take notes on the board, making sure to capture the major elements of their version. I lead a class discussion on the stories' similarities and differences. Common phrases usually include "once upon a time," "the big bad wolf," "I'll huff and I'll puff," and "not by the hair of my chinny chin chin." The building materials also exhibit commonality, albeit with some variety. Is the first house made of hay or straw? Is the second house constructed from wood or sticks? Students commonly refer to the third and final house as a brick house or a house made with bricks. Sometimes, however, a student from the northeast will refer to a house of stone. The endings of the student versions exhibit even more diversity. In some, all the pigs survive and the wolf leaves, exasperated. In others, the pigs kill and sometimes eat the wolf. In a few, only the third pig survives. I point out that the diverse endings of the story compare to the postresurrection accounts in the gospels.

Once I have compared and contrasted four or more versions of the fairy tale, I am ready to lead the class in examining the Synoptic problem. Typically, the class concludes that all versions are based on an original story. The similarities provide evidence for an original tale. In the retelling, certain details stay the same. The differences probably evolved as the story was passed down or because the storyteller wished to make a particular point.

The activity requires a fair amount of time—about twenty-five to thirty minutes—but to quote McKeachie again, "The enemy of learning is the teacher's need to cover the content at all costs."[2] I choose to sacrifice content for comprehension. In the end, my students pay attention to detail, analyze and evaluate the differences between texts, and understand the Synoptic problem. They are prepared to evaluate solutions, such as the

---

2. McKeachie and Svinicki, *McKeachie's Teaching Tips*, 64.

two-source theory. Moreover, by the end of the exercise, students seem less anxious.

Bibliography

McKeachie, Wilbert J., and Marilla D. Svinicki. *McKeachie's Teaching Tips: Strategies, Research, and Theory for College and University Teachers.* Belmont, CA: Wadsworth Cengage Learning, 2014.

QUICK TIP
HELPING STUDENTS NEGOTIATE THE
VARIETY OF JESUSES

CALLIE CALLON

A third of the way through my Introduction to the New Testament class, students have just finished studying the Synoptic Gospels. They have come to realize how each of these authors offers a unique portrayal of Jesus. Then we encounter the Gospel of John, whose representation of Jesus is vastly different from those of the synoptic authors. They are now confronted with four distinct Jesuses.

This understandably distresses some students. Many of them have never read all four gospels in their entirety, nor have they compared the gospels with each other. Most have encountered them in isolated excerpts, such as in popular culture or worship contexts, neither of which tends to address the diversity (or perhaps the plurality) of Jesuses. To help students approach this issue, therefore, I have developed two complementary exercises.

I implement the first exercise by assigning two short newspaper articles. Each covers the same event featuring the same person but with different biases: one politically conservative, the other politically liberal.[1] I ask students to identify similarities and differences between the articles, including the choice of headline, quotations used to characterize the event, and the overall tone taken by the respective authors. These

---

1. I have found articles published immediately after Donald Trump's 2016 presidential election to be particularly fruitful for this assignment. For a liberal-leaning article, I have used Daniel Dale, "Donald Trump Wins, America Elects an Unthinkable President," *Toronto Star*, 9 November 2016, https://tinyurl.com/SBL03108bt. To represent the conservative side, I have used the editorial piece "Trump Has the Last Laugh," *Toronto Sun*, 9 November 2016, https://tinyurl.com/SBL03108bu.

observations then inform our class discussion. Students readily articulate that, although each article describes the same event, it does so in distinctive ways, employing different language and including different details. Students further contextualize the differences, noting that they occur because each author writes from a different perspective in order to appeal to a different audience. Students realize that they can apply the analogy to the four evangelists. The exercise helps them understand and appreciate the practice of selective reporting.

After this discussion, I implement a second exercise. It involves a visual analogy based on ancient artistic depictions of Jesus. The analogy demonstrates how artistic and theological perspectives can and do inform the representation of a figure. Using PowerPoint, I show students a variety of third- and fourth-century images of Jesus. I choose ancient representations not only because of their historical proximity to the time of the evangelists but also because of their striking diversity. Each image presents a different type of Jesus. One portrays Jesus as the good shepherd, carrying a lamb across his shoulders.[2] Others depict Jesus as the healer of the hemorrhaging woman, the rod-holding wonderworker who raises Lazarus, the lawgiver bearing a scroll, and a hero or deity modeled after traditional Greco-Roman figures such as Orpheus and Helios.

Students learn that, like the painters of the third and fourth centuries, the evangelists were autonomous artists. They were not concerned with objective representation. Instead, they crafted images of Jesus predicated on their own theological perspectives and the interests of their communities. Students also recognize that, like all artists, the evangelists expressed their understanding of Jesus by including certain elements and excluding others. I highlight the necessity of doing so in an artistic work by suggesting that the representation of Jesus as lawgiver would be less coherent if the same image depicted him with a lamb slung over his shoulder, and that the miracle-worker portrait would be rather confusing if he held a scroll in his hand rather than a rod.

Finally, I bring the discussion back to John, whose gospel was the catalyst for the exercise. I quote John 21:25: "But there are also many other things that Jesus did; if every one of them were written down, I suppose that the world itself could not contain the books that would be written"

---

2. This depiction was likely modeled after ancient representations of Hermes. It serves as another example of an artist's decision to assimilate Jesus to a Greco-Roman archetype. I point this out in class.

(NRSV). The Fourth Evangelist himself admits to discretion in his selection of certain events and sayings for his depiction of Jesus.

While these exercises do not address the question as to which version of Jesus is more historically credible, they do help students feel more comfortable with the variety of Jesuses. They also make students more receptive to other aspects of course material that might similarly cause distress. For example, I have found that students who have accepted historical-critical explanations for a variety of Jesuses are more willing to consider historical-critical explanations for Paul's lack of interest in Jesus's teachings. Students appreciate directly confronting the plurality of Jesuses in the New Testament. They benefit from navigating it in class with the help of analogies from news reporting and visual arts. The plurality of Jesuses becomes less of a distressing issue and more of an opportunity to understand the unique theological perspectives of the evangelists.

Bibliography

Dale, Daniel. "Donald Trump Wins, America Elects an Unthinkable President." *Toronto Star*, 9 November 2016. https://tinyurl.com/SBL03108bt.

"Trump Has the Last Laugh." *Toronto Sun*, 9 November 2016. https://tinyurl.com/SBL03108bu.

Quick Tip
Zombies in the Biblical Studies Classroom? Bingo!

KATHERINE LOW

Gen Z students recognize zombies. Known as "living dead," "reanimated undead," or "dead but bizarrely still alive," zombies permeate popular culture.[1] By my count, more than half of the zombie films ever made in the United States were released in the wake of 9/11.[2] In these films, survivors of a zombie apocalypse fight off the threat of flesh-eating reanimated corpses while navigating societal and political collapse. A zombie plague sweeps through the land, often transmitted through zombie bites; then chaos ensues.[3] A small band of human survivors remains to face an uncertain future in a preindustrial, postcivilization wasteland, sometimes with the hope of reaching a zombie-free zone or forming a safe community.

Because they reflect our fears, including those of mass infectious outbreaks and failures of government systems to protect citizens, zombies provide an opportunity for "critical reflection and cultural examination."[4] They are useful tools for teaching three broad biblical themes: political crisis and social upheaval, "walking dead" resurrection and apocalypse, and human embodiment and spirituality. I find zombies helpful not only

---

1. See Todd K. Platts, "Locating Zombies in the Sociology of Popular Culture," *SC* 7 (2013): 547–60.

2. See also Alan Edward Green Jr., "The Post-9/11 Aesthetic: Repositioning the Zombie Film in the Horror Genre" (PhD diss., University of South Florida, 2013).

3. The CDC has successfully used zombies to get people thinking about emergency preparedness. See Center for Disease Control and Prevention, Center for Preparedness and Response, "Zombie Preparedness," https://tinyurl.com/SBL03108bv.

4. John Veraeke, Christopher Mastropietro, and Filip Miscevic, *Zombies in Western Culture: A Twenty-First Century Crisis* (Open Book, 2017), 4.

for making comparisons but also for drawing contrasts, particularly regarding popular depictions of the apocalypse as opposed to depictions in biblical apocalyptic literature.

I teach biblical studies in a small residential liberal arts college. My course load includes an introduction to the Hebrew Bible in the fall and an introduction to the New Testament in the spring. Later in the semester, usually around Halloween in the fall and Easter in the spring, I play a ZOMBI bingo game as a fun break from the curriculum (fig. 5).

	Z	O	M	B	I
1	Unbinding a reanimated corpse John 11:44	An undead "death" 2 Kings 2:1–18	Blood crying out from the ground Genesis 4:10	Rising skeletons get flesh Ezekiel 37	Dead shall live Isaiah 26:19
2	Pestilence stalking in darkness Psalm 91	Boy comes back to life 1 Kings 17:17–24	ZOMBIE FREE ZONE	Dead boy sneezes 2 Kings 4	Second death: Revelation 2:11, 20:14
3	Boy falls to his death, lives again Acts 20:7–12	Rising up from Sheol 1 Samuel 28	Dead but sleeping? Mark 5:35–43	Out of tombs in Jerusalem Matthew 27:50–54	Famine, pestilence, war, and death Revelation 6:1–8
4	Rotting flesh Zechariah 14:12–13	We are all (metaphorically) spiritually dead Ephesians 1:1–10	Dead will rise first 1 Thessalonians 4:16–17	Earth creature brought to life Genesis 2:7	Eating the flesh of the children Jeremiah 19:9 (also Deuteronomy 28:53–57)

Fig. 5. ZOMBI bingo card

I shuffle the categories on the cards, divide students into groups, give a card to each student, and call out the numbers on the card, such as "Z–1" or "O–3." Whenever a student gets a ZOMBI—five spaces covered in a row—their group starts looking up the passages of their ZOMBI. They discuss how to understand the biblical event in relation to the function of zombies in popular culture. The discussions are always animated (zombie pun intended). In online settings, I have saved the ZOMBI bingo card in a Google Doc and sent it to students, after which we play all together in a synchronous session. The categories can be adjusted based on the course. For instance, if I am teaching a Hebrew Bible course, I remove the New Testament passages, thus creating cards with three rows instead of four. I include a short-answer question on the final exam to assess student recall of biblical themes they encountered in the ZOMBI exercise.

Since societal collapse accompanies a zombie apocalypse, students easily identify themes of political crisis and social upheaval in biblical prophecies. King Saul, for example, faces a threat of war and goes against his own principles to consult a medium, but Samuel offers no help or hope for the king (1 Sam 28:3–19). Vivid descriptions of war and pestilence in Zechariah 14 echo a zombie plague. To illustrate Ps 91, I play a clip from AMC's popular television series *The Walking Dead*. Hershel Greene, a farm owner and community leader, reads the psalm aloud to a group of zombie apocalypse survivors, bringing hope that God will protect them from a "walking pestilence."[5]

Students also detect themes of death and resurrection, often associated with apocalypse but not always in ways that students might expect. I evoke Sarah Baker's observation that "in recent popular culture, the language of biblical apocalypse has been deliberately removed from its religious context, and instead stands as a signifier for the end of the world as we know it."[6] The four deadly riders of Rev 6:1–8 do not end the story. While modern zombie lore features themes of a global pandemic and one man's quest to navigate the postapocalyptic world, Rev 20 tells how God defeats the powers of evil and ushers in an age of peace.[7] Silver-screen zombies haunt civilization with their satiating, all-consuming appetites; the Jesus of John 11 restores his beloved friend Lazarus to life.[8] As they study these and other passages, students notice the differences between zombie culture and biblical themes of death and resurrection.[9] They also notice some similarities. Just as zombie lore includes the sheltering of beloved zombies by their living friends and lovers, God raises believers' beloved ones (Matt 27:52–53; 1 Thess 4:13–18; Rev 2:11; 20:14).

Students engage in lively discussion about various aspects of human embodiment. They are especially interested in passages about human breath. In Gen 2:7, God animates humanity with the "breath of life," and in Ezek 37:1–14, God reanimates dry bones. Elijah and Elisha use body heat and perhaps some kind of mouth-to-mouth resuscitation to bring dead boys back to life (1 Kgs 17; 2 Kgs 4; see Acts 20:7–12). Zombies,

---

5. *The Walking Dead*, "This Sorrowful Life."

6. Sarah Baker, "Ambivalent Apocalypse: The Influence of the Book of Revelation in Films and Television," *AJPC* 6 (2017): 268.

7. Baker, "Ambivalent Apocalypse," 269.

8. Students have discussed whether Jesus, raised from the dead, eats any of the breakfast with his disciples in John 21.

9. For an argument that zombie popular culture reveals more about existentialism than about nihilism and need not be dismissed as a "hopeless march towards death," see Christopher M. Moreman, *Dharma of the Dead: Zombies, Mortality and Buddhist Philosophy* (Jefferson, NC: McFarland, 2018), 95.

reanimated corpses, still remain material humans on some level. They do not have heartbeats, but what about breath? Students love to debate this point because zombies usually emit guttural moans and groans. Do zombies have a soul, or a part of their original humanity lingering within their bodies? What if reformed zombies could live among humans once again? Abel's blood cried out for vengeance (Gen 4:10), but could we forgive reformed zombies for the blood they shed? If the reformation of zombies were similar to the physical and spiritual resurrection described in Mark 5:35–53 and Eph 1:1–10, would a zombie apocalypse be a good thing for society? Would we even recognize one if we saw it?

A game of ZOMBI bingo can inspire discussion about prophecies addressing political crisis, death and resurrection in apocalyptic literature, and human embodiment and spirituality. Because Gen Z students have grown up with zombie culture, I have found that using zombies to approach biblical themes helps students relate to ancient texts and makes the Bible come to life.

Bibliography

Baker, Sarah. "Ambivalent Apocalypse: The Influence of the Book of Revelation in Films and Television." *AJPC* 6 (2017): 263–73.

Center for Disease Control and Prevention, Center for Preparedness and Response. "Zombie Preparedness." https://tinyurl.com/SBL03108bv.

Edward Green, Alan Jr. "The Post-9/11 Aesthetic: Repositioning the Zombie Film in the Horror Genre." PhD diss., University of South Florida, 2013.

Moreman, Christopher M. *Dharma of the Dead: Zombies, Mortality and Buddhist Philosophy.* Jefferson, NC: McFarland, 2018.

Platts, Todd K. "Locating Zombies in the Sociology of Popular Culture." *SC* 7 (2013): 547–60.

Veraeke, John, Christopher Mastropietro, and Filip Miscevic. *Zombies in Western Culture: A Twenty-First Century Crisis.* Open Book, 2017.

PART 4
GOING ONLINE

"You Don't Always Die from Tobacco": Teaching with Provocative Video Clips

ERIC A. SEIBERT

It is often said that a picture is worth a thousand words—and so it is. A single image can bear unassailable witness to the truth. It can move people to action and can change hearts and minds with enormous speed and power.

Yet if a picture is worth a thousand words, a video is worth ten thousand! According to James McQuivey, it is actually worth quite a bit more. In his 2008 study "How Video Will Take Over the World," McQuivey claims that a video is worth 1.8 million words. Here's the math. If a picture equals 1,000 words and "video shoots at 30 frames per second," then each second of video is equivalent to 30,000 words, which, when multiplied by "a common explainer video length" of 60 seconds, comes to 1.8 million words.[1] Regardless of whether one agrees with the particulars of McQuivey's calculations, he is surely right to emphasize the importance of videos. Given the potential videos have to influence hearts and minds, educators would do well to incorporate them into their instructional design.

There are many benefits to teaching biblical studies with short videos and video clips. First, they take very little time to utilize. Since time is always a precious commodity in face-to-face instruction, it is helpful to have pedagogical tools that have high impact but require little time. A second reason videos are so well suited for undergraduate higher education in particular is that they appeal to the current generation of students. Traditional undergraduate students today belong to Generation

---

1. Shawn Forno, "A Video Is Worth 1.8 Million Words," *IdeaRocket*, https://tinyurl.com/SBL03108bw. See James McQuivey, "How Video Will Take Over the World: What the Rise of OmniVideo Means for Consumer Product Strategy Professionals," *Forrester*, 17 June 2008, https://tinyurl.com/SBL03108bx.

Z, a generation composed of individuals born from 1997 to the present.[2] According to a 2019 survey by Visual Objects, Gen Z is the first generation to prefer YouTube over every other website, even Facebook.[3] Given YouTube's popularity, it makes sense to use videos from this platform, in particular, when teaching biblical studies to undergraduates. Third, well-chosen videos, like carefully crafted parables, can be used to help students grasp difficult concepts or see things from new angles. Videos with visually powerful and emotional appeal can be especially useful in this regard. Fourth, videos help students retain what they have learned since videos connect with their emotions. Really good videos are not easily forgotten. They stick with students long after they are viewed, making them a highly useful teaching tool. Finally, videos not only engage visual learners but also have the potential of reengaging students whose attention has drifted.

Numerous film and video resources can be used in the biblical studies classroom with great profit.[4] These include instructional videos, movies that dramatize portions of the biblical story, and modern films with themes and ideas related to the Bible. Many educators tap into these resources in one form or another over the course of a semester.

My interest here is to consider one specific type of video that educators can use to teach biblical studies: namely, videos that are brief, provocative, easily accessible, and sometimes seemingly unrelated to the Bible. The videos discussed in this chapter range from approximately one to three minutes in length and can all be found on YouTube. In what follows, I will demonstrate how to use these videos to teach biblical studies effectively and creatively, thereby enhancing student learning. I believe videos such

---

2. Kim Parker and Ruth Igielnik, "On the Cusp of Adulthood and Facing an Uncertain Future: What We Know about Gen Z So Far," Pew Research Center, 14 May 2020, https://tinyurl.com/SBL03108a.

3. See Rhonda Bradley, "Why Generation Z Loves YouTube," *The Manifest*, 22 January 2019, https://tinyurl.com/SBL03108by; and Kelsey McKeon, "How Different Generations View and Use the Top Websites," *Visual Objects*, 16 January 2019, https://tinyurl.com/SBL03108ca.

4. See especially Matthew S. Rindge, Erin Runions, and Richard S. Ascough, "Teaching the Bible and Film: Pedagogical Promises, Pitfalls, and Proposals," *TTR* 13 (2010): 140–55; Mark Roncace and Patrick Gray, eds., *Teaching the Bible through Popular Culture and the Arts* (Atlanta: Society of Biblical Literature, 2007), 87–172. See also Adele Reinhartz, *Scripture on the Silver Screen* (Louisville: Westminster John Knox, 2003).

as these can serve as useful heuristic devices and therefore welcome additions to the pedagogical toolboxes of all who teach undergraduates.

My Institutional Context and Approach

I teach at Messiah University, a Christian liberal arts school located in south-central Pennsylvania. As part of our general education program, every student at Messiah is required to take a Bible course. Students can choose from one of three options to fulfill this requirement: Encountering the Old Testament, Encountering the New Testament, or—for those who want it all—Encountering the Bible. One of the objectives for these courses is to "recognize the Bible's variety of literary genres and discuss principles necessary for their interpretation."[5] Two of the videos discussed below relate to this objective. I have used them when teaching Encountering the Bible. The other two help students consider the problem of divine violence in the Bible. I have used them in upper-level courses. The four videos I have selected are quite different from one another and demonstrate various uses for this medium in teaching biblical studies. One is part of a stand-up comedy routine, one is a compilation of violent Bible verses with corresponding artwork, one is an antitobacco advertisement, and one is a fictional movie trailer. Each is edgy and pushes boundaries in certain ways. While the first two are directly related to the Bible, the last two are not. I would encourage watching each of these videos prior to reading my discussion of them.[6]

My primary purpose here is not to make a case for using these four videos in particular, although I think they are effective. Rather, my goal is to encourage educators to try using videos like these when teaching biblical studies by illustrating some of the pedagogical techniques that can be

---

5. Each of these courses has the same three objectives: (1) reflect on how the Bible functions as an ancient text with authority for Christian belief and practice, (2) describe important aspects of the Bible's complex formation, and (3) recognize the Bible's variety of literary genres and discuss principles necessary for their interpretation.

6. The URLs are as follows: "Tim on Noah's Ark," timhawkinscomedy, YouTube, https://tinyurl.com/SBLPress03108d2; "The Morality of God—Part 1—God's Killings," atheist48, YouTube, https://tinyurl.com/SBLPress03108d3; "You Don't Always Die from Tobacco," feeteh, YouTube, https://tinyurl.com/SBLPress03108d4; "*Gandhi II*," Movieclips, YouTube, https://tinyurl.com/SBLPress03108d5.

applied to them. Since finding these kinds of videos can be challenging, I will also make a few suggestions in that regard.

Beginning a Conversation about God's Violent Behavior in the Bible

Many undergraduate students are unaware of the enormous amount of divine violence in the Bible. There are numerous reasons for this. The most obvious is that a large percentage of undergraduates have not actually read the Bible. While many are acquainted with bits and pieces, it is the rare student indeed who has made it all the way from Genesis to Revelation. This results in a lack of familiarity with many stories of God's slaying, smiting, and slaughtering, and it leaves students ill-equipped to deal responsibly with these problematic passages.

Most places of worship do not offer their congregants very much help in this regard. Violent texts are regularly passed over for friendlier passages, passages that more easily yield a positive life lesson or contain some other inspirational content. Even clergy who mention violent stories such as the account of Noah's ark or the battle of Jericho routinely sanitize them in sermons or Sunday school lessons. The focus is on the deliverance of Noah and his family, or the victory of Joshua and the Israelites, with rarely a word said about the countless number of people suffering, bleeding, and dying outside the boat and inside the city.[7] These victims of violence remain anonymous, their stories never told. All the while, questions about God's character are seldom raised, leaving people to wonder how God, who is supposedly loving and compassionate, could behave with such violence and cruelty.

Anyone who teaches the Bible knows it is impossible to avoid the issue of divine violence. Sooner or later, a question will be asked or a text will be read that requires attention to this topic. One of the first steps toward engaging students in a constructive conversation about God's violent behavior in the Bible involves helping them to recognize it. This is where short, provocative video clips can be extremely useful. They provide a helpful point of entry into this larger conversation.

---

7. See Eric A. Seibert, *The Violence of Scripture: Overcoming the Old Testament's Troubling Legacy* (Minneapolis: Fortress, 2012), 43, 81–85, 100–103, 154.

I have used two videos that function quite well in this regard. The first is a one-minute clip from Christian comedian Tim Hawkins.[8] In a stand-up routine, Hawkins tells the audience there are some things in the Bible that are not family friendly, things that would not make it into the *Precious Moments Bible*. After briefly mentioning the account of Cain and Abel, Hawkins riffs on the well-known story of Noah's ark.

> So, like I'll never understand parents who will paint Noah's ark on their kids', little kids' bedroom walls. It doesn't make sense. Noah's ark is a great story but it's just out there, man. It's like, "Daddy, what are you doing?"
> "I'm painting Noah's ark on your wall, sweetheart. My favorite story. You know, where God sends a worldwide flood to kill every living thing. Yeah, I love it. It's awesome. Hey, grab a brush and paint some screaming people on that rock for me just to make it [the end of the sentence is difficult to hear]. It's going to be great."

In a humorous and disarming way, Hawkins enables people to see the story of Noah's ark from a different perspective. For some students, this may be the first time they ever consider the violent dimensions of the story (unless they watched Darren Aronofsky's imaginative adaptation of the story of Noah in his 2014 blockbuster film). In addition, by shining a spotlight on the horror happening outside the ark, Hawkins implicitly raises serious ethical and moral questions about God's behavior.

For a more sobering visual entry into this difficult terrain, I sometimes use a three-minute video produced by atheist48 titled "The Morality of God—Part 1—God's Killings." Bible verses containing divine violence or divinely sanctioned violence are projected on the screen, accompanied by artwork depicting some aspect of the verses on display.[9] Dramatic music plays throughout the video, adding gravitas to the visual experience. A total of twenty-two passages are covered in the span of just a few minutes.[10] Examples include God's execution of every firstborn Egyptian (Exod

---

8. "Tim on Noah's Ark."

9. Images accompany the verses in all but a few cases.

10. The passages are divided into three titled sections—God kills innocent children, God kills complainers, and God kills—and appear in the following order: Deut 32:39–42; Exod 12:29; 2 Sam 12:14–18; 2 Kgs 2:23–24; Isa 34:6; Jer 12:12; Num 11:1; 16:49; 21:5–6; Isa 66:16; Exod 32:26–28; Lev 10:1–2; Num 15:33–36; 31:17–18; Deut 2:33–36; 3:3–6; 1 Sam 6:19; 15:2–3; 2 Sam 6:7; 24:15; 1 Kgs 20:36; 2 Kgs 17:25. Sometimes only a portion of the passage is displayed.

12:29), God's command to annihilate every last Amalekite, including "child and infant" (1 Sam 15:3, NRSV), and God's use of snakes to kill Israelites in the wilderness (Num 21:5–6). The unrelenting procession of verse after violent verse, image after violent image, has a powerful and disturbing effect on many students. The video hints at the magnitude of the problem, raising serious questions about God's morality and goodness.

The classroom conversation can take several directions from here, depending on the objectives of the course and the will of the instructor. Class time could be used to process the impact of these videos. Did the passages discussed (and displayed) in these videos trouble them? Why or why not? An instructor could segue into a brief summary of what makes these passages problematic for so many.

The comedic efforts of Tim Hawkins and the hard-hitting work of atheist48 lay an important foundation for further reflection. They familiarize students with passages about divine violence and lead them to consider the disturbing aspects of those passages. They prepare students to recognize the violence and to wonder how it coheres with other depictions of a compassionate, loving God.[11]

Understanding Why Prophets Did Crazy Stuff

Prophetic literature is not easy for most undergraduates to understand. The prophets speak about faraway places, use figurative language, and deliver their oracles in poetry rather than prose. One way I try to help students understand prophetic literature is by demonstrating how prophets functioned as persuasive speakers.

Focusing specifically on the Latter Prophets, I try to disabuse students of the idea that prophets primarily spoke about far-off future events. I also try to correct mistaken notions that prophets just stood on soapboxes and spoke extemporaneously. As Terry Brensinger observes, "The prophets did more than simply stand up on street corners and deliver emotion-packed, unrehearsed speeches. On the contrary, while they undoubtedly did precisely that at times, there are other occasions when great care and planning stand

---

11. For an extended discussion of how to address the issue of divine violence in the classroom, see Eric A. Seibert, "When God Smites: Talking with Students about the Violence of God in Scripture," *TTR* 17 (2014): 323–41; two videos featured in this chapter are mentioned on 329–30.

behind both the prophetic message as well as the literary forms through which it finds expression."[12] Prophets were persuasive speakers with carefully crafted messages.[13] They desperately wanted people to hear and heed their words because they were convinced they had an authoritative message from God. Therefore, they engaged in all sorts of persuasive techniques, including rhetorical questions, similes and metaphors, and personification.

But prophets did not just speak. They also acted, and they sometimes did so in ways that strike modern readers as bizarre. Isaiah walked around nude for three years (Isa 20), Ezekiel laid on one side for 390 days and on the other for forty days (Ezek 4), and Jeremiah gathered people together to watch him break a piece of pottery (Jer 19). Why did prophets behave this way? What were they trying to accomplish, and how was their audience influenced by what they saw? These are difficult questions to answer, and scholars differ over the precise meaning of these symbolic actions.[14]

Some scholars have viewed them as dramatic means for prophets to get people's attention and effectively communicate the divine word. As Carolyn Sharp writes in her recent commentary, "Prophetic sign-acts may have served as dramatic performance art, street theater that created embodiments of the word of the Lord as tableaux in front of an audience comprised largely of folks who could not read or who may not have paid attention to complex oracular poetry."[15] If this is the correct way to view prophetic acts, or at least some of them, then the "Singing Cowboy" anti-tobacco ad provides a creative entry point into a conversation about them. The ad was produced in 2006 by "The Truth campaign, a youth-focused anti-tobacco education campaign in the United States," and was "nominated for most outstanding commercial in the Emmy Awards 2007."[16]

---

12. Terry L. Brensinger, *Simile and Prophetic Language in the Old Testament*, MBPS 43 (Lewiston, NY: Mellen, 1996), 148.

13. On this point I am greatly indebted to Dr. Herbert Huffmon's graduate class on Amos and Hosea at Drew University, in which we studied the prophets through the lens of persuasion.

14. For a helpful discussion of the complexities involved in discerning the meaning of these prophetic acts, and for a critique of some of the most commonly held views along with a new proposal, see David Stacey, *Prophetic Drama in the Old Testament* (London: Epworth, 1990), 260–82.

15. Carolyn J. Sharp, *The Prophetic Literature* (Nashville: Abingdon, 2019), 67.

16. Duncan MacLeod, "The Truth Singing Cowboy on Smoking," Inspiration Room, 11 August 2007, https://tinyurl.com/SBL03108cg. For an article providing some backstory, see "The Singing (Larry) Cowboy," https://tinyurl.com/SBL03108ch.

As the video begins, we see a congested city street. Seconds later, two cowboys come into view, riding on horseback between rows of vehicles. One has a guitar in tow. The other looks kind of like the Marlboro man, a character featured for many years in cigarette commercials and ads. After dismounting, he approaches a smoking campfire ring in the middle of the street, sits down, and takes off a bandanna that reveals a sizable hole in his neck. He then holds an electrolarynx (a microphone-like device) up to his neck and begins singing while his companion plays the guitar. As we might expect, his voice sounds stiff and robotic.

> You don't always die from tobacco.
>   Sometimes you just lose a lung.
> You don't always die from tobacco.
>   Sometimes they just snip out your tongue.
> And you won't sing worth a heck
>   with a big hole in your neck
> Cause you don't always die from tobacco.
>   No, you don't always die from tobacco.

Initially, people in the video appear to be looking forward to hearing the "Singing Cowboy" and his minstrel. But the troubled expressions that soon appear tell a different tale. They are disturbed by what they see and hear and easily comprehend the point of the ad: smoking has long-term health risks that could seriously degrade the smoker's quality of life. Don't chance it!

When I have shown this video, I would turn to the class afterwards and say something along these lines: "What the heck? Why would someone make a video like that? Why not just send out a mass mailing and give people the information they need about tobacco and tobacco-related diseases?" Students would respond by saying things like, "It makes more of an impact." "People ignore mass emails and mailings." "It drives the point home to actually see someone who is suffering from the effects of tobacco." I would use their responses as a springboard to discuss symbolic prophetic acts. Just as this antitobacco video is more powerful and persuasive than a fact sheet alone, so too are symbolic prophetic acts more powerful than written oracles. However they were intended to function, they certainly would have made an impact on those who witnessed them.

When students begin to see it this way—and I think the "Singing Cowboy" video helps immensely—they can frame these prophetic acts more constructively. They are better able to appreciate prophets as people deeply committed to conveying the word of God to their communities, not just as wacky individuals performing weird stunts.

I realize that using an ad like this might not align with some educators' understanding of prophetic actions. Some, for example, believe that these acts and their accompanying words were thought to have some degree of power to create reality.[17] These educators (and others) could use the ad for a different purpose, one unrelated to these acts. It might serve simply to illustrate the value of persuasion with regard to prophetic speech. The rhetorical power of the ad can help students think about why persuasion is so valuable when the stakes are so high. Recognizing the importance of persuasion in prophetic speech not only fosters a better understanding of prophetic literature but also offers many applications for preaching and teaching today.

Challenging Violent Interpretations of Jesus in the Book of Revelation

The final genre I address in my introductory Bible class is apocalyptic literature. We discuss numerous characteristics of this genre and consider various interpretive approaches to the book of Revelation. If class time allows, I might also talk briefly about the portrayal of Jesus in the book of Revelation. Specifically, are we to envision Jesus slaughtering countless people at the end of time?

While most Christians agree that Jesus was essentially nonviolent during the thirty-odd years he lived on earth, many believe he will behave quite differently upon his return. They base their belief on a literal interpretation of the book of Revelation, one that I think fails to account for the meaning and significance of apocalyptic literature. As C. S. Cowles puts it:

> By interpreting its highly symbolic language literally, the nonviolent Jesus of the Gospels is transformed into a violent warrior.... Thus, like Clark Kent emerging from the telephone booth as Superman, Jesus at his return will cast aside his servant garments and will disclose who he really is: a fierce, merciless, and physically violent eschatological terminator who will make the blood of his enemies flow knee-deep.[18]

---

17. For this view and a critique, see Stacey, *Prophetic Drama*, 268–75.
18. C. S. Cowles, "A Response to Tremper Longman III," in *Show Them No Mercy:*

To frame this question, it may be useful to read Rev 19:11–16 in class. The passage speaks of Jesus making war, "clothed in a robe dipped in blood," and having "a sharp sword" coming out of his mouth "to strike down the nations" (NRSV). Based on this passage (and others), many Christians envision Jesus to be something of an end-time Terminator. In the words of Mark Driscoll, "In Revelation, Jesus is a pride [*sic*] fighter with a tattoo down His leg, a sword in His hand and the commitment to make someone bleed."[19] There is a very lucrative industry built on the notion of Jesus's end-time violence. The sixteen-volume Left Behind series (1995–2007), written by Tim LaHaye and Jerry B. Jenkins—a series that has sold over eighty million copies—is predicated on this extremely violent view of Jesus.[20]

To push back against this popular (though in my view erroneous) way of understanding Jesus, I sometimes show the class a brief video clip from Weird Al Yankovic's 1989 movie *UHF*.[21] The video clip depicts a trailer for an imaginary upcoming movie, *Gandhi II*, to be shown on the television station U62.

Four Views on God and Canaanite Genocide, ed. Stanley N. Gundry (Grand Rapids: Zondervan, 2003), 193. Cowles's remarks are a response to Tremper Longman's essay in *Show Them No Mercy*, though they are apropos to all who read Revelation literally.

19. "7 Big Questions: Seven Leaders on Where the Church Is Headed," *Relevant Magazine*, October 10, 2007, https://tinyurl.com/SBL03108ci.

20. Ann Byle, "LaHaye, Co-author of Left Behind Series, Leaves a Lasting Impact," *Publisher's Weekly*, 27 July 2016, https://tinyurl.com/SBL03108cj. For a discussion and critique of the violence in the Left Behind series, see Loren L. Johns, "Conceiving Violence: The Apocalypse of John and the Left Behind Series," *Direction* 34 (2005): 194–214. For a summary of the violent view of Jesus in the final book of the series, see 195–96.

21. Rotten Tomatoes describes the movie as follows: "When a desperate UHF station gives the seriously odd George the job of manager, he proves to be a programming genius, turning the station around—and attracting the attention of an unscrupulous competitor. This comedy focuses most of its creative attention on numerous bizarre television parodies featured throughout." See "*UHF*," Rotten Tomatoes, https://tinyurl.com/SBL03108ck. The violent interpretation of Jesus in Rev 19 is routinely based on a more literal reading of the passage. Yet the book of Revelation, a work of apocalyptic literature, is meant to be read symbolically. For a brief discussion of Rev 19:11–21 that rejects interpreting Jesus as a violent warrior, see Eric A. Seibert, *Disturbing Divine Behavior: Troubling Old Testament Images of God* (Minneapolis: Fortress, 2009), 254–57. For an extended argument that Jesus was nonviolent, see Eric A. Seibert, *Disarming the Church: Why Christians Must Forsake Violence to Follow Jesus and Change the World* (Eugene, OR: Cascade, 2018), 60–113.

As the trailer begins, we see a "bad guy" shooting a gun as a stereotypical movie-trailer voice says, "Next week, on U62. He's back. And this time, he's mad. *Gandhi II*." The shooter stumbles and falls to the ground, only to look up and see "Gandhi" standing there. Gandhi looks very much like the images familiar to many of us. He is bald, wears a pair of Coke-bottle glasses, and is dressed in his signature white khadi wrap. What is surprising, however, is that he has a steel pipe in one hand, which he menacingly taps into the other.

The scene then shifts to four tough guys who, in slow motion, approach Gandhi. One pulls a knife as he moves closer. But these thugs are no match for Gandhi. He makes short work of them, giving them a beating they will not soon forget. Gandhi throws one guy into a dumpster and punches another so hard that his fist goes through the man's body and comes out the other side blood-red. As this melee is underway, the narrator's booming voice declares, "No more Mr. Passive Resistance. He's out to kick some butt. This is one bad mother you don't want to mess with." The fight scene ends with Gandhi holding a knife to the throat of one of the ruffians, warning, "Don't move, slimeball!"

In the brief nighttime scene that follows, Gandhi drives into a back alley. After bringing his red sports car to a stop, he immediately hops out and manhandles a would-be assailant, repeatedly smashing his face on the roof of the car. "He's a one-man wrecking crew," says the narrator. "But he also knows how to party."

The final scene of the video features Gandhi entering a fancy restaurant, flanked by two attractive, well-dressed young women. As the waiter leans in for Gandhi's order, we hear Gandhi say, "Give me a steak, medium rare." At that point, we hear an unidentified voice from somewhere in the restaurant exclaim, "Hey, baldy!" The narrator then declares, "There is only one law, his law," as Gandhi flips over his table and grabs a weapon. Everyone dives to the floor as Gandhi shoots up the place with a machine gun. The final words of the narrator, "*Gandhi II*," appear on the screen, made to look as though they were shot from the automatic weapon Gandhi is firing.

The entire video runs just under a minute. After it ends, I ask the class: "Is that Gandhi?" This is, essentially, a rhetorical question. Even people who know very little about Mahatma Gandhi realize that he was deeply committed to nonviolence. The video's portrayal of an aggressive, violent, meat-eating party animal is nothing like the man who brought independence to twentieth-century India. It is so obvious it hardly needs to be said. And this is what makes it such an excellent entrée into a conversation about the nonviolent nature of Jesus.

What sense does it make to view Jesus, the one who taught love of enemies and forgiveness, as one who returns smiting, slaying, and slaughtering at the end of time? Just as *Gandhi II* does not accurately reveal the true character of India's nonviolent liberator, interpretations of Jesus based on violent readings of Revelation do not accurately reflect the character of Jesus as portrayed in the Gospels. Jesus consistently helped and healed people. He did not hurt them. If we want to teach students to read Revelation responsibly, we must help them interpret Rev 19:11–16 (and similar passages) in ways that are consistent with the image of Jesus as the slaughtered lamb.[22] This is, after all, the defining image of Jesus in the book of Revelation. As Brian McLaren observes:

> Revelation celebrates not the love of power, but the power of love. It denies, with all due audacity, that God's anointed liberator is the Divine Terminator, threatening revenge for all who refuse to honor him, growling "I'll be back!" It asserts, instead, that God's anointed liberator is the one we beat up, who promises mercy to those who strike him, whispering, "Father, forgive them; for they do not know what they are doing" (Luke 23:34).[23]

Much more could be done with this video to extend the discussion in various directions, but I hope enough has been said to illustrate how a video such as this can function as an excellent conversation starter by challenging traditional understandings of the apocalyptic Jesus as a purveyor of violence.

---

22. See Ted Grimsrud, *To Follow the Lamb: A Peaceable Reading of the Book of Revelation* (Eugene, OR: Cascade, 2022); Michael J. Gorman, *Reading Revelation Responsibly: Uncivil Worship and Witness; Following the Lamb into the New Creation* (Eugene, OR: Cascade Books, 2011); Mark Bredin, *Jesus, Revolutionary of Peace: A Nonviolent Christology in the Book of Revelation* (Carlisle, UK: Paternoster, 2003); Loren L. Johns, *The Lamb Christology of the Apocalypse of John: An Investigation into Its Origins and Rhetorical Force* (Tübingen: Mohr Siebeck, 2003); and Sylvie T. Raquel, "Blessed Are the Peacemakers: The Theology of Peace in the Book of Revelation," in *Essays on Revelation: Appropriating Yesterday's Apocalypse in Today's World*, ed. Gerald Stevens (Eugene, OR: Pickwick, 2011), 55–71.

23. Brian D. McLaren, *A New Kind of Christianity: Ten Questions That Are Transforming the Faith* (New York: HarperOne, 2010), 126.

Finding Short, Provocative Videos

While the four videos considered in this chapter illustrate various ways to use this medium to teach biblical studies, they are only the tip of the iceberg. There are many more waiting to be discovered and repurposed for use in the biblical studies classroom. To my knowledge, however, there is no quick and easy way to find them. I came across each of this chapter's videos differently and mostly by accident. I was introduced to the Tim Hawkins clip by one of my relatives. I may have found "The Morality of God" video on the internet while intentionally searching for something like it, but I really cannot remember. I initially saw the "Singing Cowboy" antitobacco ad at the beginning of a movie my wife and I first watched many years ago. Though I am not entirely sure, I think it was *Becoming Jane*, a film that tells the life story of Jane Austen. A short version of the ad precedes the feature presentation on the DVD we own. I honestly cannot recall how I first became aware of *Gandhi II*. It is quite possible I was introduced to it by a colleague of mine who, in turn, may have seen it in a footnote.[24]

My suggestion for finding videos like these is to be on the lookout for them. When watching YouTube videos, notice the possibilities for teaching biblical studies. Think about how they might illuminate a challenging concept. Those who want to be more proactive and who have a student assistant at their disposal could ask the student to spend a few hours looking for short videos that hold promise for teaching biblical studies. This will probably be most effective if the student worker is majoring in biblical studies (or a related field) or has already taken a Bible class or two. Then, once the student has compiled a list of suggested videos, view them to determine which ones are most likely to work well in class.

Instructors might also consider creating a course assignment that requires students to identify two or three YouTube videos—like the ones discussed in this essay—that they believe have good potential for teaching biblical studies.[25] As part of this assignment, students would write a short paper describing the videos and explaining how they envision them being used to teach the Bible. This would enhance student learning by helping students think creatively about the Bible and its themes as they attempt to make connections to the digital world. In addition, it would be

---

24. McLaren, *New Kind of Christianity*, 274–75.
25. I am grateful to Dr. J. Blair Wilgus for this suggestion.

an excellent way to develop a repertoire of videos that could be useful for classroom instruction in the future.

Finally, I would note that some online sites are designed to help users locate specific clips that can be used in a variety of creative ways. One such site is wingclips.com. On this site, movie clips can be located by title, category, theme, or Scripture reference, making it easy to find appropriate clips for instructional purposes. While all of these clips can be previewed freely and some can be downloaded and used without cost, many of them must be purchased for full-screen use. A similar site, movieclips.com, allows viewers to access videos for free via YouTube.

When selecting videos to use in the classroom, instructors need to exercise caution by considering the impact certain images might have on students. I have sometimes wondered how the "Singing Cowboy" commercial affects students who may have lost a parent, friend, or other loved one to some kind of tobacco-related illness. And the *Gandhi II* movie trailer might need a trigger warning. It is certainly not G-rated! It contains gratuitous violence, particularly in the scene where Gandhi's fist goes all the way through his assailant's stomach and comes out bloody on the other side. It helps to show provocative videos, but it also pays to remember that provocation is a means to an end. Ultimately, I seek to illustrate some aspect of biblical studies or to encourage students to consider a particular interpretive approach. I want to avoid getting stuck on the video. If the imagery is too disturbing, students might fixate on it and miss the point. I think carefully about what I share with my students and take extra precautions to prevent the videos I use from hijacking student learning or triggering posttraumatic stress.

Conclusion

Brief, provocative videos have the power to engage students in ways that more conventional teaching methods lack. Carefully chosen clips make useful additions to the biblical studies professor's pedagogical toolbox. Most students welcome the change to the regular classroom routine. Audiovisual presentations mix things up and provide an alternative to more traditional modes of instruction. Used well, they will help students learn to read the Bible more responsibly—a worthy objective for all who have the good fortune of teaching biblical studies.

Bibliography

"7 Big Questions: Seven Leaders on Where the Church Is Headed." *Relevant Magazine*, October 10, 2007. https://tinyurl.com/SBL03108ci.

Bradley, Rhonda. "Why Generation Z Loves YouTube." The Manifest, 22 January 2019. https://tinyurl.com/SBL03108by.

Bredin, Mark. *Jesus, Revolutionary of Peace: A Nonviolent Christology in the Book of Revelation*. Carlisle, UK: Paternoster, 2003.

Brensinger, Terry L. *Simile and Prophetic Language in the Old Testament*. MBPS 43. Lewiston, NY: Mellen, 1996.

Byle, Ann. "LaHaye, Co-author of Left Behind Series, Leaves a Lasting Impact." *Publisher's Weekly*, 27 July 2016. https://tinyurl.com/SBL03108cj.

Cowles, C. S. "A Response to Tremper Longman III." Pages 191–95 in *Show Them No Mercy: Four Views on God and Canaanite Genocide*. Edited by Stanley N. Gundry. Grand Rapids: Zondervan, 2003.

Forno, Shawn. "A Video Is Worth 1.8 Million Words." IdeaRocket. https://tinyurl.com/SBL03108bw.

"Gandhi II." Movieclips. YouTube. https://tinyurl.com/SBLPress03108d5.

Gorman, Michael J. *Reading Revelation Responsibly: Uncivil Worship and Witness; Following the Lamb into the New Creation*. Eugene, OR: Cascade Books, 2011.

Grimsrud, Ted. *To Follow the Lamb: A Peaceable Reading of the Book of Revelation*. Eugene, OR: Cascade, 2022.

Johns, Loren L. "Conceiving Violence: The Apocalypse of John and the Left Behind Series." *Direction* 34 (2005): 194–214.

———. *The Lamb Christology of the Apocalypse of John: An Investigation into Its Origins and Rhetorical Force*. Tübingen: Mohr Siebeck, 2003.

MacLeod, Duncan. "The Truth Singing Cowboy on Smoking." Inspiration Room, 11 August 2007. https://tinyurl.com/SBL03108cg.

McKeon, Kelsey. "How Different Generations View and Use the Top Websites." Visual Objects, 16 January 2019. https://tinyurl.com/SBL03108ca.

McLaren, Brian D. *A New Kind of Christianity: Ten Questions That Are Transforming the Faith*. New York: HarperOne, 2010.

McQuivey, James. "How Video Will Take Over the World: What the Rise of OmniVideo Means for Consumer Product Strategy Professionals." Forrester, 17 June 2008. https://tinyurl.com/SBL03108bx.

"The Morality of God—Part 1—God's Killings." atheist48. YouTube. https://tinyurl.com/SBLPress03108d3.

Parker, Kim, and Ruth Igielnik. "On the Cusp of Adulthood and Facing an Uncertain Future: What We Know about Gen Z So Far." Pew Research Center, 14 May 2020. https://tinyurl.com/SBL03108a.

Raquel, Sylvie T. "Blessed Are the Peacemakers: The Theology of Peace in the Book of Revelation." Pages 55–71 in *Essays on Revelation: Appropriating Yesterday's Apocalypse in Today's World*. Edited by Gerald Stevens. Eugene, OR: Pickwick, 2011.

Reinhartz, Adele. *Scripture on the Silver Screen*. Louisville: Westminster John Knox, 2003.

Rindge, Matthew S., Erin Runions, and Richard S. Ascough. "Teaching the Bible and Film: Pedagogical Promises, Pitfalls, and Proposals." *TTR* 13 (2010): 140–55.

Roncace, Mark, and Patrick Gray, eds. *Teaching the Bible through Popular Culture and the Arts*. Atlanta: Society of Biblical Literature, 2007.

Seibert, Eric A. *Disarming the Church: Why Christians Must Forsake Violence to Follow Jesus and Change the World*. Eugene, OR: Cascade, 2018.

———. *Disturbing Divine Behavior: Troubling Old Testament Images of God*. Minneapolis: Fortress, 2009.

———. *The Violence of Scripture: Overcoming the Old Testament's Troubling Legacy*. Minneapolis: Fortress, 2012.

———. "When God Smites: Talking with Students about the Violence of God in Scripture." *TTR* 17 (2014): 323–41.

Sharp, Carolyn J. *The Prophetic Literature*. Nashville: Abingdon, 2019.

"The Singing (Larry) Cowboy." https://tinyurl.com/SBL03108ch.

Stacey, David. *Prophetic Drama in the Old Testament*. London: Epworth, 1990.

"Tim on Noah's Ark." timhawkinscomedy. YouTube. https://tinyurl.com/SBLPress03108d2.

"*UHF*." Rotten Tomatoes. https://tinyurl.com/SBL03108ck.

"You Don't Always Die from Tobacco." feeteh. YouTube. https://tinyurl.com/SBL03108ce.

Picturing Textual Criticism: Using Digital Images to Capture Student Attention

Seth Heringer

After years of tweaking how I taught textual criticism in introductory New Testament courses, it became clear that I needed to make substantive revisions because many students were uninterested in manuscripts and scribal changes. Some grew bored after they understood the basics: that differences exist among the Greek manuscripts that comprise our modern New Testament. They viewed the supporting information, such as details in the manuscripts and theories of transmission, as superfluous. Others showed skepticism. Because they were unable to integrate manuscript variations into their understanding of an inspired Bible, they wondered whether they were real. English translations did not satisfy them because they could not see the original differences for themselves.

To address student boredom and doubt, I applied a new pedagogical methodology. I shifted from regarding my students as passive recipients of information to treating them as discoverers of knowledge by giving them two tools to practice textual criticism. First, I showed students high-resolution images of important Greek manuscripts. These images of ancient and tattered documents, written in the simultaneously strange yet familiar Greek alphabet, sustained student attention and curiosity. The images also reified the differences among manuscripts as students compared the Greek texts. Second, I created an English-translation worksheet that reproduced the differences among these manuscripts, allowing students to assume the role of a text critic by considering which manuscript was closest to the original. Taken together, these practices created a learning experience that incorporated all six characteristics of "sticky" learning.

Sticky Learning

The concept of sticky learning was developed by Chip and Dan Heath in their book *Made to Stick: Why Some Ideas Survive and Others Die*. Heath and Heath delineate the characteristics that make some ideas easy to remember and others easy to forget.[1] Their research shows that simple, unexpected, concrete, credible, emotional, and story-based ideas are most easily retained. I applied these principles to teaching textual criticism in order to increase student knowledge retention while making textual criticism more interesting.

For Heath and Heath, a simple idea is one that reveals the core of a concept. This core is not found by merely removing all complexity; rather, one must "relentlessly prioritize."[2] For instructors, simplicity means cutting even interesting and important ideas that are not directly related to the essence of a topic. I simplified my teaching by removing information that did not serve my core purpose of demonstrating that textual variants exist and that text critics compare them in an attempt to reconstruct the original text. I retained complexity by using a schema.[3] Like analogies, schemas serve as anchors that tie a simple concept to its complex implications. Schemas allow students to build on a clear structure. In my class, the worksheet serves as a schema by grounding students in the existence of textual variants while displaying Greek texts in chronological order.

Sticky ideas, like the solutions to mysteries and riddles, are unexpected. Heath and Heath posit that surprise revelations attract attention.[4] They also warn, however, that "surprise doesn't last. For our idea to endure, we must generate interest and curiosity."[5] When ideas tap into our innate curiosity and leave us in wonder, they endure. Heath and Heath suggest that speakers can generate curiosity by creating gaps in knowledge and then filling them.[6] In my experience, students are surprised when they

---

1. Chip Heath and Dan Heath, *Made to Stick: Why Some Ideas Survive and Others Die* (New York: Random House, 2007). The authors have also written "Teaching That Sticks," an essay that applies the six principles of *Made to Stick* to pedagogy. It is available for free on their website: https://tinyurl.com/SBL03108cl.

2. Heath and Heath, *Made to Stick*, 16.

3. Heath and Heath, *Made to Stick*, 53–55.

4. Heath and Heath, *Made to Stick*, 65.

5. Heath and Heath, *Made to Stick*, 16.

6. Heath and Heath, *Made to Stick*, 84.

realize that the exact wording of some biblical passages is not known with certainty. Their surprise turns into curiosity when they acknowledge their inability to assess and synthesize ancient manuscripts, revealing a gap in their understanding. I then fill in that gap by teaching them how to account for textual variants with the practices of textual criticism.

Sticky ideas are also concrete. Heath and Heath define a concrete idea as something "you can examine with your senses." They identify this characteristic as important because "abstraction makes it harder to understand an idea and to remember it."[7] They recommend using physical examples and experiments when explaining ideas. Conversely, my original approach to teaching textual criticism was hindered by layers of abstraction. Students were unable to see the manuscripts and had to trust my English translation of the variants. I therefore increased concreteness by using digital images to allow students to examine the Greek manuscripts directly. They could see the fibers, the missing pieces, and the faded writing. This strategy has an added extra layer of concreteness when students take on the role of a text critic. As Susan Ambrose and colleagues suggest, an important principle of teaching and learning is to "provide authentic, real-world tasks" for students by creating "problems and tasks that allow students to vividly and concretely see the relevance and value of otherwise abstract concepts and theories."[8] As students complete the worksheet and theorize which manuscript reflects the original, they act as if they were in a virtual lab, attempting to solve a real text-critical problem.

Simple, unexpected, and concrete ideas will not stick unless they are credible. Students will not remember anything about textual criticism if they do not believe in textual variants. Heath and Heath acknowledge that overcoming student incredulity presents a challenge. "If we're trying to persuade a skeptical audience to believe a new message," they say, "the reality is that we're fighting an uphill battle against a lifetime of personal learning and social relationships."[9] I faced such skepticism when I relied only on English examples of textual variants. Some students wanted to see the evidence for themselves. Therefore, I incorporated digital images of the manuscripts in order to let students corroborate their existence with their own eyes.

---

7. Heath and Heath, *Made to Stick*, 100, 104.

8. Susan A. Ambrose et al., *How Learning Works: Seven Research-Based Principles for Smart Teaching* (San Francisco: Jossey-Bass, 2010), 83.

9. Heath and Heath, *Made to Stick*, 133.

Ideas that evoke emotions can stick especially well. Heath and Heath describe how people care about ideas when "we make them feel something."[10] Emotions in response to learning about textual criticism will differ based on the students and their context. Nonreligious students may feel a range of emotions from vindication to bewilderment. Students who hold the Bible as the authoritative word of God often feel disoriented. They may doubt their faith, disbelieve the evidence, or become angry that nobody had told them about textual variants before. I will offer suggestions on ways to engage fruitfully these emotions in the example class below.

The power of stories is well known, so Heath and Heath encourage their readers to harness stories as they communicate their ideas. Storytelling draws hearers in and sustains their attention. Stories entertain while they teach. Heath and Heath claim that storytelling acts as mental simulation. It combines story and imagination to prompt thoughts "of things that we might otherwise have neglected," "problem-solving," and "building skills."[11] I now teach the textual history of the New Testament as a story that begins with the writing of an original document, continues through its copying and transmission, and ends with modern translations. As students follow this story, they mentally simulate scribal involvement with the process, pondering what would cause those scribes to change the text.

Making Textual Criticism Stick with Digital Images

I have developed a strategy for sticky learning that makes textual criticism simple, surprising, concrete, and credible. It engages students' emotions while telling a story. I will demonstrate it by describing a lesson that can be presented in two fifty-minute class sessions.

I begin the lesson by introducing my students to the end of the story of textual transmission: the Bibles they brought to class. I have students read Luke 11:2 and consider how the publisher knew what specific words to put on the page. Some speculate that the text passed through a line of translations before it arrived in their own Bibles; others believe that the New International Version was directly inspired by God. Pursuing the idea of an original text, I ask whether, like the American Constitution, an original copy of the New Testament is stored somewhere behind sealed glass.

---

10. Heath and Heath, *Made to Stick*, 17.
11. Heath and Heath, *Made to Stick*, 212–13.

This question allows me to introduce the idea that the New Testament is a collection of books written in Greek by a variety of authors. Each of these books, like the Constitution, has its own history of transmission but, unlike the Constitution, developed variants over time.

The discussion of textual variants creates a gap in students' knowledge. They wonder how these variants are synthesized into the unified text that appears in their Bibles. I begin to fill this gap by telling the story of how manuscripts were created and transmitted. To emphasize the physicality of these manuscripts, I show pictures of papyrus and parchment, describing how these writing materials were made. Next, I have students consider how manuscripts written on such fragile materials could have survived. Students often surmise that an original autograph must have been copied many times. I use this answer to discuss how some textual variants arose from unintentional scribal mistakes such as skipping a line or word. I also discuss intentional changes attributed to theological preferences or desire for harmonization.

After these introductory discussions, I have students analyze specific textual variants of Luke 11:2 by completing a worksheet (fig. 6). The worksheet invites them to compare Luke 11:2 across four manuscripts by marking similarities and differences among their English translations.

This worksheet has three purposes. First, it presents an opportunity to give a short history of some of the most important manuscripts for textual criticism. Second, it encourages students to discover variants for themselves.[12] Third, it serves as a schema that can add complexity to the simple idea of textual differences by collecting manuscripts, chronology, and variations into one chart. Additionally, it bridges the English and Greek languages, giving students a reference point for examining the digital image of a specific manuscript.

If the lesson had ceased here, students would have learned useful information about textual variants, but the story would not be complete, credible, or concrete. I therefore continue the presentation by displaying digital images of each manuscript from the worksheet. In order to prepare students to survey Greek texts, I introduce five letters of the Greek uncial alphabet, focusing on the word ΠΑΤΕΡ. Concentrating on one word provides a reference point for students scanning a confusing jumble of Greek letters. Before turning to the Greek, however, I have students guess the

---

12. Students can complete this task before coming to class.

Luke 11:2: Translation and Greek Text

P.Bodm. XIV–XV (late second or early third century), Codex Vaticanus (fourth century)

He said to them, "When you pray, say: Father, hallowed be your name. Your kingdom come."

Ειπεν δε αυτοις Οταν προσευχεσθε λεγετε Πατερ αγιασθητω το ονομα σου ελθετω η βασιλεια σου.

Codex Sinaiticus (fifth century)

He said to them, "When you pray, say: Father, hallowed be your name. Your kingdom come. Your will be done on earth as in heaven."

Ειπεν δε αυτοις Οταν προσευχησθε λεγετε Πατερ αγιασθητω το ονομα σου ελθατω η βασιλια σου Γενηθητω το θελημα σου ως εν ουρανω ουτω και επι γης.

Codex Alexandrinus (fifth century)

He said to them, "When you pray, say: Our Father who is in heaven, hallowed be your name. Your kingdom come, your will be done on earth as in heaven.

Ειπεν δε αυτοις Οταν προσευχεσθε λεγετε ΠΕΡ ημων ο εν τοις ΟΥΝΟΙΣ αγιασθητω το ονομα σου Ελθετω η βασιλεια σου Γενηθητω το θελημα σου ως ως εν Ο ΥΝΩ και επι γης. Τον αρτον

Codex Bezae (fifth century)

He said to them, "Do not babble, then, like the others; for some people think that by their much speaking, they will be justified (heard); but rather, praying say: Our Father who is in Heaven hallowed be your name. Let your kingdom come upon us, let your will be done on earth as in heaven."

Ο δε ειπεν Οταν προσευχησθε μη βαττολογειτε ως οι λοιποι δοχουσιν γαρ τινες οτι εν τη πολυλογεια αυτων εισακουσθησονται αλλα προσευχομενοι λεγετε Πατερ ημων ο εν τοις ουρανοις αγιασθητω ονομα σου Εφ ημας ελθετω σου η βασιλεια Γενηθητω το θελημα σου ως ως εν ουρανω και επι γης

Fig. 6. A worksheet with the Greek text and English translation of textual variants in Luke 11:2

Greek word for "father" by thinking of words related to fatherhood. The class will usually supply a cognate such as *paternity* or *paternal*. I then teach the individual letters of ΠΑΤΕΡ, sounding each out and writing it on the board. I also display a paleographical chart, exposing students to the Greek alphabet with variations in ancient letter formation.[13]

Students are now ready to view the Greek manuscripts. Referring them back to their worksheet, I display an image of Luke 11:2 in Bodmer Papyrus XIV-XV. The image, complete with reconstructed lacunae, immediately concretizes the manuscript by showing its physicality and fragility.[14] I give students a minute to survey the manuscript before having them identify the word ΠΑΤΕΡ. Once they have located it, I change the image to one that includes typed Greek words with their English translations (fig. 7). I then translate the Greek text slowly for the students, allowing them to confirm that the Bodmer Papyrus XIV–XV Greek on their worksheet matches the digital image.

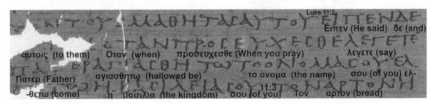

Fig. 7. An image of Luke 11:2 in P.Bodm. XIV–XV with inserted Greek and English translation. Reproduced with permission from Biblioteca Apostolica Vaticana, https://digi.vatlib.it/view/MSS_Pap.Hanna.1(Mater.Verbi)/0028.

The existence of textual variants becomes more credible as I proceed down the worksheet, displaying the digital images for each text in turn. As we observe each image, I emphasize the Greek variants. For example, when the discussion moves from Bodmer Papyrus XIV-XV to Codex Sinaiticus (fig. 8), I point out the additional sentence following ΒΑΣΙΛΕΙΑ ΣΟΥ.

---

13. See chart by Robert Waltz, *Table of Scripts Used in Various Uncials*, http://waltzmn.brainout.net/UncialScript.html.

14. The Bodmer papyri comprise "twenty-seven almost perfectly preserved sheets" that "marked another revolution in our understanding of how the New Testament text developed" because of their similarities to Codex Vaticanus. Kurt Aland and Barbara Aland, *The Text of the New Testament: An Introduction to the Critical Editions and to the Theory and Practice of Modern Textual Criticism*, 2nd ed. (Grand Rapids: Eerdmans, 1989), 87.

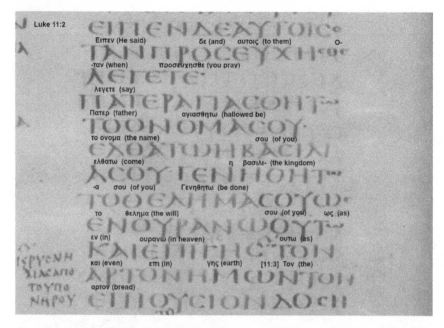

Fig. 8. An image of Luke 11:2 in Codex Sinaiticus with inserted Greek and English translation. Reproduced with permission from The British Library, https://www.codexsinaiticus.org/en/manuscript.aspx?book=35&chapter=11.

Similarly, for Codex Alexandrinus (fig. 9), I first point to the abbreviation ΠΕΡ for ΠΑΤΕΡ, indicating that it is one of many *nomina sacra*, common abbreviations used for divine names or titles in ancient Greek manuscripts. Next, I identify ΗΜΩΝ as another deviation from the previous manuscripts.

Fig. 9. An image of Luke 11:2 in Codex Alexandrinus with inserted Greek and English translation. Used with permission. © British Library Board, Royal MS 1 D VIII, f.30r, http://www.bl.uk/manuscripts/Viewer.aspx?ref=royal_ms_1_d_viii_fs001r.

If there is time, I introduce Codex Bezae (fig. 10) because it shows how difficult it can be to discern the letters on a manuscript. As I zoom closely into the manuscript, students quickly notice that some of the letters fade into the background, making them hard to perceive. Additionally, Bezae exhibits a lengthy interpolation from Matt 6:7 and serves as a good example for discussing intentional scribal changes for the purpose of harmonization.

Fig. 10. An image of Luke 11:2 in Codex Bezae with inserted Greek and English translation. Reproduced by kind permission of the Syndics of Cambridge University Library. MS Nn.2.41, https://cudl.lib.cam.ac.uk/view/MS-NN-00002-00041/441.

Next, I ask students to imagine themselves as scribes in the story of textual transmission. What sort of mistakes might they make? Why might they intentionally change the text? I direct students to ponder this question before forming them into small groups to discuss their conclusions. If the groups do not discover that the later versions are influenced by the parallel passage in Matt 6, I suggest that possibility. My institution's confessional context allows me to ask students to recite the Lord's Prayer. Because they are familiar with Matthew's version, students add to Luke's version just as the later manuscripts do. They recognize their own familiarity with Matthew's version and so understand why some copyists might have changed Luke's.

The recitation of the Lord's Prayer concludes the discussion of textual copying and transmission. I tell students that we are now moving to the final chapter of our textual transmission story with the work of modern text critics. Here, I teach how text critics assess textual variants and reconstruct the most likely original text. They apply criteria such as manuscript age and quality, moderate preference for shorter and more difficult readings, and consideration of the kinds of changes scribes were likely to have made, such as harmonizing passages and replacing uncommon words with more familiar ones.[15] I then assign small groups to apply these principles to the variants of Luke 11:2 in order to determine which manuscript might reflect the original. The exercise concludes with a full class discussion where I review the entire textual transmission story beginning with original writings, continuing through copying and transmission, and ending with the reasons for deciding that the variant from Bodmer Papyrus XIV-XV is closest to the original text. I then point them back to Luke 11:2 in their Bibles and have them recall how those specific words got on the page.

Although our study of textual criticism has ended, students will still need time to process emotional and spiritual issues. Instructors working in nonconfessional contexts should be prepared to field a variety of responses, from attacks on the Bible's reliability to questions about long-held beliefs and trenchant defenses of biblical authority. Managing a fruitful conversation about these responses can be both challenging and rewarding. In my institutional context, I conduct a final discussion on biblical authority. I address student discomfort over variants and scholarly reconstructions by pointing to Martin Heide's statistical analysis of the "most important papyri of the second and third centuries" that finds them to agree over 90 percent of the time. Based on this analysis he concludes, "The history of the text of the New Testament is not characterized by error and alteration, but far more by a high degree of stability. Despite an abundance of variants, the text of the New Testament is good and reliable."[16] I conclude by discussing the role the Holy Spirit plays in sustaining the text and guiding the church in its reading.

The strategy of using digital images to practice textual criticism of Luke 11:2 incorporates the six characteristics of sticky learning into an engaging classroom experience. It uses a story line to trace the creation,

---

15. Aland and Aland, *Text of the New Testament*, 280–81; Bruce M. Metzger and Bart D. Ehrman, *The Text of the New Testament: Its Transmission, Corruption, and Restoration*, 4th ed. (New York: Oxford University Press, 2005), 300–305. The recent developments from the *Editio Critica Maior* have furthered our knowledge of the original text through technological advancements and search algorithms, but these findings are unnecessary to include at this introductory level.

16. K. Martin Heide, "Assessing the Stability of the Transmitted Texts of the New Testament and the *Shepherd of Hermas*," in *The Reliability of the New Testament: Bart D. Ehrman and Daniel B. Wallace in Dialogue*, ed. Robert B. Stewart (Minneapolis: Fortress, 2011), 132–38, 154.

copying, and transmission of manuscripts across time. The story remains simple even as it expands to include textual variants and the decisions of text critics. It surprises students with the idea that the Greek behind the New Testament is derived from multiple manuscripts spanning four centuries and full of textual variants. This surprise creates gaps in knowledge that are filled with a display of concrete digital images of various manuscripts of Luke 11:2 that lets students see the manuscripts and variants for themselves. It consistently involves students in the process of discovery, ending the story of textual transmission by describing the work of text critics and giving students an opportunity to practice textual criticism of Luke 11:2. The emotions evoked by viewing Greek manuscripts and practicing textual criticism make the lesson memorable. The strategy turns what could be a boring recitation of documents and differences into an active, visual, and sticky exploration of textual criticism.

Bibliography

Aland, Kurt, and Barbara Aland. *The Text of the New Testament: An Introduction to the Critical Editions and to the Theory and Practice of Modern Textual Criticism*. 2nd ed. Grand Rapids: Eerdmans, 1989.

Ambrose, Susan A., Michael W. Bridges, Marsha Lovett, Michele DiPietro, and Marie K. Norman. *How Learning Works: Seven Research-Based Principles for Smart Teaching*. San Francisco: Jossey-Bass, 2010.

Heath, Chip, and Dan Heath. *Made to Stick: Why Some Ideas Survive and Others Die*. New York: Random House, 2007.

Heath, Dan, and Chip Heath. "Teaching That Sticks." https://tinyurl.com/SBL03108cl.

Heide, K. Martin. "Assessing the Stability of the Transmitted Texts of the New Testament and the *Shepherd of Hermas*." Pages 125–59 in *The Reliability of the New Testament: Bart D. Ehrman and Daniel B. Wallace in Dialogue*. Edited by Robert B. Stewart. Minneapolis: Fortress, 2011.

Metzger, Bruce M., and Bart D. Ehrman. *The Text of the New Testament: Its Transmission, Corruption, and Restoration*. 4th ed. New York: Oxford University Press, 2005.

Turning Dung into Fertilizer:
The Pedagogical Utility of Free e-Bible Tools

CARL N. TONEY

When knowledge was centered on universities and their libraries, the academy held the keys to the kingdom. Now, with the advent of the digital age, information is increasingly open-sourced. Both instructors and students need new skills to navigate the current digital landscape. For instructors and students in biblical studies, that landscape features free e-Bible tools. Free and open resources may seem like dung to many academics. They can, however, be used as fertilizer. Free e-Bible tools have the potential to contribute to a broader liberal arts education by developing the digital literacy of students and instructors alike as we learn to make constructive use of them. In addition, free e-Bible tools can serve as sustainable, cost-effective resources for enhancing students' learning beyond the classroom.

Learning a New Skill: Digital Literacy

Digital literacy is a nebulous concept with a wide variety of definitions.[1] Paul Gilster, one of the earliest proponents of digital literacy, defined it as "the ability to understand and use information in multiple formats from a wide range of sources when it is presented via computers."[2] Allan Martin's definition provides even greater nuance:

---

1. See the surveys and evaluations of Maria Spante et al., "Digital Competence and Digital Literacy in Higher Education Research: Systematic Review of Concept Use," *CE* 5 (2018), https://tinyurl.com/SBL03108cm; Robin Goodfellow, "Literacy, Literacies, and the Digital in Higher Education," *THE* 16 (2011): 131–44; Colin Lankshear, "Digital Literacy and Digital Literacies: Policy, Pedagogy and Research Considerations for Education," *NJDL* 4 (2015): 8–20.

2. Paul Gilster, *Digital Literacy* (New York: Wiley Computer, 1997), 1.

Digital literacy is the awareness, attitude and ability of individuals to appropriately use digital tools and facilities to identify, access, manage, integrate, evaluate, analyze and synthesize digital resources, to construct new knowledge, create media expressions, and communicate with others, in the context of specific life situations, in order to enable constructive social action; and to reflect upon this process.[3]

We instructors often take digital literacy for granted.[4] For example, we tend to distinguish between digital natives and digital immigrants. Digital natives were born into the digital environment. They feel comfortable using computers, social media, web browsers, cell phones, video games, digital cameras, and other modern technological toys and tools. Digital immigrants, on the other hand, grew up without technological saturation. Regardless, we must resist assuming that digital immigrants are the only ones who lack digital literacy.[5] By the same token, we cannot assume that digital natives naturally make constructive use of digital resources because they grew up speaking digital language.[6]

Both instructors and students often overestimate the digital literacy of undergraduate students.[7] There is little correlation between students'

---

3. Allan Martin, "A European Framework for Digital Literacy," *NJDL* 1 (2006): 155–56. Martin understands digital literacy to develop through three stages: digital competence, digital usages, and digital transformation.

4. Meg Coffin Murray and Jorge Pérez, "Unraveling the Digital Literacy Paradox: How Higher Education Fails at the Fourth Literacy," *IISIT* 11 (2014): 95; Jill D. Jenson, "It's the Information Age, So Where's the Information? Why Our Students Can't Find It and What We Can Do to Help," *CT* 52.3 (2004): 107–8.

5. Marc Prensky, who coined these terms, considers the gap between digital natives and digital immigrants to be the most pressing problem facing education. See Prensky, "Digital Natives, Digital Immigrants Part 1," *OH* 9.5 (2001): 1–6; Prensky, "Digital Natives, Digital Immigrants Part 2: Do They Really Think Differently?," *OH* 9.6 (2001): 1–6. For a helpful alignment of this model with education theory, see Charles Kivunja, "Theoretical Perspectives of How Digital Natives Learn," *IJSHE* 3 (2014): 94–109. Sue Bennett, Karl Maton, and Lisa Kervin represent critics with their conclusion that "there is no evidence of widespread and universal disaffection, or of a distinctly different learning style the like of which has never been seen before." See Bennett, Maton, and Kervin, "The 'Digital Natives' Debate: A Critical Review of the Evidence," *BJET* 39 (2008): 783. See also the helpful review and analysis of Neil Selwyn, "The Digital Native—Myth and Reality," *AP* 61 (2009): 364–79.

6. See Sylvie T. Raquel's essay in this volume.

7. William Magrino and Peter Sorrell, "Teaching the New Paradigm: Social Media inside and outside the Classroom," *W&P* 5 (2014): 358. According to Melinda Messineo

proficient personal use of technology and proficiency in digitally based academic research.[8] As Andrew Keen frames the problem, we need to educate students who take "search-engine results as gospel [thus enabling] a younger generation of intellectual kleptomaniacs, who think their ability to cut and paste a well-phrased thought or opinion makes it their own."[9] Instead, everyone—both digital natives and digital immigrants—must learn digital literacy, including more robust skills for searching, analyzing, and creating their own content.

Over the last several years, I have searched and analyzed several free e-Bible tools in undergraduate biblical studies classrooms. By researching and introducing these unfamiliar tools, I have exposed digital illiteracy in myself and my students. I have also created new opportunities to develop digital literacy. I have turned what some might call dung into fertilizer.

In the Beginning: GreekBible.com

I first encountered e-Bible resources through GreekBible.com.[10] Anthony J. Fisher designed this website in 2002 as a supplement for his coursework in New Testament Greek. The site allows users to search the twenty-sixth edition of Nestle-Aland for words and phrases. Users can also look up basic definitions and parsing for Greek words. GreekBible.com thus functions as a

---

and Ione Y. DeOllos, students self-report that using technology for academic applications (library, online courses, etc.) is far more challenging than using it for personal applications (internet, email, word processing, etc.). See Messineo and DeOllos, "Are We Assuming Too Much? Exploring Students' Perceptions of Their Computer Competence," *CT* 53.2 (2005): 52–53.

8. Jenson, "It's the Information Age," 107–12. Murray and Pérez note, "Many students entering the university today have a high level of exposure to digital technologies and media. However, they are not prepared to cross the bridge between personal and academic use of technology. As academic knowhow is gained through formal education, so too must technological prowess be gained through structured learning experiences" ("Unraveling the Digital Literacy Paradox," 88). Andrej Šorgo et al. discovered that "personal ownership of smartphones, portable computers and desktop computers has no direct effect on information literacy, while ownership of a tablet computer is actually a negative predictor." See Šorgo et al., "Attributes of Digital Natives as Predictors of Information Literacy in Higher Education," *BJET* 48 (2017): 749.

9. Andrew Keen, *The Cult of the Amateur* (London: Brealey, 2007), 93, 25. See also Tara Brabazon, *The University of Google* (Aldershot, UK: Ashgate, 2007), 16, 39.

10. Greek Bible, http://greekbible.com.

quick and simple digital readers' edition of the New Testament. It promotes fluency by encouraging daily Greek reading without the impediments of limited vocabulary or the need to keep consulting lexicons.[11] These daily reading habits help Greek students to extend their learning outside the classroom.[12] In addition, students benefit from the ability to cut and paste the unicode-based Greek text into their papers without needing to install fonts and with less worry about improper spelling or accents.

Unfortunately, most of my undergraduate students found this resource unhelpful because it lacks an English translation. It also neglects the entire Hebrew Bible and Septuagint, making it useless for engaging with Jewish writings. Despite these shortcomings, GreekBible.com put both online and free biblical resources on my pedagogical radar as feasible options for my students. It drew my attention to similar resources, such as the open-access Society of Biblical Literature Greek New Testament.[13] It also taught me that instructors who use open educational resources such as Greek-Bible.com (or any free e-Bible tool) make an important ethical response to the price of textbooks, which rose by 90 percent from 1998 to 2016.[14]

Bible Websites Gain Popularity: StudyLight.org

My next engagement with an e-Bible resource involved StudyLight.org, one of the more popular free e-Bible websites at the time of this writing.[15] StudyLight.org has the advantage over GreekBible.com because it includes

---

11. Benjamin Merkle, *Greek for Life: Strategies for Learning, Retaining, and Reviving New Testament Greek* (Grand Rapids: Baker Academic, 2017).

12. Open-source vocabulary-building websites or apps such as Anki also help students build language fluency.

13. The Society of Biblical Literature Greek New Testament represents the most recent modern critical edition of the Greek New Testament that uses a unicode font (see the justification in the work's preface). Available at http://sblgnt.com.

14. P. Blessinger and T. J. Bliss, eds., *Open Education: International Perspectives in Higher Education* (Cambridge: Open Book, 2016); Mark Perry, "Chart of the Day: The Astronomical Rise in College Textbook Prices vs. Consumer Prices and Recreational Books," *AEIdeas*, 1 September 2016, https://tinyurl.com/SBL03108cn.

15. StudyLight, https://www.studylight.org. Jeff Garrison created StudyLight. org in 2001. A similar resource is Bible Study Tools, https://www.biblestudytools. com, which provides access to English translations, such as ESV, KJV, LEB, NIV, and translations in several languages, such as Spanish, Portuguese, French, and Chinese. The parallel Bible feature allows for side-by-side comparisons. The interlinear uses the

resources for both the Hebrew Bible and the New Testament. Its collection of primary resources helps students understand the cultural context of the New Testament and early Christianities. These primary resources include the writings of Flavius Josephus, the church fathers, the major creeds, and significant confessions and catechisms. Other websites supplement these sources. For example, EarlyChristianWritings.com gives access to early Christian literature such as the writings of the apostolic fathers and selections from the New Testament Apocrypha.[16]

The site also features biblical reference tools including over one hundred commentaries, six concordances, twenty-seven dictionaries, and eight encyclopedias.[17] As with most publicly available resources that exploit copyright expiration, these secondary resources are not always current, relevant, authoritative, accurate, or written for academic purposes.[18] This drawback requires instructors to teach their students how to determine a source's usefulness.[19] StudyLight.org provides users with the provenance of cited material, which aids in resource evaluation. Students can learn to appreciate the value of historical scholarship through their access to works such as John Calvin's and J. B. Lightfoot's commentaries. Students can also learn not to base their research on the works of Matthew Henry (1708–1710), whose writings are older than the United States of America.[20] Likewise, they learn not to rely on Albert Barnes's *Notes on the Old and New Testament* (1884), collected shortly after the Civil War.[21] By comparing these older resources to newer works found in their school's library, students discover

---

English text of the NASB or KJV. It uses *BHS* for the Hebrew and NA[26] for the Greek. As with StudyLight.org, most of the free resources are available due to their age.

16. Early Christian Writings, http://www.earlychristianwritings.com.

17. Bible Hub is another site that contains a large number of old commentaries. See Bible Hub, https://biblehub.com/. It also has an extensive library of early Christian literature, including works of the church fathers and the New Testament Apocrypha. The interlinear is more user-friendly and includes the original language, transliteration, basic definition, and parsing.

18. See Steve Jung's essay in this volume.

19. See Tapio Varis, "European and Global Approaches to Digital Literacy," *DK* 1.3 (2008): 58; Ana Isabel Santos and Sandro Serpa, "The Importance of Promoting Digital Literacy in Higher Education," *IJSSS* 5.6 (2017): 90–93.

20. Matthew Henry, *Complete Commentary on the Whole Bible* (New York: Revell, 1708–1710). Henry died in 1714, and his work was expanded and completed by 1896.

21. Albert Barnes, *Notes on the Old and New Testaments* (London: Blackie & Son, 1884). The notes were originally published separately in the 1830s.

how modern critical methods have led to new insights about the biblical text. They also learn about the impact of discoveries of ancient documents such as the Dead Sea Scrolls and Nag Hammadi writings.

Student-centered digital literacy assignments might include active learning in which students must discern the usefulness of information for themselves. For example, students can research secondary resources, choosing appropriate criteria to rank their quality. Alternatively, instructors can create case studies by selecting passages such as the creation accounts, the flood stories, or the household codes. Students can then research and evaluate the history of scholarship on these passages. They might supplement material from StudyLight.org using the Society of Biblical Literature's Bible Odyssey, where "the world's leading scholars share the latest historical and literary research on key people, places, and passages of the Bible."[22]

Instructors can help students probe behind the English text using StudyLight.org's multiple Bible translations (e.g., LEB, ESV, KJV, NASB, NIV, NRSV) to perform simple interlinear searches with basic definitions and parsing. In this way, students can examine a text such as Rom 3:22, comparing translations of πίστεως Ἰησοῦ Χριστοῦ as either "faith of Jesus Christ" (KJV) or "faith in Jesus Christ" (LEB, NASB, NIV, NRSV, etc.). Students can also read the Bible in Hebrew (*BHS*) or Greek (NA[26], translations by Tischendorf and Westcott-Hort, the Textus Receptus, and the Byzantine text).[23] The variety of Greek manuscripts creates an opportunity to teach students about textual criticism by comparing Greek texts.[24] To promote further engagement with primary languages, the website also offers pronunciation guides and transliterations.

StudyLight.org also enables some limited lemma searches. These searches create opportunities to discuss effective digital searching and strategies for searching databases. Students also have access to a wide variety of Hebrew and Greek lexicons, including the *Enhanced Brown-Driver-Briggs*

---

22. Bible Odyssey, https://www.bibleodyssey.org/.

23. Constantin von Tischendorf, *Novum Testamentum Graece*, 8th ed. (Lipsiae: Giesecke & Devrient, 1869–1872); Brooke Foss Westcott and Fenton John Anthony Hort, *The New Testament in the Original Greek* (Cambridge: Macmillan, 1881).

24. See Bruce Metzger, *A Textual Commentary on the Greek New Testament*, 2nd ed. (New York: United Bible Societies, 1994); Kurt Aland and Barbara Aland, *The Text of the New Testament: An Introduction to the Critical Editions and to the Theory and Practice of Modern Textual Criticism*, 2nd ed. (Grand Rapids: Eerdmans, 1989); Bart Ehrman and Michael Holmes, eds., *The Text of the New Testament in Contemporary Research: Essays on the "Status Quaestionis,"* 2nd ed., NTTSD 42 (Leiden: Brill, 2014).

Hebrew and English Lexicon.[25] Location aids for words in the *Theological Wordbook of the Old Testament*, Liddell-Scott-Jones (8th ed.), and the *Theological Dictionary of the New Testament* help instructors to encourage students to use these physical resources in their school's library.[26]

On the whole, StudyLight.org lacks an attractive, intuitive interface.[27] For instructors teaching students to work with primary language tools, however, this website serves quite well. Its dated resources, such as Henry's commentaries or Barnes's *Notes*, provide case studies for discussing the evolution of biblical studies. By comparing older and newer resources, students can learn to discern the value of advances in critical methodology or the increasing inclusion of diverse perspectives.[28]

A Whole New World:
BibleWebApp.com and NetBible.org

Newer websites offer simplified and more intuitive interfacing. Premiere sites in this category include BibleWebApp.com and NetBible.org.[29] Both

---

25. Francis Brown, Samuel Rolles Driver, and Charles Augustus Briggs, *Enhanced Brown-Driver-Briggs Hebrew and English Lexicon* (Oxford: Clarendon, 1977); Jeff A. Benner, *Ancient Hebrew Lexicon of the Bible* (College Station, TX: Virtual Bookworm, 2005).

26. R. Laird Harris, Gleason L. Archer, Jr., and Bruce K. Waltke, eds., *Theological Wordbook of the Old Testament*, 2 vols (Chicago: Moody, 1980); *LSJ*; Joseph Henry Thayer, *A Greek-English Lexicon of the New Testament* (New York: Harper & Brothers, 1889); George Abbott-Smith, *A Manual Greek Lexicon of the New Testament* (New York: Scribner's Sons, 1922); James Hope Moulton and George Milligan, *Vocabulary of the Greek New Testament* (London: Hodder and Stoughton, 1930); Gerhard Kittel and Gerhard Friedrich, eds., *Theological Dictionary of the New Testament*, 10 vols., trans. Geoffrey W. Bromiley (Grand Rapids: Eerdmans, 1964–1976).

27. Another similar website is Bible Gateway, https://www.biblegateway.com. A prominent limiting feature of this website is the lack of a Hebrew interlinear. The site is also geared toward evangelical Protestants. One potentially useful feature is free access to the IVP New Testament Commentary Series, allowing students to engage with a newer work by evangelical scholars. Bill Mounce's reverse interlinear of the Greek New Testament, which offers a transliterated text, is another helpful feature. Greek definitions are linked to an adaptation of William D. Mounce's *Concise Greek-English Dictionary of the New Testament*. Unfortunately, no parsing information is provided.

28. See John Hayes and Carl Holladay, *Biblical Exegesis*, 3rd ed. (Louisville: Westminster John Knox, 2007).

29. BibleWebApp, https://biblewebapp.com/study; NET Bible, https://netbible.org.

use side-by-side windows to display English-Hebrew and English-Greek parallel Bibles. This format allows users to highlight English words in order to view the corresponding words, with parsing, from the West-minster Leningrad Codex and the Society of Biblical Literature Greek New Testament.

Both BibleWebApp.com and NetBible.org include the NET Bible and its 60,932 textual and translation notes. The NET Bible is the first modern English translation designed for the internet. Like many modern English translations, it has its own app (formerly called Lumina) for smartphones and tablets.[30] The NET Bible also provides some limited discussion on notable textual variants, such as the long endings of Mark. Unfortunately, it also omits without explanation some variants, such as the conclusion of the Lord's Prayer in Matt 6:13.

Both websites make word searches easy. Users simply click on a word and follow hyperlinks. Greek and Hebrew word searches can help students learn the relationship among cognates such as πιστεύω (believe) and πίστις (faith). Unfortunately, neither website provides transliterations when users view either the original text or the Hebrew and Greek lexicons. To help address this problem, instructors can require students to memorize the Hebrew and Greek alphabets (with the qualification that the ability to sound out words does not amount to language literacy).

Both sites also lack access to the more robust lexicon and commentary selection of websites such as StudyLight.org. Instead, NetBible.org fea-tures a library tab that provides links to a curated set of scholarly articles written for Bible.org.[31] Other articles are accessible with a paid subscrip-tion to Galaxie Software. This paywall raises digital-literacy awareness by prompting discussions about the current trend of raising paywalls that hinder access, the value of curated materials, and the biases that influence curated collections.[32] Instructors might encourage students to bypass the paywall by using their institution's digital library.

With BibleWebApp.com, students have access to nine English transla-tions (e.g., ESV, KJV, NASB, NET, NIV) as well as translations in Spanish,

---

30. The NET Bible launched two beta translations in 2001 and 2003, which solic-ited user feedback before the release of the first edition in 2006 and the second edition in 2017. See "Preface to the NET Bible," NET Bible, https://tinyurl.com/SBL03108co.

31. Bible.org, https://bible.org.

32. Adithya Pattabhiramaiah, S. Sriram, and Puneet Manchanda, "Paywalls: Monetizing Online Content," *JM* 83 (2018): 19–36.

Arabic, Chinese, French, and Turkish. As with StudyLight.org, students can use this variety to compare translations. BibleWebApp.com also includes the NET Bible's notes. Students researching the differences between "faith/ faithfulness of Jesus Christ" and "faith in Jesus" can look up the notes' brief introduction (with suggested articles) to the scholarly debate. In addition, they can improve their digital literacy by finding articles on the NET Bible and then searching their institution's library database for availability.

BibleWebApp.com also includes an audio Bible as well as the Deaf Bible, which features sign language from various countries.[33] These features assist hearing-impaired students and may prompt interest in disability studies as it relates to biblical literature.[34] In addition, the limited inclusion of translations in languages other than English may be of help to native speakers of those languages. Bilingual students may appreciate the expanded opportunities to compare translation choices. For example, while the NASB renders κρίνω as "judge" in both John 3:17 and 5:22, the Spanish Reina Valera (1909) chooses *condenar* and *juzgar*, respectively.

In sum, the simplified approach of websites such as BibleWebApp.com and NetBible.org may appeal to instructors teaching introductory courses. Students can easily undertake some basic lexical work. The lack of older resources may appeal to instructors who do not wish to expose students to dated material. Translations in various languages open discussions about how language and culture affect meaning.[35] Sign language and audio files offer access to students who might otherwise feel marginalized.

Computer Software: Accordance, OliveTree, and Logos

Not all free e-Bible tools are web-based. For years, some have been available for downloading. Cross-platform integration gives students similar

---

33. Deaf Bible, https://deaf.bible.

34. E.g., Hector Avalos, Sarah Melcer, and Jeremy Schipper, eds., *This Abled Body: Rethinking Disabilities in Biblical Studies*, SemeiaSt (Atlanta: Society of Biblical Literature, 2007); Amos Yong, *The Bible, Disability, and the Church: A New Vision of the People of God* (Grand Rapids: Eerdmans, 2011); Candida Moss and Jeremy Schipper, *Disability Studies and Biblical Literature* (New York: Palgrave Macmillan, 2011).

35. See Mark Brett, ed., *Ethnicity and the Bible* (New York: Brill, 1996); Randall Bailey, Tat-siong Benny Liew, and Fernando Segovia, eds., *They Were All Together in One Place? Toward Minority Biblical Criticism* (Atlanta: Society of Biblical Literature, 2009).

experiences on PC, Mac, and Chrome operating systems. As of this writing, major providers of Bible software include Accordance, OliveTree, and Logos (BibleWorks was discontinued in 2018).[36] Each offers a free version that users can upgrade by purchasing digital library resources.

Accordance offers free access to the ESV and KJV translations along with severely limited demo versions of the MT and NA[28] (the NA[28] demo stops with Matt 3). These limitations make Accordance's free version not a useful resource for undergraduate education.

OliveTree provides free access to more English Bibles including the ASV, ESV, KJV, NIV, and NKJV along with other translations such as Reina Valera. It makes the Westminster Leningrad Codex and Society of Biblical Literature Greek New Testament available, but not in interlinear format or linked to lexicons. OliveTree allows users to compare two Bibles in side-by-side windows. Users can also download public domain resources such as Matthew Henry's commentaries and Matthew G. Easton's *Illustrated Bible Dictionary*. Again, lack of access to newer resources raises concerns regarding the quality of this free e-Bible.

Most of Logos's free resources involve their proprietary works. The English Bibles include only its Lexham translation and the KJV. Similar to StudyLight.com and BibleWebApp.com, Logos presents the LEB in parallel with a Hebrew or Greek text. Unfortunately, students must navigate a complicated process in order to set up this feature. The parallel display features basic parsing and definitions. For English readers, Logos improves on the user experience of other e-Bible tools by including an interlinear with English transliterations of the Hebrew and Greek texts. It also includes pronunciation tools that help students speak the words in class discussions and presentations.

Logos offers more sophisticated word studies than do other web-based tools. A basic search begins by clicking on a word in the biblical text or typing the word in the search bar. Alternatively, students can use a "Bible Word Study" step-by-step guide to walk through the process. They can also look up multiple words in a Boolean search (e.g., "faith" AND "grace") and search for specific phrases (e.g., "kingdom of God"). By searching with

---

36. "Accordance 13 Lite," Accordance, https://www.accordancebible.com/accordance-lite; "Free Resources for the Olive Tree Bible App," Olive Tree Bible Software, https://www.olivetree.com/store/home.php?cat=259&free=y&bible-category=free-items&source=topnav; "Logos Academic Basic," Faithlife, https://academic.logos.com/free-completely-free-logos-academic-basic.

Boolean operators such as AND, NOT, OR, *, (), and "", students improve their digital literacy.

Logos users can limit the range of a word study to specific biblical books. A search for γεννάω in Matt 1 lets students connect its thirty-nine translations as "became the father of" with other translations in statements about Jesus being "conceived" (Matt 1:20) and "born" (Matt 1:16; 2:1, 4). Students can also use Logos's list of γεννάω cognates to discover Matthew's "genesis" wordplays in the opening chapter, such as the "genealogy [*genesis*]" of Jesus (1:1) and "birth [*genesis*]" of Jesus (Matt 1:18). They add to their digital literacy skills as they learn to expand a search's scope by looking for related terms.

For text-critical purposes, Logos takes advantage of the Society of Biblical Literature Greek New Testament apparatus. It also includes Rick Brannan's and Israel Loken's *Lexham Textual Notes on the Bible*, which offers a brief and user-friendly discussion of variants in both the Hebrew Bible and the New Testament.[37] Instructors can help students appreciate textual criticism by dividing a class into teams and letting them explore a few significant textual variants related to passages such as the Trinity formula (1 John 5:7–8), Mark's long ending (Mark 16:9–20), the story of the woman caught in adultery (John 7:53–8:11), the matter of Junia's gender (Rom 16:7), or the identity of audience for Ephesians (Eph 1:1).

Logos also includes the Septuagint with an English translation. This translation allows students to access the Old Testament Apocrypha, an important resource for learning about Second Temple Judaism. It also allows them to discuss the different recensions of writings such as Jeremiah. They can explore the movement of Jer 25:15–38 in the MT to Jer 32 LXX or wrestle with the fact that Jer 33:14–26 in the MT never appears in the LXX. Alternatively, they can engage with issues of arrangement and versification by comparing Hebrew Psalms with LXX Psalms.

Word studies automatically link to a few basic (but unfortunately old) lexicons, including *The Abridged Brown-Driver-Briggs Hebrew-English Lexicon of the Old Testament* (1906) and George Abbott-Smith's *A Manual Greek Lexicon of the New Testament* (1922).[38] Logos's commentary resource selection is also ancient and somewhat narrow. It includes

---

37. Rick Brannan and Israel Loken, *The Lexham Textual Notes on the Bible* (Bellingham, WA: Lexham, 2014).

38. These resources are also found on StudyLight.org, which has a more expansive collection.

Jamieson-Fausset-Brown's *Commentary Critical and Explanatory on the Whole Bible* (1871) and Gore-Goudge-Guillaume's *A New Commentary on Holy Scripture: Including the Apocrypha* (1942).[39] A more useful feature is its Faithlife Study Bible Notes, which includes hyperlinks to more detailed articles.

Overall, the free computer versions of Bible software often offer more features than do web-based e-Bibles. Logos in particular contains tools that help students engage with the biblical text with lemma searches and word studies. These powerful search features are not always user-friendly, however. Instructors will need to devote time to helping students set up their Logos digital libraries. Since Logos users can purchase additional resources from Logos's extensive library, training students to use Logos introduces them to a software ecosystem.

There's an App for That: YouVersion and BlueLetterBible

As of this writing, the digital frontier for biblical resources is mobile devices. NET Bible, Accordance, OliveTree, and Logos all have corresponding apps. They make up for their paucity of features with ease of use on tablets and smartphones, and continue to catch up with the functionality of web-based and computer platforms. Meanwhile, the accessibility of e-Bible apps has shifted the audience of e-Bible tools from academics, experts, and pastors to laypeople. This shift in audience has been accompanied by a corresponding shift of app resources away from commentaries and lexicons to devotional and spiritual publications.

This shift is evident in YouVersion.[40] The app began with fifteen Bible versions in two languages but soon grew to feature over 2,100 versions in more than 1,400 languages. It has been installed on over 430 million

---

39. Another interesting opportunity to teach digital literacy involves showing students how Logos has abbreviated Jamieson-Fausset-Brown's work and given it a newer publication date. See Robert Jamieson, Andrew Fausset, and David Brown, *A Commentary Critical and Explanatory on the Whole Bible* (Oak Harbor, WA: Logos Research Systems, 1997). Charles Gore, Henry Leighton Goudge, and Alfred Guillaume, eds., *A New Commentary on Holy Scripture: Including the Apocrypha* (New York: Macmillan, 1942).

40. The app was launched on July 10, 2008, by Life.Church. See "YouVersion Bible App," https://www.youversion.com/the-bible-app.

devices.[41] Its versions of the NET Bible and NASB include their translation and textual notes. Many versions also offer an audio option. Users can
compare two translations side-by-side and access multimedia resources
from the Bible Project, Lumo Project, and BibleSeries.tv. YouVersion does
not include primary language versions or tools. Students might compare
YouVersion's resources to those of other e-Bibles in order to evaluate
their purposes and biases. YouVersion encourages social interactions
whereby users connect with one another to discuss the Bible. It promotes
daily engagement through "verse of the day" notifications and uses Bible-
reading reminders to help form new habits. Students can benefit from
YouVersion's social features by engaging in community discussions outside the classroom.

A growing number of apps are more conducive to academic study. They
include PARALLEL PLUS Bible-study app, Tecarta Bible, BibleGateway,
and e-Sword.[42] BlueLetterBible, with over eight and a half million users,
integrates web-based services with mobile platforms.[43] It permits side-
by-side comparisons of multiple modern translations including the ESV,
KJV, NET, NIV, Chinese Traditional Bible, and the Spanish Reina Valera.
Hebrew and Greek texts include the Westminster Leningrad Codex, the
Textus Receptus, the Westcott-Hort translation, and the Byzantine text.[44]
Online Hebrew-English or Greek-English interlinear versions provide
basic English definitions, parsing, transliteration, and pronunciation.

BlueLetterBible's word studies, based on Strong's numbers, direct
users to the print editions of the *Theological Wordbook of the Old Testament*
and the *Theological Dictionary of the New Testament*. Users can expand
word studies with Boolean searches and look up definitions in Gesenius's
Hebrew-Chaldee Lexicon and Thayer's *Greek-English Lexicon*.[45] They can
also access a large collection of older references such as commentaries by
John Calvin, John Edwards, Matthew Henry, Jamieson-Fausset-Brown,

---

41. "YouVersion Bible App Celebrates Tenth Anniversary," YouVersion, https://
tinyurl.com/SBL03108cq.

42. In addition, all major Bible translations have their own apps with their own
curated collection of resources including study Bibles and other resources. Note: while
e-Sword is free to download for PCs, the apps and Mac software are not.

43. Blue Letter Bible, https://www.blueletterbible.org.

44. Westcott and Hort, *New Testament in the Original Greek*.

45. Heinrich W. F. Gesenius, *Hebrew-Chaldee Lexicon to the Old Testament*, trans.
Samuel P. Tregelles (London: Bagster, 1860).

J. B. Lightfoot, and Martin Luther as well as other resources such as the *Illustrated Bible Dictionary, International Standard Bible Encyclopedia, Nave's Topical Bible,* and *Vine's Expository Dictionary of New Testament Words.*[46] In addition, the app teaches digital literacy by explaining the significance of resources and offering guidance for use.

Due to the ubiquity of mobile devices, apps allow even greater accessibility than do computers. Students can use resources without concerns for internet connectivity. Because the interfaces differ among web-based resources, apps, and downloaded e-Bibles, instructors should evaluate and choose the best interface for student learning goals and ease of use, keeping in mind that ease of use tends to limit functionality. Allowing students to choose their own e-Bibles might lead to problems, since not all features may be found in each interface. On the other hand, it might also lead to an opportunity to teach digital literacy. Instructors might ask students to form groups and undertake a project such as performing a word study. Students can debrief afterwards and share their experiences about the strengths and weaknesses of each tool.

Conclusion

Just as the undergraduate classroom continues to evolve, so do online resources. Biblical studies instructors would be wise to consider using free e-Bible tools. They cost nothing, they allow for easy access, and they include Hebrew and Greek versions as well as various translations and secondary sources. Some enable translation comparisons, word searches, and social interaction. All provide opportunities for improving digital literacy, equipping students and instructors alike for biblical studies in an online world.

Bibliography

Abbott-Smith, George. *A Manual Greek Lexicon of the New Testament.* New York: Scribner's Sons, 1922.

---

46. Orville J. Nave, *Nave's Topical Bible: A Digest of Holy Scriptures* (Lincoln, NE: Topical, 1905); William Vine, *Expository Dictionary of New Testament Words* (New York: Revell, 1940).

"Accordance 13 Lite." Accordance. https://www.accordancebible.com/accordance-lite.

Aland, Kurt, and Barbara Aland. *The Text of the New Testament: An Introduction to the Critical Editions and to the Theory and Practice of Modern Textual Criticism.* 2nd ed. Grand Rapids: Eerdmans, 1989.

Avalos, Hector, Sarah Melcer, and Jeremy Schipper, eds. *This Abled Body: Rethinking Disabilities in Biblical Studies.* SemeiaSt. Atlanta: Society of Biblical Literature, 2007.

Bailey, Randall, Tat-siong Benny Liew, and Fernando Segovia, eds. *They Were All Together in One Place? Toward Minority Biblical Criticism.* Atlanta: Society of Biblical Literature, 2009.

Barnes, Albert. *Notes on the Old and New Testaments.* London: Blackie & Son, 1884.

Benner, Jeff A. *Ancient Hebrew Lexicon of the Bible.* College Station, TX: Virtual Bookworm, 2005.

Bennett, Sue, Karl Maton, and Lisa Kervin. "The 'Digital Natives' Debate: A Critical Review of the Evidence." *BJET* 39 (2008): 775–86.

Bible Gateway. https://www.biblegateway.com.

Bible Hub. https://biblehub.com/.

Bible Odyssey. https://www.bibleodyssey.org/.

Bible Study Tools. https://www.biblestudytools.com.

Bible Web App. https://biblewebapp.com/study.

Bible.org. https://bible.org.

Blessinger, P., and T. J. Bliss, eds. *Open Education: International Perspectives in Higher Education.* Cambridge: Open Book, 2016.

Blue Letter Bible. https://www.blueletterbible.org.

Brabazon, Tara. *The University of Google.* Aldershot, UK: Ashgate, 2007.

Brannan, Rick, and Israel Loken. *The Lexham Textual Notes on the Bible.* Bellingham, WA: Lexham, 2014.

Brett, Mark, ed. *Ethnicity and the Bible.* New York: Brill, 1996.

Brown, Francis, Samuel Rolles Driver, and Charles Augustus Briggs. *Enhanced Brown-Driver-Briggs Hebrew and English Lexicon.* Oxford: Clarendon, 1977.

Deaf Bible. https://deaf.bible.

Early Christian Writings. http://www.earlychristianwritings.com.

Ehrman, Bart, and Michael Holmes, eds. *The Text of the New Testament in Contemporary Research: Essays on the "Status Questionis."* 2nd ed. NTTSD 42. Leiden: Brill, 2014.

"Free Resources for the Olive Tree Bible App." Olive Tree Bible Software. https://www.olivetree.com/store/home.php?cat=259&free=y&bible-category=free-items&source=topnav.

Gesenius, Heinrich W. F. *Hebrew-Chaldee Lexicon to the Old Testament.* Translated by Samuel P. Tregelles. London: Bagster, 1860.

Gilster, Paul. *Digital Literacy.* New York: Wiley Computer, 1997.

Goodfellow, Robin. "Literacy, Literacies, and the Digital in Higher Education." *THE* 16 (2011): 131–44.

Gore, Charles, Henry Leighton Goudge, and Alfred Guillaume, eds. *A New Commentary on Holy Scripture: Including the Apocrypha.* New York: Macmillan, 1942.

Greek Bible. http://greekbible.com.

Harris, R. Laird, Gleason L. Archer Jr., and Bruce K. Waltke, eds. *Theological Wordbook of the Old Testament.* 2 vols. Chicago: Moody, 1980.

Hayes, John, and Carl Holladay. *Biblical Exegesis.* 3rd ed. Louisville: Westminster John Knox, 2007.

Henry, Matthew. *Complete Commentary on the Whole Bible.* New York: Revell, 1708–1710.

Jamieson, Robert, Andrew Fausset, and David Brown. *A Commentary Critical and Explanatory on the Whole Bible.* Oak Harbor, WA: Logos Research Systems, 1997.

Jenson, Jill D. "It's the Information Age, So Where's the Information? Why Our Students Can't Find It and What We Can Do to Help." *CT* 53.2 (2004): 107–12.

Keen, Andrew. *The Cult of the Amateur.* London: Brealey, 2007.

Kittel, Gerhard, and Gerhard Friedrich, eds. *Theological Dictionary of the New Testament.* 10 vols. Translated by Geoffrey W. Bromiley. Grand Rapids: Eerdmans, 1964–1976.

Kivunja, Charles. "Theoretical Perspectives of How Digital Natives Learn." *IJSHE* 3 (2014): 94–109.

Lankshear, Colin. "Digital Literacy and Digital Literacies: Policy, Pedagogy and Research Considerations for Education." *NJDL* 4 (2015): 8–20.

"Logos Academic Basic." Faithlife. https://academic.logos.com/free-completely-free-logos-academic-basic.

Magrino, William, and Peter Sorrell. "Teaching the New Paradigm: Social Media inside and outside the Classroom." *W&P* 5 (2014): 357–73.

Martin, Allan. "A European Framework for Digital Literacy." *NJDL* 1 (2006): 151–61.

Merkle, Benjamin. *Greek for Life: Strategies for Learning, Retaining, and Reviving New Testament Greek*. Grand Rapids: Baker Academic, 2017.

Messineo, Melinda, and Ione Y. DeOllos. "Are We Assuming Too Much? Exploring Students' Perceptions of Their Computer Competence." *CT* 53.2 (2005): 50–55.

Metzger, Bruce. *A Textual Commentary on the Greek New Testament*. 2nd ed. New York: United Bible Societies, 1994.

Moss, Candida, and Jeremy Schipper. *Disability Studies and Biblical Literature*. New York: Palgrave Macmillan, 2011.

Moulton, James Hope, and George Milligan. *Vocabulary of the Greek New Testament*. London: Hodder & Stoughton, 1930.

Murray, Meg Coffin, and Jorge Pérez. "Unraveling the Digital Literacy Paradox: How Higher Education Fails at the Fourth Literacy." *IISIT* 11 (2014): 85–100.

Nave, Orville J. *Nave's Topical Bible: A Digest of Holy Scriptures*. Lincoln, NE: Topical, 1905.

NET Bible. https://netbible.org.

Pattabhiramaiah, Adithya, S. Sriram, and Puneet Manchanda. "Paywalls: Monetizing Online Content." *JM* 83 (2018): 19–36.

Perry, Mark. "Chart of the Day: The Astronomical Rise in College Textbook Prices vs. Consumer Prices and Recreational Books." *AEIdeas*, 1 September 2016. https://tinyurl.com/SBL03108cn.

"Preface to the NET Bible." NET Bible. https://tinyurl.com/SBL03108co.

Prensky, Marc. "Digital Natives, Digital Immigrants Part 1." *OH* 9.5 (2001): 1–6.

———. "Digital Natives, Digital Immigrants Part 2: Do They Really Think Differently?" *OH* 9.6 (2001): 1–6.

Santos, Ana Isabel, and Sandro Serpa. "The Importance of Promoting Digital Literacy in Higher Education." *IJSSS* 5.6 (2017): 90–93.

SBL Greek New Testament. http://sblgnt.com.

Selwyn, Neil. "The Digital Native—Myth and Reality." *AP* 61 (2009): 364–79.

Šorgo, Andrej, Tomaž Bartol, Danica Dolničar, and Bojana Boh Podgornik. "Attributes of Digital Natives as Predictors of Information Literacy in Higher Education." *BJET* 48 (2017): 749–67.

Spante, Maria, Sylvana Sofkova Hashemi, Mona Lundin, and Anne Algers. "Digital Competence and Digital Literacy in Higher Education Research: Systematic Review of Concept Use." *CE* 5 (2018). https://tinyurl.com/SBL03108cm.

StudyLight. https://www.studylight.org.

Thayer, Joseph Henry. *A Greek-English Lexicon of the New Testament*. New York: Harper & Brothers, 1889.

Tischendorf, Constantin von. *Novum Testamentum Graece*. 8th ed. Lipsiae: Giesecke & Devrient, 1869–1872.

Varis, Tapio. "European and Global Approaches to Digital Literacy." *DK* 1.3 (2008): 53–60.

Vine, William. *Expository Dictionary of New Testament Words*. New York: Revell, 1940.

Westcott, Brooke Foss, and Fenton John Anthony Hort. *The New Testament in the Original Greek*. Cambridge: Macmillan, 1881.

Yong, Amos. *The Bible, Disability, and the Church: A New Vision of the People of God*. Grand Rapids: Eerdmans, 2011.

"YouVersion Bible App." https://www.youversion.com/the-bible-app/.

"YouVersion Bible App Celebrates Tenth Anniversary." YouVersion. https://tinyurl.com/SBL03108cq.

The Course Site, Interpretation, and Community in Online Biblical Studies

Timothy Luckritz Marquis

In a 2014 blog post published on the peer-reviewed website Hybrid Pedagogy, instructional designer Glen Cochrane makes the case that writing was the first asynchronous learning technology.[1] Throughout his piece, Cochrane explores the importance of balancing synchronous and asynchronous learning modalities as a matter of balancing the experiences of our students with the mechanisms, networks, and technologies that both support and hinder their lives.

In a sense, the terrain Cochrane traverses in his blog post was visited once before by Socrates and Phaedrus by the river under the plane tree, communing directly with each other, nature, and the gods themselves while discussing truth, rhetoric, and writing. Socrates laments the priority of writing over speech, citing the myth of an Egyptian pharaoh. The pharaoh, who reluctantly accepted the god Thoth's gift of writing, called it a technology for forgetting (*Phaedr.* 274b–278d). For Jacques Derrida, Plato's demotion of writing would itself create a sort of mythic understanding of synchronous language as the ground of all true meaning, an understanding Derrida called the logocentrism of the West.[2]

One might understand the balance between synchronous and asynchronous learning—a tension that permeates all discussions of face-to-face, hybrid, and fully online learning—as a case study in the Western struggle over speech and writing, presence and absence, remembering and forgetting. This struggle is familiar to biblical studies. Biblical scholars

---

1. Glen Cochrane, "Synchronous and Asynchronous Technologies: When Real Worlds Collide," Hybrid Pedagogy, 1 September 2014, https://tinyurl.com/SBL03108cr.

2. Jacques Derrida, *Dissemination*, trans. Barbara Johnson (Chicago: University of Chicago Press, 1981), 63–71.

know that texts can serve not only to bolster memory but also to inculcate certain memory practices in a way that forms communities of readers (such as biblical studies classes) through their interaction with the text. The text becomes a location for the community.

We know all this about the way texts, memory, and interpretation work and try to impart these ideas to our students. With our disciplinary convictions about texts in mind, then, I would like to consider another technology: the course site. Our attitudes toward our course sites are subsets of our attitudes toward all sorts of current debates about teaching and learning, including those over the efficacy of online learning. Whether in a learning management system or in a content management system, the way we use our course sites reinforces our approaches to reading and learning, and how we use those approaches to form our learning spaces and communities.[3] Most often, we use the course site as a repository for readings, making it a collection of texts. When we post announcements and grades, we make it a channel for communication. When we add discussion boards or blogs, it becomes a venue for out-of-class interactions. And especially when we design and build more complex virtual spaces for learning experiences, the course site conditions both how our students interpret the texts around which our classes gather as well as how they engage in other types of learning. The course site can reflect the interpretive and epistemological practices that form our students as readers of biblical literature.

In what follows, I consider what the course site is and can be, and I discuss the ways in which we might use the course site to reflect how we talk to our students about texts. I do so from my own recent professional experience, having transitioned from a decade of teaching New Testament studies to undergraduates and seminarians into my current role as an instructional designer for a large state university. This new career path has allowed me to learn a great deal from faculty and designers about how to imagine and build the course site as a learning space. How faculty imagine their course sites depends on their disciplines, so as a biblical scholar and course designer, I draw from my understanding of the skills and values of our field to examine how the course site can form and be formed by the ways in which we interpret texts with our students.

---

3. Common examples of learning management systems include Blackboard Learn or Ultra, Canvas, Brightspace, and Moodle. Course sites can also be created on content management systems such as WordPress or Wix.

The concept of needing a system to manage learning clearly derives from a number of historical moments and various social impulses within the modern history of education. The first digital learning management systems attempted to aggregate various tools to create a digital classroom. These tools included platforms for student posts and responses.[4] For thirty years, however, most faculty have used learning management systems for just a few purposes. A 2008 study showed that most faculty limited their learning management system use to text delivery—that is, sending and receiving lectures, readings, and student papers.[5] Educause's Center for Analysis and Research survey for 2017 found that over 75 percent used their learning management system to "post a syllabus," "push out course material," display grades, and "push out and collect assignments," while fewer than 50 percent used the learning management system for online courses or discussion boards.[6] A 2020 study reflects similar findings.[7] For most faculty, the course site serves as a repository in the service of teaching and learning rather than an extension of the teaching and learning that happens in the classroom.[8]

Since biblical studies relies on interpretation and thus communities of interpretation, however, the use of the course site in biblical studies as a container for texts does not reflect our understanding of the nature of texts, reading, and teaching. We have not used course sites to their full potential. As we all know, most learning management systems and content

---

4. Most accounts cite SoftArc's 1990 platform, FirstClass, as the earliest example of the type. See Martin Weller, "Chapter 9: The Learning Management System," in *Twenty-Five Years of Ed Tech* (Athabasca, Canada: Athabasca University Press, 2020), https://tinyurl.com/SBL03108cs.

5. Grainne Conole et al., "'Disruptive Technologies,' 'Pedagogical Innovation': What's New? Findings from an In-Depth Study of Students' Use and Perception of Technology," *CompEd* 50 (2008): 511–24.

6. Jeffrey Pomerantz and D. Christopher Brooks, "ECAR Study of Faculty and Information Technology, 2017," Educause, 2017, https://tinyurl.com/SBL03108ct. Educause is a professional organization that supports and studies technology issues in higher education.

7. Malcolm Brady and Naoimh O'Reilly, "Learning Management Systems and Their Impact on Academic Work," *TPE* 29 (2020): 251–68.

8. That videoconferencing seemed to dominate the crisis-induced adaptations during the 2020–2021 COVID-19 pandemic shows that, in a pinch, faculty are understandably trying to simulate as closely as possible the physical classroom. The move off campus has also increased experimentation in digital learning spaces and asynchronous modalities.

management systems contain tools that facilitate communication around and even within a digital text itself. But more importantly, the course site as a whole can be designed as a primary or complementary learning space as we combine these tools to serve our learning goals.

Because most course sites contain texts, the ability to host a curated collection of primary and secondary literature is one of the course site's most valuable functions. If the learning management system serves simply for storage, as a container for texts, then it does display some affinity with the concept of scriptural canon—but only if the canon is understood in a flat sense, like a mere list. Apart from the texts that make up course content, other texts in a course site—such as the syllabus and course policies—pertain to the more problematic term in the phrase "learning management system": management.[9] The rules and guidelines we lay down for learning are necessary, but our students often mistake attaining grades or adhering to a rubric as the goal of learning. As with legal texts in the Bible, the regulations and laws necessary for learning should be understood not only as regulations but also as indications of the learning community's goals and values.

The creation of a course site that functions as a venue for more active and communal reading entails more than just using the tools contained in a learning management system. It also involves considering the nature of the course site as a whole. As a way of imagining a different type of course site, I would like to examine one of its close cousins: the electronic textbook, especially if that textbook is interactive—that is, if it includes learning activities such as videos or quizzes. Part of the challenge of creating a digital learning environment involves designing a means for giving and receiving feedback. A recorded lecture simulates the instructor's presence but does not allow the instructor to entertain clarifying questions.[10] Similarly, students cannot gather around a textbook or a PDF file to engage in communal interpretation without help from other materials or tools. An interactive e-textbook, however, can combine text, illustrations, videos, presentations, questions or quizzes, and links to other tools in a way that

---

9. I do not address controversial aspects of learning management systems, such as student surveillance through analytics or proctoring, except to say that the controversies themselves speak to how the community that gathers around the course site deals with the sorts of social factors that affect people everywhere else.

10. It does if the lecturer has institutional access to a video platform such as Kaltura or H5P that allows for the embedding of questions.

guides students through their learning, allowing them to interact directly with the text. Many platforms for creating an interactive digital textbook are at instructors' disposal today. I created a couple of short textbooks for my seminary-level New Testament courses using iBooks Author (the functions of which have recently been included in Apple's word processing program, Pages), but other platforms (such as WordPress's Pressbooks) offer free or low-cost digital spaces for authoring and hosting personal e-textbooks.

In my e-textbooks, each chapter began with an introduction orienting students to the chapter's topic and assessments.[11] Usually, illustrations or embedded external videos supported this introduction. For example, in a chapter discussing the oral and written nature of Scripture, students could not only read about the subject but also view video clips of Christian and Jewish liturgical readings. A hyperlink took them to an online tool called Quran Explorer to hear recitations of the Qur'an.[12] A recorded lecture often followed the introduction, as did links to other readings. The text could refer students to specific biblical passages linked to Bible websites or apps. Alternatively, as has become a popular practice in our field, I could embed or link to texts from interactive platforms such as Google Docs or add annotation tools such as Hypothesis.[13] By immediately following direct instruction with embedded formative assessments, students can quickly apply the knowledge they have gained in a way that mirrors active classroom learning. It allows them to do so either individually or in small groups. The textbook itself becomes the learning space, as the ebook structures the student's learning outside of a face-to-face classroom. In many ways, the e-textbook is not so much a book as its own type of course site. This "book-that-is-not-a-book" uses interactivity to question implicitly the ebook's nature as a book and thus begins to decenter how students read.

Most instructors already decenter student textbook reading to some extent. We facilitate active learning and an understanding of how knowledge is constructed by not "teaching the textbook." We do not want students to think something is true because it is in the textbook but rather because a community of inquiry came to certain understandings based on

---

11. By assessments, I mean a wide variety of means to engage students and gauge their learning.

12. Quran Explorer, https://quranexplorer.com.

13. See Kimberly Bauser McBrien's essay in this volume.

shared values and questions. An e-textbook can duplicate this process by asking students to answer questions or engage in group annotation of a text. An interactive digital environment can evoke the kind of interactive interpretation we are trying to teach.

Instructors usually do not design their own e-textbooks. They do, however, have access to standard learning management systems that can be used to create course sites that mediate interactive interpretation just as well as an e-textbook. When my previous institution switched from Blackboard to Canvas, I transferred the contents of my e-textbook to Canvas. Later, in other institutional contexts, I moved it to the content management system environment of WordPress (under a free account). I was able to create the same kind of interactive interpretation in a course site as I had created in an e-textbook.

Just as many instructors could benefit from reimagining what a course site is, students also do not fully understand their roles in the digital learning environment. As we design e-textbooks and interactive course sites, we need to keep in mind that students require guidance for using them. They are accustomed to navigating the various course sites of all their instructors, most of whom use only a few of the available tools. At the same time, course sites are not the same as the websites or apps they are used to navigating. The ways in which many learning management systems guide learning—including stored PDFs, discussion boards, quizzes, and submitted assignments—result in functionality that does not resemble anything else on the open web. The myth of Gen Zers as digital natives hides the fact that their expertise extends only to the websites familiar to them, and not all young people visit the same sites for the same reasons. Some have more access than others. There is no digital monoculture, and there are no digital natives.[14] There are only students, many of whom come to us after having endured standardized testing for the past thirteen years of their lives. The interactive online learning environment presents them with diverse online experiences in which they are able to engage with the instructor, the content, and each other as fellow learners—different from a classroom, and different from any other online environment.[15]

---

14. Anoush Margaryan, Allison Littlejohn, and Gabrielle Vojt, "Are Digital Natives a Myth or Reality? University Students' Use of Digital Technologies," *CompEd* 56 (2011): 429–40.

15. Understanding engagement in online learning as involving the interaction among instructor, student, and course content is known as the "community of

Since many undergraduates will experience the course site as a unique type of website, then, instructors need to design a site that guides students through course learning. Many course sites begin with a welcome page with an introductory video from the instructor followed by a link to the syllabus and basic information about the course, how best to contact the instructor, and how to navigate the site. The first few learning activities should introduce the content of the course and the tools that the students will use frequently. For example, if students will be annotating texts in Google Docs, they can get used to the practice in an initial Google Doc by posting responses to an icebreaker prompt.

The patchwork of activities and interfaces makes the course site resemble the biblical canon, but in a more dynamic fashion than simply understanding either as a collection of texts. An authentic biblical theology, argues Paul Ricoeur, would accommodate the different voices produced by the Bible's various genres.[16] Similarly, the varieties of tools and platforms in an interactive course site facilitate different types of learning experiences. They create space for interpretation, and we can invite students into that space if we lay out the tools and resources so that students know how, when, and why to use them.

If we are transparent about our reasons for choosing certain tools and resources, we can even teach students about navigating the digital world outside their coursework. For example, I have sometimes asked my students to work in learning spaces that combined platforms such as Google, Apple, Microsoft, Adobe, and Amazon. I had to warn them that these combinations can often lead to technical difficulties. Google Drive might refuse to open an Apple iBook. It might request permission to open a PDF file as a Google Doc and, if permission is given, essentially destroy the PDF format. I explained we were working with products developed by companies who, in competing for market dominance, are trying to rule the world. They have no incentive for making their products compatible with the products of their competitors. When students experience the incompatibility and understand its causes, they develop the sort of critical-thinking skills that might allow them to recognize other powerful social and economic dynamics. They might learn to resist those dynamics even

---

inquiry" model. It structures much contemporary online course design. See D. Randy Garrison, Terry Anderson, and Walter Archer, "Critical Inquiry in a Text-Based Environment: Computer Conferencing in Higher Education," *IHE* 2 (2000): 87–105.

16. Paul Ricoeur, "Naming God," *USQR* 34 (1979): 215–27.

as they navigate them in the service of an online learning community. Just as the first Christians also adopted new technologies (such as the Roman roads and the codex) to reform and reimagine their own communities in ways that resisted social and economic power, our teaching and learning should gather diverse tools and diverse students into communities of learning that imagine new futures.

Course sites that invite students to engage together in critiques of this sort can evoke another familiar digital environment: social media. None of our students using Instagram or TikTok will mistake our course site for a social media platform. For one thing, it is firewalled off from the outside world. This makes it a much safer space than Instagram or TikTok, or at least it should. Yet just as social media enhances human endeavor by connecting people with shared interests, values, and goals, a course site connects class members across time and space in shared learning. If that learning is to be effective, the course site (much like the social media platform) should encourage students to bring their own experiences, values, and goals to bear on their learning. In advanced courses, it might be appropriate to create a connected learning framework that sheds the cocoon of the course site for engagement with the wider world through blogging or social media. In either case, the course site unites a learning community otherwise separated by distance and time. In this detail, too, the online learning environment resembles early Christian communities who used writing and travel for asynchronous connection. The act of biblical interpretation itself can be construed as a practice in asynchronous communication. Our transparency about how the course site gathers a learning community can highlight these parallels for our students.

Finally, discussing how community gathers around a digital space brings us back to the notion of asynchronous learning and asynchronous community, Like the physical technologies of the ancient world, the digital technologies of today can be used to create asynchronous communities and foster asynchronous learning, particularly in its most extreme form: the fully online course. At its best, online learning exists because our communities become impoverished to the extent that they exclude underrepresented people, communities, and ideas. A well-designed course site increases access to learning for any student with an internet connection, inviting them to a learning community that gathers outside a particular time and place. Just as ancient Jews and Christians used roads and codices to connect asynchronous communities, so too can digital learning spaces allow students to connect with their community of interpretation whenever they can and wherever they are.

Bibliography

Brady, Malcolm, and Naoimh O'Reilly. "Learning Management Systems and Their Impact on Academic Work." *TPE* 29.3 (2020): 251–68.

Cochrane, Glen. "Synchronous and Asynchronous Technologies: When Real Worlds Collide." Hybrid Pedagogy, 1 September 2014. https://tinyurl.com/SBL03108cr.

Conole, Grainne, Maarten de Laat, Teresa Dillon, and Jonathan Darby. "'Disruptive Technologies,' 'Pedagogical Innovation': What's New? Findings from an In-Depth Study of Students' Use and Perception of Technology." *CompEd* 50 (2008): 511–24.

Derrida, Jacques. *Dissemination*. Translated by Barbara Johnson. Chicago: University of Chicago Press, 1981.

Garrison, D. Randy, Terry Anderson, and Walter Archer. "Critical Inquiry in a Text-Based Environment: Computer Conferencing in Higher Education." *IHE* 2 (2000): 87–105.

Margaryan, Anoush, Allison Littlejohn, and Gabrielle Vojt. "Are Digital Natives a Myth or Reality? University Students' Use of Digital Technologies." *CompEd* 56 (2011): 429–40.

Pomerantz, Jeffrey, and D. Christopher Brooks. "ECAR Study of Faculty and Information Technology, 2017." Educause. 2017. https://tinyurl.com/SBL03108ct.

Quran Explorer. https://quranexplorer.com.

Ricoeur, Paul. "Naming God." *USQR* 34 (1979): 215–27.

Weller, Martin. *Twenty-Five Years of Ed Tech*. Athabasca, Canada: Athabasca University Press, 2020. https://tinyurl.com/SBL03108cs.

QUICK TIP
BRIDGING THE RESIDENTIAL AND ONLINE CLASSROOM

NICHOLAS A. ELDER

For pedagogues committed to active learning models, the online classroom appears to present formidable obstacles. We tend to think of asynchronous engagement as especially limiting. In asynchronous courses, the professor and the students are not physically present with one another in time and space. This necessarily changes the structure of student engagement.

Still, the online, asynchronous classroom offers as many opportunities as it does obstacles. Whatever occurs in the physical classroom can usually occur in the digital classroom. A given activity may require modifications to work asynchronously, but one does not need to start from scratch when refitting a unit or entire course for the online modality. When reimagined, discussion forums have the potential to broaden students' engagement with course content.

In the standard format for asynchronous discussion forums, instructors pose a prompt, ask students to respond to it by mid-week, and then require that they further respond to two peers by the end of the week. While this format has its advantages, other formats open new possibilities for duplicating and even expanding face-to-face discussions. Instead of merely posing questions, professors might also ask students to create digital artifacts that relate to the week's content.

Since most Gen Z students are digital natives, their learning has always been mediated by electronic media. Asynchronous platforms offer students more access to the full palette of digital media through which they experience the world. In the digital classroom, they have the time and opportunity to engage with course content and produce artifacts using familiar tools. In my own digital classrooms, I find that students learn more thoughtfully and thoroughly than they do in the physical classroom.

In my New Testament courses, for example, students visually depict a scene from Revelation. For face-to-face classes, I bring media such as crayons or Play-Doh and give students approximately fifteen minutes to create their scenes, keeping in mind that, as an apocalyptic text, Revelation is not meant as a guide for predicting the future. We then proceed to a discussion about whether and how students incorporated this insight into what they created. When I ask asynchronous students to perform the same activity and share their results in a forum, they take advantage of their familiarity with digital media. As a result, they produce very different pieces than do synchronous students. In asynchronous forums, my students have posted time-lapse drawings, handbell performances, movie trailers, embroideries, self-portraits, and original slam poetry.

Another activity in both face-to-face and asynchronous classes introduces New Testament letters by comparing them with personal papyri letters. After a short lecture about personal letters and ancient-letter writing conventions, I ask students to identify those conventions in select papyri letters. They then translate these letters and their conventions into a modern medium. The activity teaches that conventions vary with time and medium.

In face-to-face classes, students almost always choose to write a pen-and-paper letter. This choice leads to a simple exercise of recognizing and altering ancient conventions. In asynchronous classes, however, students tend to alter the medium altogether, recasting the letters as tweets, snaps, emails, and text messages. In the end, translating the ancient conventions to modern media serves as a springboard for addressing how New Testament authors work within these conventions while creatively modulating them.

One final example demonstrates how I refit a face-to-face activity for the asynchronous mode. The activity seeks to help students understand how scholars use criteria to determine whether certain writings are pseudonymous. I ask them to produce an email in my name. Their goal is to fool other students into thinking that I actually wrote that email, as the next step in the activity is for students to ascertain which emails are authentic and which are pseudepigraphic. They also identify the criteria by which they make their determinations. In the physical classroom, students are able to imitate many features of my emails. They emulate my salutations, conclusions, and general tone. In the asynchronous online classroom, however, students do much more. They will include sender and recipient information as mock metadata. They include sentences from my authentic emails in their pseudepigraphic creations.

All three activities work perfectly well in a face-to-face class. In fact, each one was originally designed for that modality. But they work just as well, if not better, when adapted for asynchronous learning. Students employ a wider range of digital media in the asynchronous mode. Because they can present their work in a familiar digital environment, they create technologically sophisticated artifacts. We ought therefore to increase our awareness of digital platforms and tools and to stay attuned to new developments. We ought to create environments for students to utilize those tools. We will gain opportunities for refitting face-to-face teaching for asynchronous online instruction, and they will learn more in both face-to-face and online classrooms.

QUICK TIP
ALIGNING LEARNING OUTCOMES, TEACHING, AND ASSESSMENTS IN AN ONLINE COURSE

JOHN HILTON III

Recently I was navigating a tricky driving situation. My front driver's side tire hit the side of a curb, causing the tire to go out of alignment. The car was still drivable, but the driving experience was not optimal. Just as it is important for car wheels to be aligned, it is vital for course learning outcomes to be aligned with the teaching and assessment that takes place. Otherwise, teaching will drift off target, just as my car pulled to the right.

One of the central tenets of instructional design involves clearly defined learning outcomes.[1] In many instances, a given department standardizes learning outcomes for a specific course. It is often incumbent on individual instructors, however, to translate these course-level outcomes into specific learning outcomes for individual class periods. Consider the case of a faculty member teaching an introductory course on the New Testament to a large class of students. One of the department-dictated learning outcomes in her course is "demonstrate knowledge of the unique characteristics of each gospel." While she has likely shared the outcome on the course syllabus, her students need a clear understanding of how they can achieve her objectives in a given class period. For example, when teaching about Luke, the faculty member might decide that, among other outcomes, students should be able to articulate specific ways in which the narrative highlights the role of women. In doing so, they will have demonstrated knowledge of a unique characteristic of Luke's Gospel.

---

1. See Declan Kennedy, Áine Hyland, and Norma Ryan, *Writing and Using Learning Outcomes: A Practical Guide* (Cork, Ireland: University College Cork, 2007), https://tinyurl.com/SBL03108cu.

Instructors can communicate the specific learning outcomes for a class period in many ways. I have recently experimented with one approach that many students seem to appreciate. I created a Google Doc with hyperlinks leading to the specific learning outcomes for each class period of the semester. When students enter my classroom on a given day, they see on the screen the title of the class (e.g., "The Gospel according to Luke") and a QR code that takes them directly to the Google Doc. They then click on the appropriate class period and have before them the specific objectives of the class. In this manner, I am able to communicate the class-level learning outcomes to students who can then copy and paste the outcomes into their own document and use them to structure their class notes.

Once they have clearly communicated the learning outcomes, instructors must also ensure they teach to the outcomes they expect students to achieve. Few experiences are more discouraging for students than walking out of a class without understanding important concepts. If an instructor tells students they need to be able to articulate specific ways in which Luke highlights the role of women but never addresses the issue in class, students will not learn. Clear alignment takes place when faculty members teach to the specific class-level learning outcomes that they communicated to students.

After identifying and teaching specific learning outcomes, the next step is to assess student learning. An instructor might use an exam. A multiple-choice question might read, "Which of the following is a unique way in which Luke highlights the role of women?" Answers could include, "(a) Only Luke speaks of women at the empty tomb, (b) Only Luke speaks of women helping to finance Jesus' ministry, (c) Only Luke speaks of Martha, (d) Only Luke speaks of women being among the group traditionally called 'the wise men.'" A short-answer question might ask students to identify which gospel focuses specifically on women and to provide three examples. Other possible assessment instruments include papers and projects.

To be clear, I am not advocating for the importance of this particular learning outcome or these particular questions. I am arguing for the importance of clearly identifying and communicating class-level learning outcomes and aligning those outcomes with teaching and assessments. Generation Z, perhaps more than previous generations, may expect clarity in what they are expected to learn plus alignment of teaching and assessment with the communicated expectations.

After my driving incident, I took my car to a tire shop and was able to get my wheels aligned. Just as we periodically align our car tires, faculty members can periodically examine their teaching practices by asking themselves the following questions: Have I identified specific class-level learning outcomes? Have I clearly communicated these learning outcomes to students? Is my teaching aligned with my outcomes? Are my assessments aligned with my specified outcomes and teachings? As we answer yes to the above questions, our teaching will be in alignment, and our students will be more likely to recall the most valuable lessons from the course.

Bibliography

Kennedy, Declan, Áine Hyland, and Norma Ryan. *Writing and Using Learning Outcomes: A Practical Guide*. Cork, Ireland: University College Cork, 2007. https://tinyurl.com/SBL03108cu.

Quick Tip
Putting the Pieces Together
in an Asynchronous Jigsaw

JOCELYN MCWHIRTER

In the spring of 2020, I (along with many others) pivoted from classroom to online instruction. I spent the next six weeks fumbling with unfamiliar teaching tools while trying to meet unexpected student needs. The experience drove me to devote part of the summer to earning a Certificate in Effective Online Teaching from the American Association of College and University Educators.

As part of my training, I had to design a small group discussion. I chose to create a jigsaw exercise. A jigsaw exercise turns small groups of students into experts on some aspect of a broader topic. As groups share their findings with the whole class, the pieces come together and the big picture emerges. I have used jigsaws in class nearly every week of my teaching career. I was eager to adapt the exercise for an asynchronous online environment.

I searched my jigsaw collection for an appropriate subject. Episodes in the Joseph cycle? Various genres of prophecy or psalms? Topics in Pauline ethics? In the end, I chose a jigsaw involving some of Luke's unique parables. It focuses on the parables of the two debtors, the good Samaritan, the prodigal son, and the rich man and Lazarus, along with two short parables about prayer (the friend at midnight plus the widow and the unjust judge; see Luke 7:36–50; 10:25–37; 11:5–8; 15:11–52; 16:19–31; 18:1–8). Since students have already interpreted some of Mark's and Matthew's parables, engaged in redaction criticism of Matthew, and become acquainted with Luke, they are ready to interpret Luke's unique parables and understand how they serve his narrative agenda. They are also prepared to ask questions that propel class discussion and observe respectful etiquette.

The exercise begins with small group meetings. Each group, whose members will have worked together with mutual support and account-ability since the beginning of the semester, arranges a forty-minute synchronous meeting. Before the group meetings, students read all the jigsaw parables. Then, when they go online together, they bring their Bibles and paste discussion prompts (prepared by me) into the chat. The prompts first explain the purpose of the exercise: to interpret an assigned parable (or set of two parables) within its literary context and to relate its main point to one or more of Luke's themes.[1]

The prompts then instruct students to read their assigned parable(s) out loud and to answer these questions:

- To whom does Jesus speak the parable?
- What issue does he address?
- In light of the parable's context, what do the details of the parable represent?
- What main point does it make?
- How does that point address the issue to which Jesus is respond-ing?
- How does it relate to one or more of Luke's themes?

As students discuss their answers over the next twenty minutes, they take notes for future reference.

Once they finish their discussion, they have become the class experts on their parable(s). They spend the rest of their meeting on the final task: to share their interpretation with the class by creating, recording, and posting a five-minute video interview of their parable's main characters. The interview takes place on the grid of the video-conferencing screen. The prodigal son might explain what he hoped to achieve by returning to his father. The widow might describe her desperate circumstances. In the end, the interviewer summarizes the main point of the group's parable(s) and relates it to Luke's themes.

The jigsaw pieces come together when the videos are posted to our learning management system discussion board and asynchronous class dis-cussion begins. Each student views the other groups' videos and responds

---

1. Themes might include salvation through repentance and the forgiveness of sins, Jesus as an authoritative interpreter of Moses and the prophets, and the necessity for prayer.

to at least two of them with an open-ended question about how the video interprets the parable(s). Each group member then replies to one question about their parable(s), referring to evidence from Luke's Gospel as necessary. I, too, offer my feedback, affirming student insights and encouraging them to rethink dubious conclusions. I also grade the exercise. I award points for participation in small group and class discussion, questions that prompt further reflection and new ideas, and answers that demonstrate basic comprehension and critical thinking.

I like this online exercise as much as I like its face-to-face version, which involves students in parable skits instead of character interviews. The discussion-board component makes the online version even better, since all students participate in the conversation. The online jigsaw enables student collaboration in active learning, critical thinking, and creative interpretation. Students take a step toward the course goal of interpreting the New Testament thoroughly and persuasively. And (let's hope) we all have fun reading Luke's parables and viewing his themes through the perspectives of their characters.

Contributors

Kimberly Bauser McBrien, Trinity University, San Antonio, TX

George Branch-Trevathan, Thiel College, Greenville, PA

Callie Callon, University of St. Michael's College, Toronto, ON

Lesley DiFransico, Loyola University Maryland, Baltimore, MD

Nicholas A. Elder, University of Dubuque Theological Seminary, Dubuque, IA

Timothy A. Gabrielson, Sterling College, Sterling, KS

Kathleen Gallagher Elkins, St. Norbert College, De Pere, WI

Susan E. Haddox, University of Mount Union, Alliance, OH

Seth Heringer, Toccoa Falls College, Toccoa Falls, GA

John Hilton III, Brigham Young University, Provo, UT

Melanie A. Howard, Fresno Pacific University, Fresno, CA

Christopher M. Jones, Washburn University, Topeka, KS

Steve Jung, Azusa Pacific University, Azusa, CA

Katherine Low, Mary Baldwin University, Staunton, VA

Timothy Luckritz Marquis, Virginia Commonwealth University, Richmond, VA

Kara J. Lyons-Pardue, Point Loma Nazarene University, San Diego, CA

Jocelyn McWhirter, Albion College, Albion, MI

Sylvie T. Raquel, Trinity International University, Deerfield, IL

Eric A. Seibert, Messiah College, Mechanicsburg, PA

Hanna Tervanotko, McMaster University, Hamilton, ON

Carl N. Toney, Hope International University, Fullerton, CA

John Van Maaren, Ruprecht-Karls-Universität, Heidelberg, Germany

Robby Waddell, Southeastern University, Lakeland, FL

Name Index